Odoo 12 Development Essentials
Fourth Edition

Fast-track your Odoo development skills to build powerful business applications

Daniel Reis

BIRMINGHAM - MUMBAI

Odoo 12 Development Essentials
Fourth Edition

Commissioning Editor: Pavan Ramchandani
Acquisition Editor: Alok Dhuri
Content Development Editor: Manjusha Mantri
Technical Editor: Abin Sebastian
Copy Editor: Safis Editing
Project Coordinator: Prajakta Naik
Proofreader: Safis Editing
Indexer: Priyanka Dhadke
Graphics: Jisha Chirayil
Production Coordinator: Shraddha Falebhai

First published: April 2015
Second edition: November 2016
Third edition: March 2018
Fourth edition: December 2018

Production reference: 1271218

Published by Packt Publishing Ltd.
Livery Place
35 Livery Street
Birmingham
B3 2PB, UK.

ISBN 978-1-78953-247-0

www.packtpub.com

mapt.io

Mapt is an online digital library that gives you full access to over 5,000 books and videos, as well as industry leading tools to help you plan your personal development and advance your career. For more information, please visit our website.

Why subscribe?

- Spend less time learning and more time coding with practical eBooks and Videos from over 4,000 industry professionals

- Improve your learning with Skill Plans built especially for you

- Get a free eBook or video every month

- Mapt is fully searchable

- Copy and paste, print, and bookmark content

Packt.com

Did you know that Packt offers eBook versions of every book published, with PDF and ePub files available? You can upgrade to the eBook version at www.packt.com and as a print book customer, you are entitled to a discount on the eBook copy. Get in touch with us at customercare@packtpub.com for more details.

At www.packt.com, you can also read a collection of free technical articles, sign up for a range of free newsletters, and receive exclusive discounts and offers on Packt books and eBooks.

Foreword

When I joined Odoo (a long time ago!), my first challenge was to deliver training courses for consultants, including technical sessions for new Odoo developers. Daniel's *Odoo Development Essentials* is the realization of my wishes from these sessions; the companion book I wish I could have given to the participants to kick-start their first contact with Odoo. Chapter after chapter, he walks you through the creation of your first Odoo app, following best practices at every step. Starting with a solid development environment, you'll soon feel comfortable with your Odoo system, and quickly shape up a typical app. From the model groundwork upwards, you'll learn about each framework layer, including the latest frontend features and the RPC API. In this cloud era, integration is key, and Odoo features a very comprehensive API, opening up endless integration options.

Daniel also includes reference documentation for the most important API areas, and before you know it, you will have grasped the fundamental design properties of Odoo—minimalism, modularity, extensibility, and scalability. Understanding this will be invaluable for any task you set out to accomplish. It is what sets apart good Odoo developers.

Thanks to the yearly updates, the book is great even for more experienced developers, highlighting new features and changes in the Odoo framework. This edition does not fail to deliver, introducing Odoo 12 and the updated API, including coverage of the optimized batch create method, the new super-admin mechanisms, the enhanced debug menu, and much more.

The book also includes a wealth of pro tips, acquired through years of experience, that should make a seasoned Odoo developer out of you in no time, without the extra gray hair! Daniel's natural talent will make you enjoy the *Odoo Development Essentials* journey!

Olivier Dony
R&D Engineer, Odoo Belgium

Contributors

About the author

Daniel Reis has had a long career in the IT industry, mostly as a consultant implementing business applications in variety of sectors, and today works for Securitas, a multinational security services provider.

He has been working with Odoo since 2010, is an active contributor to Odoo Community Association projects, is currently a member of the board of the Odoo Community Association, and collaborates with ThinkOpen Solutions, a leading Portuguese Odoo integrator.

I would like to thank my wife, Maria, for all her patience and support.

My thanks also to Olivier Dony for agreeing to be part of this project and for all the valuable feedback given.

About the reviewer

Parth Gajjar has a degree in computer engineering. He loves programming and designing complex applications in Odoo. He has more than 6 years of experience with Odoo.

In 2012, he joined the Indian branch of Odoo, S.A. He has expertise in both the Python and the JavaScript framework of Odoo. At Odoo, he started working in the offshore department and then moved to R&D department. At Odoo, he has worked on features such as marketing automation, surveys, website forums, Odoo Mobile App, QWeb Report Engine, CSS Editor, and Domain Selector.

Currently, he is active as a code reviewer at Odoo and helps developers with architectural decisions. He often gives technical training to Odoo partners and prospects. He also assists the recruitment department with technical interviews.

Packt is searching for authors like you

If you're interested in becoming an author for Packt, please visit `authors.packtpub.com` and apply today. We have worked with thousands of developers and tech professionals, just like you, to help them share their insight with the global tech community. You can make a general application, apply for a specific hot topic that we are recruiting an author for, or submit your own idea.

Table of Contents

Preface

Odoo is a fully-featured open source platform for building applications. Based on this core framework, a suite of integrated applications was built, covering all business areas from CRM and sales to stocks and accounting.

Beyond these out-of-the-box features, Odoo's framework was built with extensibility in mind. Modifications can be implemented as extension modules, to be applied as a layer on top on the existing modules being changed, without actually changing the original code. This provides a clean and easy-to-control customization approach.

This capability to combine several modules into feature-rich applications, along with the open source nature of Odoo, are probably important factors in the growth of the community around Odoo. In fact, there are thousands of community modules available for Odoo covering virtually every topic, and the number of people getting involved has been steadily growing every year.

Odoo 12 Development Essentials provides a step-by-step guide to Odoo development, allowing readers to quickly climb the learning curve and become productive in the Odoo application platform. At the same time, it tries to provide good reference materials, to be kept close to hand every time you are working with Odoo.

Who this book is for

This book was written for developers with minimal programming knowledge but a strong will to learn. We will often use the Python language and explain how to run Odoo in an Ubuntu/Debian system, but little previous knowledge of them is assumed. The code examples are kept simple and clear, and they are accompanied by appropriate explanations.

Experienced developers who are already familiar with Odoo should also benefit from this book. Not only does it allow them to consolidate their knowledge, but it also provides an easy way to get up to date with all the details that changed with Odoo 12.0. In fact, special care was taken to highlight all the relevant changes between the different Odoo versions since 8.0.

Finally, this book should provide a solid reference to be used daily, both by newcomers and experienced developers. The documentation of the relevant differences between the several Odoo versions should also be a good resource for any developer working with different Odoo versions at the same time or who is porting modules to other versions.

What this book covers

This books contains 14 chapters, organized into five parts: introduction, models, business logic, views, and deployment.

The **first part** introduces the Odoo framework, explains how to set up your development environment, and provides a tutorial including a thorough, step-by-step creation of a new Odoo module:

Chapter 1, *Quick Start Using the Developer Mode*, visually introduces the Odoo development concepts by walking through the creation of an Odoo application directly from the user interface, a simple to-do tracking application. Instructions are given to set up Odoo in our workstation, but an existing Odoo installation, or an Odoo.com instance, can be used, so no local setup is required.

Chapter 2, *Preparing the Development Environment*, explains how to install Odoo from source code and how to set up the development environment to be used throughout the book. We choose to install Odoo in an Ubuntu environment, and, with Windows 10, we can use the **Windows Subsystem for Linux (WSL)** to achieve this.

Chapter 3, *Your First Odoo Application*, provides a step-by-step guide to the creation of our first Odoo module, a book catalog for a Library app. While the example is simple, it covers all the different layers and components that can be involved in an Odoo application: models, business logic, backend views, and web frontend views.

Chapter 4, *Extending Modules*, explains the available inheritance mechanisms and how to use them to create extension modules, adding or modifying features from other existing add-on modules.

The **second part** of the book introduces the models responsible for the data model structures around which the application is built:

Chapter 5, *Import, Export, and Module Data*, addresses the usage of data files in Odoo and their role in modules to load data and configurations to the database. It covers the XML and CSV data file formats, the external identifier concept, how to use data file in modules, and data import/export operations.

Chapter 6, *Models – Structuring the Application Data*, discusses the model layer in detail, introducing the framework's **Object-Relational Mapping** (**ORM**), the different types of models available, and the field types, including relational and computed fields.

In the **third part**, we explain how to write the business logic layer on top of the models—the controller component of the architecture. This includes the built-in ORM functions, used to manipulate the data in the models, and social features used for messages and notifications:

Chapter 7, *Recordsets – Working with Model Data*, introduces the concepts and features of ORMs, how to query and ready to read data from models, how to manipulate recordsets, and how to write changes on model data.

Chapter 8, *Business Logic – Supporting Business Processes*, explores programming business logic on the server side to manipulate data and implement specific business rules. It also explains how to use wizards for more sophisticated user interaction. The built-in social features, messages, chatter, followers, and channels, are addressed, as well as testing and debugging techniques.

Chapter 9, *External API – Integrating with Other Systems*, shows how to implement external Odoo applications by implementing a command-line client that interacts with our Odoo server. There are several alternative client programming libraries available, which are introduced and used to implement our showcase client utility.

The **fourth part** explores the view layer and the several technologies that can be used for the user interface:

Chapter 10, *Backend Views – Design the User Interface*, covers the web client's view layer, explaining the several types of views in detail and all the elements that can be used to create dynamic and intuitive user interfaces.

Chapter 11, *Kanban Views and Client-Side QWeb*, keeps working with the web client, but introduces Kanban views and explains the QWeb templates used to design the Kanban board elements.

Chapter 12, *Reports and Server-Side QWeb*, discusses using the QWeb-based report engine and everything needed to generate printer-friendly PDF reports.

Chapter 13, *Creating Website Frontend Features*, introduces Odoo website development, including web controller implementations and using QWeb templates to build frontend web pages.

Finally, the **fifth part** covers deployment and maintenance practices. Some special considerations, not relevant to development environments, need to be taken into account when deploying for production use:

Chapter 14, *Deploying and Maintaining Production Instances*, shows us how to prepare a server for production use, explaining what configuration should be taken care of and how to configure an NGINX reverse proxy for improved security and scalability.

By the end of the book, the reader should have a solid understanding of all the steps and components involved in the Odoo application development cycle, from the drawing board to the production, deployment, and maintenance of these applications.

To get the most out of this book

Odoo is built using the Python programming language, so it is a good idea to have a good knowledge of it. We also choose to run Odoo in an Ubuntu host, and will do some work on the command line, so it will help to be familiar with it.

To get the most out of this book, we recommend that you do some complementary reading on the Python programming language, the Ubuntu/Debian Linux operating system, and the PostgreSQL database.

While we will run Odoo in an Ubuntu host (a popular cloud hosting option), we will provide guidance on how to set up our development environment in a Windows system using the **Windows for Linux Subsystem** (**WSL**), available in recent Windows 10 builds. Of course, working from an Ubuntu/Debian native system is also a good choice.

All the required software is freely available, and the instructions on where to find it will be given.

Download the example code files

You can download the example code files for this book from your account at www.packt.com. If you purchased this book elsewhere, you can visit www.packt.com/support and register to have the files emailed directly to you.

You can download the code files by following these steps:

1. Log in or register at www.packt.com.
2. Select the **SUPPORT** tab.
3. Click on **Code Downloads & Errata**.
4. Enter the name of the book in the **Search** box and follow the onscreen instructions.

Once the file is downloaded, please make sure that you unzip or extract the folder using the latest version of:

- WinRAR/7-Zip for Windows
- Zipeg/iZip/UnRarX for Mac
- 7-Zip/PeaZip for Linux

The code bundle for the book is also hosted on GitHub at **https://github.com/PacktPublishing/Odoo-12-Development-Essentials-Fourth-Edition**. We also have other code bundles from our rich catalog of books and videos available at https://github.com/PacktPublishing/. Check them out!

Download the color images

We also provide a PDF file that has color images of the screenshots/diagrams used in this book. You can download it here: https://www.packtpub.com/sites/default/files/downloads/9781789532470_ColorImages.pdf.

Conventions used

There are a number of text conventions used throughout this book.

CodeInText: Indicates code words in text, database table names, folder names, filenames, file extensions, pathnames, dummy URLs, user input, and Twitter handles. Here is an example: "The ~ symbol is a shortcut for the user's home directory, such as /home/daniel."

A block of code is set as follows:

```
<search>
 <filter name="item_not_done"
 string="Not Done"
 domain="[('x_is_done', '=', False)]" />
</search>
```

When we wish to draw your attention to a particular part of a code block, the relevant lines or items are set in bold:

```
<search>
 <filter name="item_not_done"
 string="Not Done"
 domain="[('x_is_done', '=', False)]" />
</search>
```

Any command-line input or output is written as follows:

```
$ createdb MyDB
$ createdb --template=MyDB MyDB2
```

Bold: Indicates a new term, an important word, or words that you see on screen. For example, words in menus or dialog boxes appear in the text like this. Here is an example: "Click on the debug icon and select the **Edit Action** option. This will open the **Window Actions** used to open the current **Views**."

Warnings or important notes appear like this.

Tips and tricks appear like this.

Get in touch

Feedback from our readers is always welcome.

General feedback: Email customercare@packtpub.com and mention the book title in the subject of your message. If you have questions about any aspect of this book, please email us at customercare@packtpub.com.

Errata: Although we have taken every care to ensure the accuracy of our content, mistakes do happen. If you have found a mistake in this book, we would be grateful if you would report this to us. Please visit www.packt.com/submit-errata, selecting your book, clicking on the Errata Submission Form link, and entering the details.

Piracy: If you come across any illegal copies of our works in any form on the internet, we would be grateful if you would provide us with the location address or website name. Please contact us at copyright@packt.com with a link to the material.

If you are interested in becoming an author: If there is a topic that you have expertise in, and you are interested in either writing or contributing to a book, please visit authors.packt.com.

Reviews

Please leave a review. Once you have read and used this book, why not leave a review on the site that you purchased it from? Potential readers can then see and use your unbiased opinion to make purchase decisions, we at Packt can understand what you think about our products, and our authors can see your feedback on their book. Thank you!

For more information about Packt, please visit packt.com.

Quick Start Using the Developer Mode

1

Odoo provides a rapid application development framework that's particularly suited to building business applications. This type of application is usually concerned with keeping business records, centered around **create, read, update, and delete (CRUD)** operations. Not only does Odoo makes it easy to build this type of application, it also provides rich components to create compelling user interfaces, such as kanban, calendar, and graph views.

This book is organized into five parts. We start by providing an overview of the Odoo framework, setting up a development environment, and building our first Odoo application. Being generally familiar with the main Odoo components, we will dive, in more detail, into each of the three main application layers—models, business logic, and views. Finally, our application will need to be deployed to a production environment and maintained. That's what is covered in the final chapter of the book.

In this chapter, we will quickly get into the action, exploring the Odoo internals directly from the web user interface, even before having set up our local development environment.

In this chapter, we will do the following:

- Introduce the learning project used in this chapter, the to-do application.
- Understand the Odoo architecture, editions, and releases, to have the essential context and insights relevant to working with Odoo.
- Prepare a basic Odoo work environment, so that we can work on an example project and learn by experience. Several options are proposed:
    - Using Odoo online
    - Using the Windows all-in-one installer
    - Using Docker

- Enable the developer mode, to make available in the user interface the tools we will be using.
- Modify an existing model to add a field, a quick introduction to a common customization.
- Create a custom data model, to add new data structures for your applications.
- Configure access security, to allow specific user groups to access the application features.
- Create menu items, to make the new data model available in the user interface.
- Create list, form, and search views, the basic building blocks for the user interface.

We will learn by example, and the next section will introduce the project we will use for this.

Technical requirements

The minimal requirement for this chapter is to have a modern web browser, such as Firefox, Chrome, or Edge. With this you can follow the chapter using an Odoo SaaS trial database, as explained in the *Preparing a basic work environment* section.

You may go a little further and use a packaged Odoo distribution to have it locally installed on your computer. For that, you only need an operating system such as Windows, macOS, Debian-based Linux (such as Ubuntu), or Red Hat-based Linux (such as Fedora). Windows, Debian, and Red Hat have installation packages available. Another option is to use Docker, available for all these systems and for macOS. The *Preparing a basic work environment* section will guide us in any of these installation scenarios.

In this chapter, we will mostly have point-and-click interaction with the user interface. You will find the code snippets used and a summary of the steps performed in the book's code repository, at `https://github.com/PacktPublishing/Odoo-12-Development-Essentials-Fourth-Edition`, under the `ch01` folder.

Introducing the to-do list project

The TodoMVC (`http://todomvc.com/`) project provides a comparison between multiple JavaScript frameworks by implementing the same simple to-do application in each of them. Inspired by this, we will go through the experience of building a simple to-do application with Odoo.

It should allow us to add new to-do items, and then mark them as completed. For example, you could add to-do items to the list, such as *Buy eggs*, and then check an *Is Done?* box once they are completed. The **To-do Items** should be private to the current user, so that you will only be able to access your own to-do items.

This should be enough for a simple to-do application, but to make it a little more interesting we will introduce a couple of complications. Our to-do list items should be able to include a list of people involved in the task, the *work team*.

It is useful to think about our application by considering several layers involved:

- **The data tier**: Implemented through models
- **The logic tier**: Implemented through automation code
- **The presentation tier**: Implemented through views

For the data tier, we need a **To-do Item** model. We will also make use of the built-in partner (or contacts) model to support the work team feature. We must not forget to configure the access control security for our new model.

The logic tier used here will be the basic CRUD operations handled by the framework, and we don't have in our requirements any additional automation to support. To access the full power of the framework, we need to use Python code in developer modules. While we can't do that yet, the developer menu does provide some tools for us to implement some business logic from the user interface, the automate actions. We will work on a simple example of how to use them.

Finally, for the presentation tier we will add the menu option for our application, and the views for the to-do item model. The essential views for a business application are the list view, where we can browse the existing records, and the form view, where we can zoom in to a record and see all the details. For better usability, we can also add preconfigured filters to the search box, available in the list view. The available search options are also considered a view, so this can be done through a search view.

The following are the steps to create a to-do list:

1. First, we will create a new model for to-do items, and then make it available to users by adding a to-do top menu for it.
2. Next, we will create the list and form views for the **To-do Items** model. This new model should have these fields:
   - **Description** text field
   - `Is Done?` flag (a Boolean field)

Our specification for the application includes the ability to select a list of people that will be working on the task, so we need a Model to represent people. Fortunately, Odoo includes out of the box a model for this—the partner model (res.partner is its technical name), used to store individual people, companies, and addresses.

And only particular persons are selectable for this work team. This means that we need to modify the partner model to add this new Is Work Team? flag.

So, the **To-do Items** model should also include the work team field, with a list of people. The linked people are selectable from the partners/contacts that have the Is Work Team? flag enabled.

As a summary, this is what we will need to do:

- Add a field to the partner model and form view
- Create a **To-do Item** model
- Create a to-do application menu item
- **Create a to-do Item user interface**: List and form view, and UI search options
- **Create access security**: **Group**, **access control lists** (ACL), and **Record Rules**

Before we go into the actual implementation, we will first discuss a few basic concepts about the Odoo framework, and then learn how to prepare an environment to work with.

Basic concepts

It is useful to understand the several layers involved in the Odoo architecture, and the role of each type of component we will use. So we will have a pragmatic overview of the Odoo application architecture, with a focus on helping application development by decomposing work into several components.

Also, Odoo publishes two different product editions, community and enterprise, and regularly releases new versions for both. It is important to understand the differences we can expect between the editions, and what a new major release can mean for our development and deployment. For this, we have an overview of the differences between CE and EE, and on the Odoo major version stability policy.

Let's start looking at the Odoo application architecture.

The Odoo architecture

Odoo follows a multi-tier architecture, and we can identify three main tiers—data, logic, and presentation:

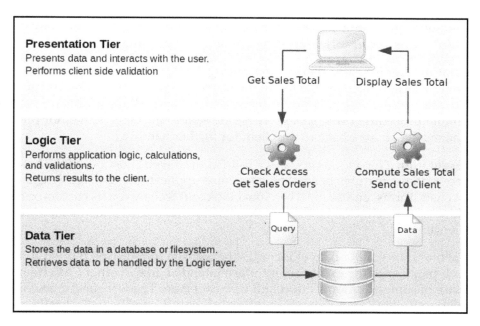

The **Data Tier** is the lowest-level layer, and is responsible for data storage and persistence. Odoo relies on a PostgreSQL server for this. PostgreSQL is the only supported database server, and this is a design choice. So, other databases such as MySQL are not supported. Binary files, such as attachments of documents or images, are usually stored in the filesystem, in a directory referred to as the `filestore`.

> This means that a full backup of an Odoo instance needs both a database dump and a copy of the `filestore`.

The **Logic Tier** is responsible for all the interactions with the data layer, and is handled by the Odoo server. As a general rule, the low-level database should only be accessed by this layer, since it is the only way to ensure security access control and data consistency. At the core of the Odoo server, we have the **object-relational mapping** (**ORM**) engine for this interface. The ORM provides the **application programming interface** (**API**) used by the add-on modules to interact with the data.

For example, the partner data entity, such as a customer or a supplier, is represented in the ORM by a model. This model is a Python object class supporting several interaction methods, such as `create()` to create new partner records, or `read()` to query existing records and their data. These generic methods can implement specific business logic in particular models. For example, the `create()` method might implement default values or enforce validation rules; the `read()` method might support some automatically computed fields, or enforce access controls depending on the user performing that action.

The **Presentation Tier** is responsible for presenting data and interacting with the user. It is implemented by a client responsible for all the user experience. The client interacts with the ORM API to read, write, verify, or perform any other action, calling ORM API methods through **remote procedure calls** (**RPCs**). These are sent to the Odoo server for processing, and then the results are sent back to the client for further handling.

For the **Presentation Tier**, Odoo provides a full-featured web client out of the box. The web client supports all the features needed by a business application: login sessions, navigation menus, data lists, forms, and so on. The global look and feel are not as customizable as a frontend developer might expect, but it makes it easy to create a functional and consistent user experience.

A complementary presentation layer includes the website framework. It gives full flexibility to create web pages with the exact user interface intended, like in other CMS frameworks, at the expense of some additional effort and web expertise. The website framework supports web controllers to implement code for presenting specific logic, keeping it separate from the model's intrinsic logic. Frontend developers will probably feel very much at home in this space.

The Odoo server API is very open, and all server functions are available through it. The server API used by the official web client is the same as the one available to any other application. So, other client implementations are possible, and could be built in almost any platform or programming language. Desktop and smartphone applications can be built to provide specific user interfaces, leveraging the Odoo data and logic tiers for business logic and data persistence.

Odoo community versus Odoo enterprise

Odoo is the name of the software product, and also the name of the company that builds it. Odoo follows an open core business model, where the **community edition** (**CE**) is free and open source, and the **enterprise edition** (**EE**) is a paid product, providing income for the company.

The CE provides all the framework features plus the essential features for most of the business applications bundled with Odoo. It is licensed under an LGPL license, chosen to allow adding proprietary extensions on top of open source modules.

The EE is built on top of the CE, providing all its features plus some additional exclusive ones. Notably, it includes an improved and mobile-friendly user interface, although the user interface underlying the organization is essentially the same in both editions.

The Odoo online SaaS service uses Odoo enterprise, and may have deployed intermediate versions released after the latest Odoo enterprise major version.

Odoo version policy

At the time of writing, Odoo's latest stable version is version 12, marked on GitHub as **branch 12.0**. This is the version we will work with throughout the book. In recent years, major stable versions have been released on a yearly schedule, in October, at the annual Odoo experience conference.

The last three stable versions are supported. With the release of 12.0, versions 11.0 and 10.0 are still supported, and version 9.0 stopped being supported. This means it will stop receiving bug and security fixes.

It's important to note that Odoo databases are incompatible between Odoo major versions. If you run an Odoo 11 server against a database created for a previous major version of Odoo, it won't work. Non-trivial migration work is needed before a database can be used with a later version of the product.

The same is true for add-on modules: as a general rule, an add-on module developed for an Odoo major version will not work on other versions. When downloading a community module from the web, make sure it targets the Odoo version you are using.

On the other hand, major releases (10.0, 11.0) are expected to receive frequent updates, but these should be mostly bug fixes. They are assured to be API-stable, meaning that model data structures and view element identifiers will remain stable. This is important because it means there will be no risk of custom modules breaking due to incompatible changes in the upstream core modules.

The version in the `master` branch will result in the next major stable version, but until then, it's not API-stable and you should not use it to build custom modules. Doing so is like moving on quicksand—you can't be sure when some changes will be introduced that will break your custom module.

Preparing a basic work environment

The first thing we need is to have an Odoo instance that we can use for our learning project.

For the purpose of this chapter, we just need a running Odoo instance, and the particular installation method is not relevant. To quickly get up and running, we can use a prepackaged Odoo distribution, or even just use an Odoo SaaS trial database (`https://www.odoo.com/`).

Using an Odoo SaaS trial database

This can be the simplest way to get started. No need to actually install anything for now, just go to `https://www.odoo.com/` and create a free trial database. The Odoo Cloud **software as a service (SaaS)** is based on the **enterprise edition (EE)**, with additional, exclusive, intermediate version releases. Other than the trial, at the time of writing it also offers a free plan: databases with only one application installed are free to use. The SaaS service runs vanilla Odoo enterprise and custom modules are not allowed. For cases where customizations are needed, the `Odoo.sh` service can be used, providing a full-featured development platform to customize and host solutions based on Odoo enterprise. See `https://www.odoo.sh/` for more information.

 Changes in Odoo 12
In previous Odoo versions, the menu structure of the web client was significantly different between the CE and EE. In Odoo 12, the menus in both editions follow a similar structure.

To create a new database on the Odoo Cloud SaaS, you will probably be asked to select a starting application. No specific application is required to follow this chapter, but if you're unsure on what to pick, **customer relationship management (CRM)** would be fine.

Also worthy of note is that the EE, on the Odoo SaaS, has the Odoo Studio application builder available. We won't be using it, since it is not available for the CE, which is used as a reference in this book. Odoo Studio provides a user-friendly user interface for the developer features introduced in this chapter, along with a few extra features, such as the ability to export the customizations made in a convenient module package. But the main capabilities are similar to what we can get by using the basic developer mode.

Installing Odoo on Windows

Ready-to-install Odoo packages can be found at `https://download.odoo.com`, available for any of the currently supported Odoo versions, as well as for the master branch (the latest development version). You can find the Windows (`.exe`) installers, alongside the Debian (`.deb`) and CentOS (`.rpm`) packages.

To install on Windows, find the latest `.exe` build in the `nightly` directory and install it. The all-in-one installation is straightforward, as it provides all that you will need to run Odoo; Python 3, a PostgreSQL database server, the Odoo server, and all Odoo additional dependencies. A Windows service is also created to automatically start the Odoo and PostgreSQL services when your machine starts.

Installing Odoo using Docker containers

Docker provides a convenient multi-platform solution to run applications. It can be used to run applications on macOS, Linux, and Windows. The container technology is simple to use and resource-efficient when compared to classic virtual machines.

You must first have Docker installed in your system. The Docker CE is free of charge, and can be downloaded from `https://www.docker.com`. It's worth referring to Docker's website for the latest installation details.

In particular, keep in mind that virtualization must be enabled in your BIOS setup. Also, the Docker CE for Windows requires Hyper-V, only available in Windows 10 Enterprise or Education releases (see `https://docs.docker.com/docker-for-windows/install`), and Docker CE for mac requires OS X El Capitan 10.11 and newer macOS releases.

For other Windows and macOS versions, you should instead install Docker Toolbox, available at `https://docs.docker.com/toolbox/overview`. Docker Toolbox bundles VirtualBox and provides a preconfigured shell that should be used as the command-line environment to operate Docker containers.

The Odoo Docker images are available in the Docker store at `https://store.docker.com/ images/odoo`. There, we can find the versions available, and the basic instructions to get started with them. To run Odoo, we will need two Docker containers, one for the PostgreSQL database, and another for the Odoo server.

The installation and operation is done from a command-line window. To install the PostgreSQL Docker container, run this:

```
$ docker run -d -e POSTGRES_USER=odoo -e POSTGRES_PASSWORD=odoo --name db
postgres:10
```

It will download the latest PostgreSQL image from the internet, and start a container for it running as a background job.

Next, install and run the Odoo server container, linking it to the PostgreSQL container we just started, and exposing it on port `8069`:

```
$ docker run -t -p 8069:8069 --name odoo --link db:db odoo:12.0 -d odoo12
```

With this, you will see the live Odoo server log in your terminal window, and can access the Odoo instance by opening `http://localhost:8069` with your favorite web browser.

 The Odoo server can fail to start if port `8069` is already in use, for example, by an already running Odoo server. In this case, you might look for and stop the running service (for example, by looking at the list of running services), or try to start this Odoo server on a different port by changing the `-p` option. For example, to use port `8070`, use `-p 8070:8069`. In that case, you probably also want to change `-d <dbname>` to set the database name that instance should use.

There are a few basic commands you should know to help manage these Docker containers:

- `docker stop <name>` stops a container
- `docker start <name>` starts a container
- `docker start -a <name>` starts a container, and attaches the output, such as the server log, to the terminal window
- `docker attach <name>` reattaches a container's output to the current terminal window
- `docker ps` lists the current Docker containers

These are the basic commands needed to operate our Docker containers.

In case you get in trouble running the containers, here is a recipe to start over:

```
$ docker container stop db
$ docker container rm db
$ docker container stop odoo
$ docker container rm odoo
```

The Docker technology has more potential, and it might be interesting to learn more about it. The Docker website has good learning documentation. A good place to get started is https://www.docker.com/get-started.

Other installation options

It is worth noting that installation packages are also available for Debian-based (such as Ubuntu) and Red Hat-based (such as CentOS and Fedora) Linux systems.

We won't be able to go into much detail on how to install them, but if you are familiar with Debian or Red Hat, this is also an option to consider. The installation packages are available from https://download.odoo.com, and the official documentation provides a good explanation on how to install them at https://www.odoo.com/documentation/master/setup/install.html.

Regarding the source code installation, it is the most complex, but also the most versatile of the installation alternatives, and it will be explained in detail in Chapter 2, *Preparing the Development Environment*.

Creating a work database

By now, we should have a PostgreSQL database server and an Odoo server instance running. We now need to create an Odoo database before we can start working on our project.

If you installed Odoo locally, keeping the default configuration options, the server should be available at `http://localhost:8069`. When we access it for the first time, since there are no Odoo databases available yet, we should see an assistant to create a new database:

The information you need to provide is the following:

- The **Database Name** is the identifier name to use for this database. You can have several databases available on the same server.
- **Email** is the login username to use for the special Administrator super user. It doesn't have to be an actual email address.
- **Password** is your secret password to log in as the Administrator.
- **Language** is the default language to use for the database.
- **Country** is the country set in the database's company data. It is optional, and is relevant for localization features in some apps, such as Invoicing and Accounting.
- The load demonstration data checkbox allows you to create the database with demonstration data, instead of creating a clean database. This is usually desirable for development and test environments.

A master password field might also be asked for, if one was set in the Odoo server configuration. This allows you to prevent unauthorized people from performing these administrative tasks. But by default it is not set, so you probably won't be asked for it.

After pushing the create database button, the new database will be bootstrapped, a process that can take a couple of minutes, and once ready you are redirected to the login screen.

The login screen has a manage databases link at the bottom to access the database manager. There, you can see the list of available databases; back up, duplicate, or delete them; and also create new ones. It can also be directly accessed at `http://localhost:8069/web/database/manager`.

 The database manager allows for privileged administration operations, and by default is enabled and unprotected. While it is a convenient feature for development, it can be a security risk for databases that have real data, even if they are test or development environments. Consider setting a strong master password, or even better, disabling it. This is done by setting `list_db = False` in the server configuration file.

Now that we have an Odoo instance and a database to work with, the next step is to enable the developer mode, providing the tools we need to implement our project.

Enabling the developer mode

To implement our project, we need the tools provided by the developer mode, which needs to be enabled.

The developer mode allows us to customize Odoo apps directly from the user interface. This has the advantage of being a rather quick way to make changes and add features. It can be used from small modifications, such as adding a field, to larger customizations, such as creating an application with several models, views, and menu items.

These customizations done directly from the user interface have some limitations, when compared to the customizations done with programming tools, covered throughout the rest of the book. For example, you can't add or extend the default ORM methods (although in some cases automated actions can be enough to provide an alternative to that). They also can't be easily integrated into a structured development workflow, which typically involves version control, automated tests, and deploying into several environments, such as quality assurance, pre-production, and production.

Here, we will be using the developer mode features mainly as a way to introduce how application configuration data is organized in the Odoo framework, and how the developer mode can be leveraged for simple customizations, or to quickly outline or prototype the solution to implement.

To enable the developer mode, go to **Settings | Dashboard**, and in the lower-right corner you should find the **Activate the developer mode** link. Clicking on it enables the developer mode features for this browser window. For Odoo 9.0 and before, the developer mode is activated in the **About** dialog window, available from the User menu, in the upper-right corner of the web client.

We also have available an **Activate the developer mode (with assets)** option. What it does is prevent web client asset minification. It is useful to debug the web client itself, at the expense of making the navigation a little slower.

For faster load times, the web client minifies the JavaScript and CSS assets into compact files. Unfortunately, that makes web client debugging nearly impossible. The **Activate the developer mode (with assets)** option prevents this minification and loads the web assets in individual, non-minified files.

The developer mode can also be enabled by tinkering directly with the current URL, so that you don't have to leave your current screen to open settings. Edit the URL to change the `.../web#...` part to insert `.../web?debug#...` or `.../web?debug=assets#...`. For example, `http://localhost:8069/web#home` would be changed to `http://localhost_8069/web?debug#home`.

Although there is no link to enable it, the frontend framework also supports the debug flag. To disable asset minification in a frontend web page, add `?debug=assets` to the corresponding URL. Take note that the option will probably not persist when navigating through links to other frontend pages.

There are browser extensions available for both Firefox and Chrome that provide a convenient button to enable and disable the developer mode. Look for "Odoo debug" in Firefox add-ons or the Chrome store.

Once the developer mode is enabled, we will see two additional menus available:

1. The **Developer Tools** menu, the bug icon on the right-hand side of the top menu bar, just before the username and avatar
2. The **Technical** menu item, in the **Settings** application

The following screenshot shows the two additional menus:

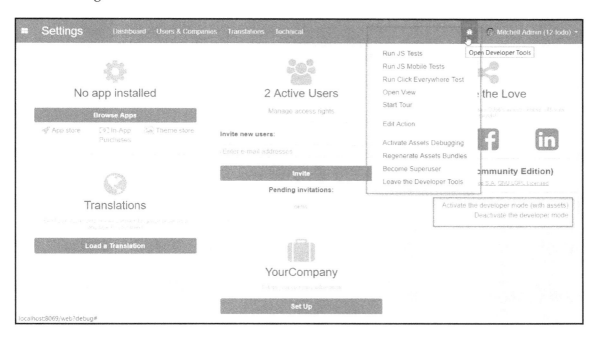

The developer mode also enables additional information on form fields; when pausing the mouse pointer over a field, a tooltip will display technical information on it.

We will be using the most relevant developer mode features in the next sections.

Modifying an existing model to add a field

Adding a custom field to an existing form is a common customization, and it can be done from the user interface, without the need to create a custom module.

For our to-do application, we want to select a group of people that will be able to collaborate on to-do items. We will identify them by setting a flag on their partner form. For that, we will add an `Is Work Team?` flag to the partner model.

The partner model is part of the Odoo core, and is available even if you haven't installed any apps yet. However, you may not have a menu option available to visit it. A simple way to add one is to install the **Contacts** application. Open the **Apps** top menu, look up this application, and install it, if you have not already done so:

After this, the **Contacts** application top menu option will be available.

Adding a field to a Model

To visit a Model's definition, with the developer mode enabled, in the **Settings** application go to the **Technical | Database Structure | Models** menu item.

Look up the **Model** having `res.partner`. The corresponding **Model Description** should be **Contact**. Click on it to open the form view, and you will see all the specific details about the partner model, including the field list:

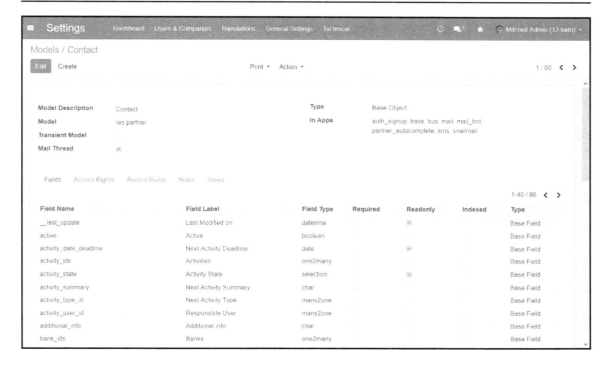

Now, **Edit** the form and click on the **Add a line** button at the bottom of the **Fields** list. A pop-up window will be presented for new field creation.

Let's fill in the configuration:

- **Field Name:** x_is_work_team
- **Field Label:** Is Work Team?
- **Field Type: boolean**

The **Field Name** must start with x_. This is mandatory for **Models** and **Fields** created directly through the user interface. Customizations made through add-on modules don't have this limitation.

That's it. Click save and close, and our new field should have been added to the **Fields** list. Chances are that this model has more than 80 fields, and so you might need to navigate to the next page of the **Fields** list to see it. To do so, use the right arrow in the upper-left corner of the **Fields** list.

Now, click on the upper-left save button to make this change permanent.

Adding a field to a form view

Our new field is now available in the partners model, but it is not yet visible to users. For that, we need to add it to the corresponding views.

Still on the **Model** having `res.partner` form, click on the **Views** tab, and we will be able to see all the view definitions for the model. As you can see, each view is a record in the database. Changing or adding view records is immediately effective, and will be visible the next time that view is reloaded:

There are a few important things to note in the **Views** list.

We can see that there are several **View Type**, such as **Form**, **Tree**, **Search**, or **Kanban**. The **Search** views are actually definitions of the filters available in the upper-right search box. The other view types are the different ways the data can be displayed. The basic ones are **Tree**, for list views, and **Form**, for the detailed form view.

 Both **Tree** and **List** can be used to refer to the same view type. They are in fact lists, and the **Tree** name exists for historical reasons—in the past, list views used to have a *tree* hierarchical mode.

You will notice that the same view type can have several definitions. If you sort the list by **View Type,** that will be clear.

Each view type, such as **Form**, can have one or more base view definitions (the ones with an empty **Inherited View** field). **Window Actions**, used by menu items, can specify the particular base view to use. If none are defined, the one with the lowest **Sequence** is used. You can think of it as being the default view. Clicking on a views line, we will see a form with the view's details, including the **Sequence** value:

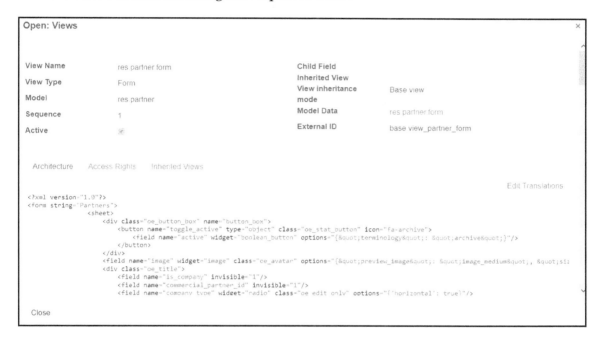

And each base view may have extensions, called **Inherited Views**. Each of these add incremental changes to the corresponding **Base view**, for example, adding a field to an existing form.

Extension views can themselves be extended by other extension views. In this case, the later extension is applied to the **Base view** after all preceding extensions have already been applied to it.

The res.partner model in particular can have a crowded view definitions list, since, like ours, many apps need to add extensions to it. An alternative is to access the particular view we want to extend, and edit it from there using the **Developer Tools** menu. This can also be used to learn what specific view is being used somewhere in the user interface.

Let's try it now:

1. Click on the **Contacts** application to be presented with a list of contact cards, then click on any of the cards, we will navigate to the corresponding **Form** view:

2. On the **Form** view, click on the **Developer Tools** menu (the bug icon in the upper-right corner) and select the **Edit View: Form** option. This will show the same view details form we saw before in **Models**, but positioned on the actual base view definition used here. As you can see, it is the res.partner.form view. We can see the owner module through the **External ID** field. In this case, it is base.view_partner_form, so we know that this view belongs to the base module. In the **Architecture** field, we can see the XML with the base view definition. We could simply edit the view architecture to add our new field, but in the long run it is not a good idea: this view is owned by an add-on module, and if some time in the future that module is upgraded, these customizations will be overwritten and lost. The proper way to modify a view is to create an **Inherited View** extension:

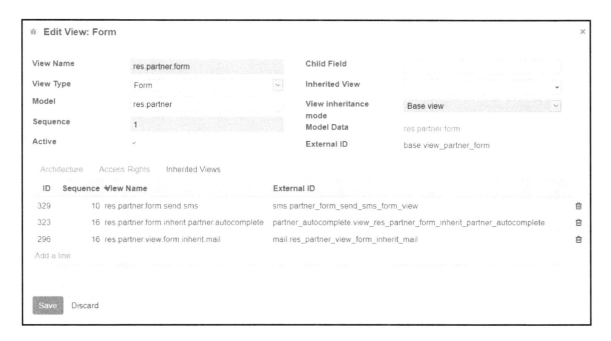

3. Using the **Inherited Views** tab, we should now create an extension view to add elements to the **Base view**:

    1. First, we need to pick an element from the original view to use as the extension point. We can do that by inspecting the **Architecture in Base view** and choosing an XML element with a `name` attribute. Most of the time, this will be a `<field>` element. Here, we will pick the `<field name="category_id" ...>` element:

    2. Now, open the **Developer Tools** menu, click on the **Edit View: Form** option, select the **Inherited Views** tab, and click on **Add a line** at the bottom of the list.

    3. A pop-up window, **Create Views which inherit from this one,** will be shown, and we should fill it with the following values:

        • **View Name:** `Contacts - Custom "Is Work Team" flag`

- **Architecture**: Use the following XML:

```
<field name="category_id"
position="after">
  <field name="x_is_work_team" />
</field>
```

- The other important fields, such as the **Model**, **View Type**, and **Inherited View**, already have the correct default values

4. We can now **Save & Close**, then, in the **Edit View: Form** window, click **Save**, and finally close it.

We will be able to see the change done once we reload the **Contacts** form view. This means reloading the page in your web browser. In most browsers, you can do that by pressing *F5*.

If we now visit again a contact form, we should see the new field on the left-hand side, below the **Tags** field:

Creating a new Model

Models are the basic components for applications, providing the data structures and storage to be used. Next, we will create the Model for the **To-do Items**. It will have three fields:

- Description
- `Is done?` flag
- Work team partner list

As we have seen earlier, Model definitions are accessed in the **Settings** app, in the **Technical** | **Database Structure** | **Models** menu.

To create a Model, follow these steps:

1. Visit the **Models** menu, and click on the upper-left **Create** button. Fill in the new Model form with these values:

    - **Model Description**: `To-do Item`
    - **Model**: `x_todo_item`

We should save it before we can properly add new fields to it.

2. So, click on **Save** and then **Edit** it again. You can see that a few fields were automatically added. The ORM includes them in all **Models**, and they can be useful for audit purposes:

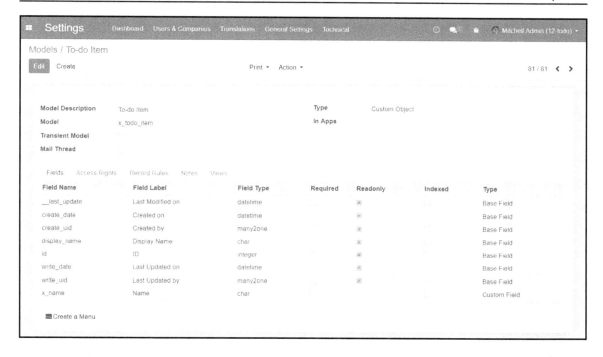

The x_name (or Name) field is a title representing the record in lists or when it is referenced in other records. It makes sense to use it for the **To-do Item** title. You may edit it and change the **Field Label** to a more meaningful label description.

Adding the Is Done? flag to the Model should be straightforward now.

3. In the **Fields** list, click on **Add a line**, at the bottom of the list, to create a new field with these values:

- **Field Name**: x_is_done
- **Field Label**: Is Done?
- **Field Type**: **boolean**

The new **Fields** form should look like this:

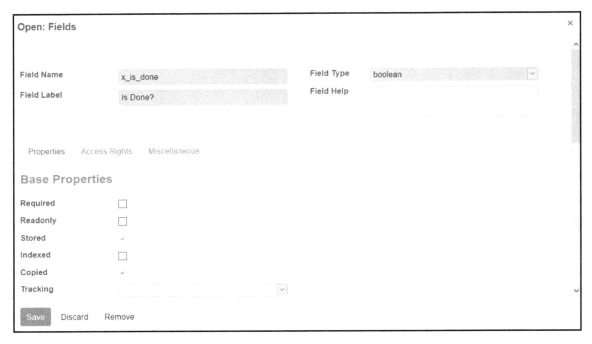

Now, something a little more challenging is to add the `Work Team` selection. Not only it is a relation field, referring to a record in the `res.partner` Model, it also is a multiple-value selection field. In many frameworks this is not a trivial task, but fortunately that's not the case in Odoo, because it supports many-to-many relations. This is the case because one to-do can have many people, and each person can participate in many to-do items.

4. In the **Fields** list, click again on **Add a line** to create the new field:

   - **Field Name**: `x_work_team_ids`
   - **Field Label**: `Work Team`
   - **Field Type**: **many2many**
   - **Object Relation**: `res.partner`
   - **Domain**: `[('x_is_work_team', '=', True)]`

The many-to-many field has a few specific definitions—**Relation Table, Column 1,** and **Column 2** fields. These are automatically filled out for you and the defaults are good for most cases, so we don't need to worry about them now. These will be discussed in more detail in Chapter 6, *Models – Structuring the Application Data.*

The domain attribute is optional, but we used it so that only eligible work team members are selectable from the list. Otherwise, all partners would be available for selection.

The **Domain** expression defines a filter for the records to be presented. It follows an Odoo-specific syntax—it is a list of triplets, where each triplet is a filter condition, indicating the **Field Name** to filter, the filter operator to use, and the value to filter against. A detailed explanation of domain expressions is given in Chapter 7, *Recordsets – Working with Model Data.*

Odoo has an interactive domain filter wizard that can be used as a helper to generate Domain expressions. You can use it at **Settings | User Interface | User-defined Filters**. Once a target **Model** is selected in the form, the **Domain** field will display an add filter button, which can be used to add filter conditions, and the text box below it will dynamically show the corresponding Domain expression code.

We now have the underlying Model for our to-do app, but we still don't have access to it. After creating a Model, we need to configure the groups that can access it. We will do that next.

Configuring access control security

Odoo includes built-in access control mechanisms. A user will only be able to use the features he was granted access to. This means that the library features we created are not accessible by regular users, even the admin user.

Changes in Odoo 12
The admin user is now subject to access control like all other users. In previous Odoo versions, the admin user was special, and bypassed security rules. This is no longer true, and we need to grant access privileges to be able to access Model data.

The central pieces for access security are the security groups, where the access rules are defined. Access for each user will depend on the groups he belongs to. For our project, we will create a to-do user group, to be assigned to the users we want to have access to this feature.

We give a group read or write access to particular **Models** using ACL. For our project, we need to add read and write access to the newly created to-do item model.

Furthermore, we can also set access rules for the record ranges users can access in a particular Model. For our project, we want the **To-do Items** to be private for each user, so to-do users should only be able to access the records created by themselves. This is done using the security record rules.

Security groups

Access control is based on groups. A security group is given access to **Models**, and this will determine the menu items available to the users belonging to that group. For more fine-grained control, we can also give access to specific menu Items, views, fields, and even data records (with **Record Rules**).

The security groups are also organized around apps, and typically each app provides at least two groups: **Users**, capable of performing the daily tasks, and **Manager**, able to perform all configurations for that app.

Let's create a new security group. In the **Settings** top menu, navigate to **Users & Companies | Groups**. Create a new record using the following values:

- **Application**: Leave empty
- **Name**: To-do User
- **Inherited** tab: Add the **User types / Internal User** item

This is how it should look like:

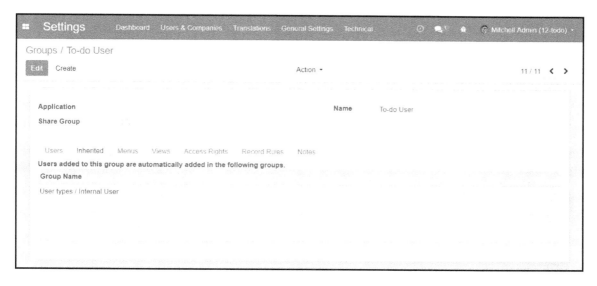

The to-do app is not available yet in the **Application** selection list, so we added it directly from the **Group** form.

We also made it inherit the **Internal User** group. This means that members of this group will also be made members of the **Inherited** groups (recursively), effectively having the permissions granted to all of them. **Internal User** is the basic access group, and app security groups usually inherit it.

Changes in Odoo 12
Before Odoo 12, the **Internal User** group was called **Employee**. This was just a cosmetic change, and the technical identifier (XML Id) is still the same as in previous versions: `base.group_user`.

Security access control lists

Now, we can grant access to specific **Models** to the **Group / To-do User**. We can use the **Access Rights** tab of the **Groups** form for this. Add an item there, using these values:

- **Name**: To-do Item User Access
- **Object**: Select **To-do Item** from the list
- **Read Access, Write Access, Create Access,** and **Delete Access**: Checked

Model access can also be managed from the **Technical | Security | Access Rights** menu item.

We don't need to add access to the **Partner** Model because the **Group** is inheriting the **Internal Users** group, which already has access to it.

We can now try these new security settings, by adding our **admin** user to this new **Group**:

1. Select the **Users & Companies | Users** menu item, select the **Mitchell Admin** user from the list, and **Edit** the form:

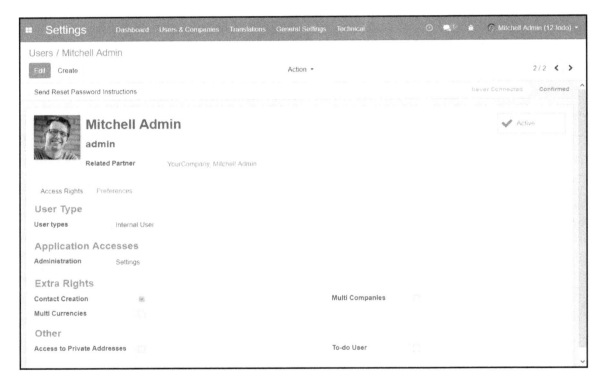

2. In the **Access Rights** tab, in the **Other** section, we can see a **To-do User** checkbox to enable the security group for this user. Select it, and **Save** the form.

If everything was done correctly, you should be able to see the to-do top menu; use it to add to-do items. We should see only our own items and won't be able to access other users'.

Security record rules

When given access to a Model, by default users will be able to access all its records. But in some cases, we need to restrict the particular records each user should be able to access. This is possible using record rules, which define domain filters to automatically be enforced when performing read or write operations.

For example, in our to-do app, the **To-do Items** are expected to be private, so we want users to only be able to see their own items. We need a record rule to filter only the records created by the current user:

- The `create_uid` field is automatically added by the framework, and stores the user that created the record, and we can use it to see who owns each record
- The current user is available in the `user` variable, a `user` variable browse object available in the context where the `domain` filter is evaluated

We can use this in a `domain` expression to achieve our goal: `[('create_uid', '=', user.id)]`.

Record rules are available in the **Settings | Technical | Security | Record Rules** menu. Navigate there and create a new **Record Rules**, with the following values:

- **Name**: A descriptive title, such as `To-do Own Items`
- **Object**: Select the Model from the list, **To-do Item** in our case
- **Access Rights**: The actions where the rule will be applied; leave all checked
- **Rule Definition**: The **Domain Filter**, `[('create_uid', '=', user.id)]`
- **Groups**: The security groups it applies to; select and add the **To-do User** group

This is how the **Record Rules** definition will look like:

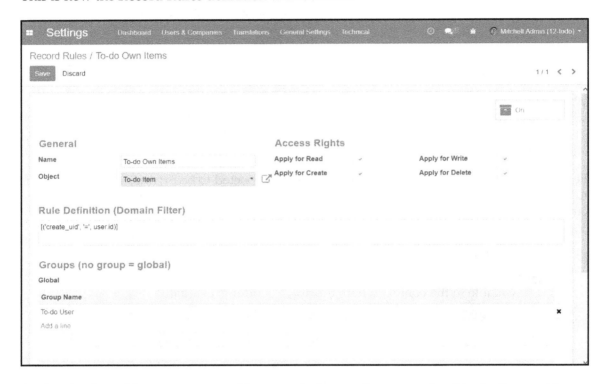

And we're done. You can now try this new rule by creating a couple of to-do items with both the **Admin** and **Demo** users. Each should be able to see only their own items. The **Record Rules** can be switched off through the box button in the upper-right corner of the form. If you try that and check the to-do item list, you should see all the items from all users.

The superuser account

In previous Odoo versions, the `admin` user was special and bypassed access security. In version 12 this has changed, and the `admin` account belongs to all app security groups, but is a regular user. We still have a superuser that bypasses access security, but it doesn't have a login.

We can still work as a superuser. When logged in as a user with the **Admin \ Setting** group, the **Become Superuser** option is in the developer menu, Or, use the **Login as superuser** hidden option in the login screen, visible if the Developer mode is enabled.

When the superuser is enabled, in the upper-right corner the current user is shown as OdooBot, and the colors in the upper-right area change to yellow and black stripes, to make it clear the superuser is enabled.

This should be used only if absolutely necessary. The fact that the superuser bypasses access security can lead to data inconsistencies, for example in a multi-company context, and should be avoided.

Creating menu items

We now have a Model to store the **To-do Items**, and want to have it available in the user interface. Adding a menu item will achieve that.

We will create a top-level menu item that directly opens the to-do list. Some apps, such as **Contacts**, can work like this, but others have submenu items, shown in the top bar.

Changes in Odoo 12
In the community edition, the menu items below the first level are now shown in the top bar, like in the EE. In previous versions, the CE presented these menu items on the left-hand side of the screen.

Menu definitions are in the **Settings** application, in **Technical** | **User Interface** | **Menu Items**:

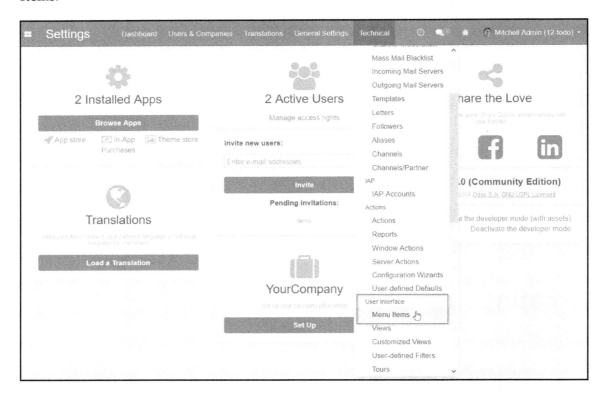

Create a new menu item using the following values:

1. **Menu**: To-do
2. **Parent Menu**: (empty)
3. In the **Action** field, select **ir.actions.act_window**, and in the selection list on the right, click **Create and Edit** to open a form for the related **Window Actions**
4. Set the following values on the **Window Actions** form:
   - **Action name**: To-do Items
   - **Object**: x_todo_item (the technical name of the target Model)

At this point the Action definition should look like this:

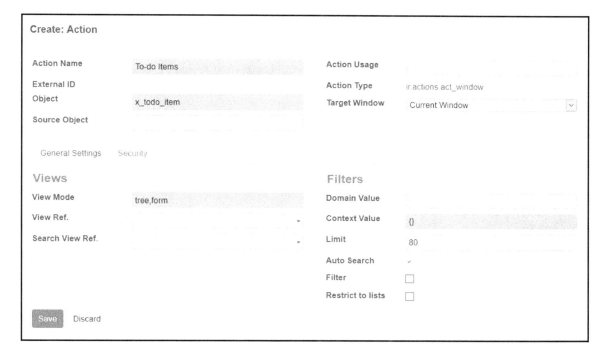

5. **Save** all the forms we opened, and the menu tree for our **To-do** application should be ready to use.

To see changes in the menu, we need to reload the web client. In most browsers, you can use the *F5* key for this. We can now use this menu item to access and interact with the to-do items model. We haven't created any view for it yet, but the Odoo framework is nice enough to automatically generate some basic views for us:

In our case, an action was added directly to a top-level menu item, with no child menu items. But menus can be a tree of menu items, with parent/child relations. The leaf menu items have a related **Action**, defining what happens when it is selected. This **Action Name** is what will be used as the title of the presented views.

There are several **Action Type** available, and the most important ones are window, reports, and server actions. **Window Actions** are the most frequent ones, and are used to present views in the web client. Report actions are used to run reports and server actions are used to define automated tasks.

At this point, we are concerned with **Window Actions** that are used to display views. The Menu Item we just created for the to-do item uses a **Window Actions**, which was created directly from the Menu Item form. We can also view and edit it from the **Settings** | **Technical** | **Actions** menu options. In this particular case, we are interested in the **Window Actions** menu option.

 In many cases, it is more convenient to use the **Edit Action** option in the **Developer Tools**, providing a convenient shortcut to edit the **Window Actions** that was used to access the current view.

Now we want to create our views, so that's what we will be working on in the next section.

Creating views

We have created the **To-do Items** Model and made it available in the user interface with a Menu Item. Next, we will be creating the two essential views for it—a list (also called a **tree**) and a form.

List views

We will now create a list view:

1. In **Settings**, navigate to **Technical** | **User Interface** | **Views** and create a new record with the following values:

    - **View Name**: To-do List View
    - **View Type**: **Tree**
    - **Model**: x_todo_item

This is how the View definition is expected to look like:

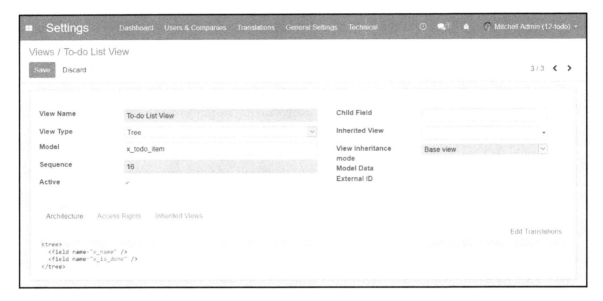

2. In the **Architecture** tab, we should write XML with the view structure. Use the following XML code:

```
<tree>
  <field name="x_name" />
  <field name="x_is_done" />
</tree>
```

The basic structure of a list view is quite simple—a `<tree>` element containing one or more `<field>` elements for each of the columns to display in the list view.

We can do a few more interesting things with list views, and will explore them in more detail in `Chapter 10`, *Backend Views – Design the User Interface.*

Form views

Next, we will create the form view:

1. Create another View record, using the following values:

    - **View Name:** To-do Form View
    - **View Type:** **Form**
    - **Model:** x_todo_item

If we don't specify the **View Type**, it will be auto-detected from the view definition.

2. In the **Architecture** tab, type the following XML code:

```
<form>
  <group>
    <field name="x_name" />
    <field name="x_is_done" />
    <field name="x_work_team_ids"
           widget="many2many_tags"
           context="{'default_x_is_work_team': True}" />
  </group>
</form>
```

The form view structure has a root `<form>` element, containing elements such as `<field>`, among others that we will learn about in `Chapter 10`, *Backend Views – Design the User Interface*. Here, we also chose a specific widget for the work team field, to be displayed as tag buttons instead of a list grid.

We added the `widget` attribute to the Work Team field, to have the team members presented as button-like tags.

By default, relational fields allow you to directly create a new record to be used in the relationship. This means that we are allowed to create new **Partner** directly from the **Work Team** field. But if we do so, they won't have the `Is Work Team?` flag enabled, which can cause inconsistencies.

For a better user experience, we can have this flag set by default for these cases. This is done with the `context` attribute, used to pass session information to the next View, such as default values to be used. This will be discussed in detail in later chapters, and for now we just need to know that it is a dictionary of key-value pairs. Values prefixed with `default_` provide the default value for the corresponding field.

So in our case, the expression needed to set a default value for the partner's `Is Work Team?` flag is `{'default_x_is_work_team': True}`.

That's it. If we now try the **To-Do** menu option, and create a new item or open an existing one from the list, we will see the form we just added.

Search views

We can also make predefined filter and grouping options available, in the search box in the upper-right corner of the list view. Odoo considers these view elements also, and so they are defined in **Views** records, just like lists and forms are.

As you may already know by now, **Views** can be edited either in the **Settings | Technical | User Interface** menu, or from the contextual **Developer Tools** menu. Let's go for the latter now; navigate to the to-do list, click on the **Developer Tools** icon in the upper-right corner, and select **Edit Search view** from the available options:

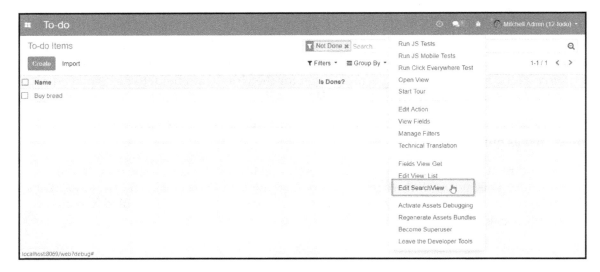

Since no search view is yet defined for the **To-do Items** Model, we will see an empty form, inviting us to create the first one. Fill in these values and save it:

1. **View Name**: Some meaningful description, such as `To-do Items Filter`
2. **View Type**: **Search**
3. **Model**: `x_todo_item`
4. **Architecture**: Add this XML code:

```
<search>
 <filter name="item_not_done"
         string="Not Done"
         domain="[('x_is_done', '=', False)]" />
</search>
```

If we now open the to-do list from the menu, so that it is reloaded, we will see that our predefined filter is now available from the Filters button below the search box. If we type **Not Done** inside the search box, it will also show a suggested selection.

It would be nice to have this filter enabled by default, and disable it when needed. Just like default field values, we can also use `context` to set default filters.

When we click on the **To-do** menu option, it runs a **Window Actions** to open the To-do list view. This **Window Actions** can set a context value, signaling the **Views** to enable a search filter by default. Let's try this:

1. Click on the **To-do** menu option to go to the **To-do** list.
2. Click on the **Developer Tools** icon and select the **Edit Action** option. This will open the **Window Actions** used to open the current **Views**. In the lower-right corner, there is a **Filter** section, where we have the **Domain** and **Context** fields.

The **Domain** allows to set a fixed filter on the records shown, which can't be removed by the user. We don't want to use that. Instead, we want to enable the `item_not_done` filter created before by default, which can be deselected whenever the user wishes to. To enable a filter by default, add a context key with its name prefixed with `search_default_`, in this case `{'search_default_item_not_done': True}`.

If we click on the **To-do** menu option now, we should see the **Not Done** filter enabled by default on the search box.

Summary

In this chapter, not only did we present an overview of how Odoo components are organized, but we also made use of the developer mode to dive into the Odoo internals and understand how these components work together to create applications.

We used these tools to build a simple application, with Models, Views, and the corresponding Menu. We also learned the usefulness of the **Developer Tools** to inspect existing applications or make quick customizations directly from the user interface.

In the next chapter, we will start getting more serious about Odoo development, and will learn to set up and organize our development environment.

Questions

1. What are the relevant layers to consider when designing an Odoo application?
2. How is the developer mode enabled?
3. Where do you create a new data model?
4. How do you make a new data model available for end users to create and edit records?
5. How do you add a field to an existing form?
6. What is a domain, and where can it be used?
7. How can you set default values on the form you are navigating to?
8. How do you give a user access to a model?
9. How can you add a Category field to the To-do Items, with possible values selectable from an options list? (The options list is editable and can be expanded by users).
10. How can you extend the to-do category model, so that the list of categories is specific for each user?

2
Preparing the Development Environment

Before we dive into Odoo development, we need to set up our development environment and learn the basic administration tasks for it.

In this chapter, we will learn how to set up the working environment where we will build our Odoo applications. We will set up an Ubuntu system to host the development server instance. This can be a cloud server, a local network server, or a subsystem in your Windows 10 computer.

We will learn how to do the following:

- Set up the host computer, either an Ubuntu system or a Windows 10 system, with the Windows Subsystem for Linux
- Install Odoo from source, including the installation of the database and the system dependencies
- Manage Odoo databases includes creating, dropping, and copying
- Configure the Odoo server options
- Find and install community add-on modules
- Use virtual environments to manage different Odoo versions and projects
- Enable the server developer mode to simplify development tasks

Technical requirements

This chapter will guide you to install Odoo from source in your development computer. Ideally, we need an Ubuntu 18.04 operating system. A Windows 10 system is also an option, since we will explain how to set up Ubuntu in the Windows Subsystem for Linux.

Some reference code for this chapter can be found in the book's GitHub repository, `https:/` `/github.com/PacktPublishing/Odoo-12-Development-Essentials-Fourth-Edition`, in the `ch02/` directory.

Setting up a host for the Odoo server

A Debian/Ubuntu system is recommended to run Odoo servers. While Odoo is multi-platform and can run on a variety of operating systems, it's also true that the Odoo R&D team considers Debian the reference deployment platform. In fact, Odoo's own SaaS operations are known to be Debian-based. It is also the most popular choice in the community. This means that it will be easier to find help or advice if you use Debian or Ubuntu. Even if you're from a Windows background, it will be important that you have some knowledge about it.

You will still be able to work from your favorite desktop system, be it Windows, Mac, or other Linux flavors, such as CentOS.

 Keep in mind that these instructions are intended to set up a new system for development. If you want to try some of them in an existing system, always take a backup ahead of time in order to be able to restore it in case something goes wrong.

Installing the Windows Subsystem for Linux

On a Windows system, the simplest solution is to use the **Windows Subsystem for Linux** (**WSL**), available on Windows 10. With it, we can have an Ubuntu system running inside Windows, capable of performing everything we need for Odoo development. More information on the WSL can be found at `https://docs.microsoft.com/en-us/windows/` `wsl/about`.

The WSL is a Windows 10 optional feature, available in recent builds, and must first be enabled. After that, we should install Ubuntu from the Windows store. The official instructions for that are at `https://docs.microsoft.com/en-us/windows/wsl/install-` `win10`.

At the time of writing, these are the steps needed to complete the installation:

- Our first step is to ensure that the WSL optional feature is enabled. Open PowerShell as administrator and run the following:

```
Enable-WindowsOptionalFeature -Online -FeatureName
        Microsoft-Windows-Subsystem-Linux
```

The preceding command should be typed in a single line. Then, restart the computer when prompted.

After this, we should install the Ubuntu Windows app. The simplest way to do that is to open the Windows store and search for Ubuntu. When writing this book, we used the latest Ubuntu **long-term support** (**LTS**) release, 18.04. Follow the installation process, including setting up a user account and corresponding password.

Running the Ubuntu application will open a Window bash command line where we can perform the same commands we would use on an Ubuntu system. Remember the user and password configured during the Ubuntu installation, since they will be prompted for whenever you need to perform actions with elevated privileges (for example, running `sudo`).

Installing a Linux server

We can also install Linux in our machine, in a computer in our network or in a cloud private server.

We will need a Debian-based server for our development Odoo server. If these are your first steps with Linux, note that Ubuntu is a Debian-based Linux distribution, so they are very similar.

Odoo is guaranteed to work with the current stable version of Debian or Ubuntu. At the time of writing, these are Debian 9 Stretch and Ubuntu 18.04 LTS Bionic Beaver.

We do recommend you choose Ubuntu, since it is easier to install than Debian. Ubuntu ISO images can be downloaded from `https://www.ubuntu.com`. It is recommended to use the latest LTS version available.

If you're just getting started with Linux, a ready-to-use image can be easier to start with. TurnKey Linux provides easy-to-use preinstalled images in several formats, including ISO. The ISO format will work with any virtualization software you choose, even on a bare-metal machine you might have. A good option might be the LAPP image, which includes Python and PostgreSQL, and can be found at `http://www.turnkeylinux.org/lapp`.

We probably want an OpenSSH server installed, to be able to remotely work on the server. Ubuntu has that option available in the setup assistant, but it can also be installed with the following command:

```
$ sudo apt-get install openssh-server
```

After this, we can use any **Secure Shell** (**SSH**) client to connect to our Odoo host. In a Windows machine, a popular option is to use PuTTY. It can be downloaded from http://www.putty.org.

We can check our server's IP address using the following:

```
$ ip addr show
```

Using an SSH client not only allows you to work on a remote server, it is also more comfortable to work with than the virtual machine console screens, providing better copy/paste support and allowing you to choose window size, font type, and so on.

Installing Odoo from source

In Chapter 1, *Quick Start Using the Developer Mode*, we discussed the different options available to quickly get Odoo running on our computer. We want to go a little deeper, and run Odoo directly from the source code.

Odoo is built using the Python programming language, and it uses the PostgreSQL database for data storage; these are the two main requirements of an Odoo host. To run Odoo from source, we will first need to install the Python libraries it depends on. The Odoo source code can then be downloaded from GitHub. While we can download a ZIP file or tarball, we will see that it's better if we get the sources using the Git version control application; it'll help us to have it installed on our Odoo host as well.

 The exact dependency installation may vary depending on your operating system and on the Odoo version you are installing. If you have trouble with any of the previous steps, make sure you check the official documentation at https://www.odoo.com/documentation/12.0/setup/install.html. Instructions for previous editions are also available there.

Installing the PostgreSQL database

Odoo needs a PostgreSQL server to work with. The typical development setup is to have PostgreSQL installed in the same machine as Odoo. We still need to install the PostgreSQL database, required to run Odoo:

```
$ sudo apt update
$ sudo apt install postgresql # Install PostgreSQL
$ sudo su -c "createuser -s $USER" postgres # Create db superuser
```

The last command creates a PostgreSQL user for the current system user. We need that so that we can create and drop the databases to be used by our Odoo instances.

If you are running Ubuntu inside the WSL, note that system services are not automatically started. This means that you may need to manually start the PostgreSQL service before running any command that needs a database connection, such as `createuser` or starting an Odoo server. To manually start the PostgreSQL service, run the following: `sudo service postgresql start`.

Installing Odoo system dependencies

To be able to run, Odoo needs some system packages and software. To get the version controlled source code, we need Git. To install and run Odoo, we need Python 3.5 or later, `pip` for Python 3, and a few system dependencies needed for some Python packages:

```
$ sudo apt update
$ sudo apt upgrade
$ sudo apt install git  # Install Git
$ sudo apt install python3-dev python3-pip # Python 3 for dev
$ sudo apt install build-essential libxslt-dev \
libzip-dev libldap2-dev libsasl2-dev libssl-dev
```

Odoo releases 9, 10, and 11 require the `less` CSS preprocessor. So, you need to install it if you need to also these Odoo versions:

```
$ sudo apt install npm  # Install Node.js and its package manager
$ sudo ln -s /usr/bin/nodejs /usr/bin/node  # node runs Node.js
$ sudo npm install -g less less-plugin-clean-css  # Install less
```

The preceding command is not required to run Odoo 12, but it is often the case that you need to also work on these versions and, if this is the case, you will end up needing it.

Changed in Odoo 12

The CSS preprocessor used changed from less to Sass. This means that less is no longer required to run Odoo. The Sass compiler does not require additional installation steps, since it is made available by libsass-python, a Python dependency of Odoo 12. The reasons for the change include: bootstrap 4 changing from less to Sass, existing Python bindings, and avoiding Node.js (or Ruby) dependencies.

Installing Odoo from source

To keep things organized, we will work in a /odoo-dev directory inside our home directory. Throughout the book, we will assume that the /odoo-dev is the directory where your Odoo server is installed.

Odoo 12 uses Python 3, specifically 3.5 or later. This means that on the command line, we should use python3 and pip3, instead of python and pip.

Changed in Odoo 11

Starting from version 11, Odoo runs on Python 3.5 or later. Odoo 11 still runs on Python 2.7, but Odoo 12 only runs on Python 3.5+. Odoo 10 and before only run on Python 2.7.

To install Odoo from source, we start by cloning the Odoo source code directly from GitHub:

```
$ mkdir ~/odoo-dev  # Create a directory to work in
$ cd ~/odoo-dev  # Go into our work directory
$ git clone https://github.com/odoo/odoo.git -b 12.0 \
  --depth=1  # Get Odoo sources
```

The ~ symbol is a shortcut for the user's home directory, such as /home/daniel.

If using Windows Subsystem for Linux, the files in the home directory are stored in a difficult to find place, inside the Windows system folder. A way to avoid this issue is to store our work files in the Windows folder of our preference, and then use a symbolic link for it (similar to a shortcut) in the Linux subsystem. For example, `mkdir /mnt/c/Users/Public/odoo-dev` creates the `C:\Users\Public\odoo-dev` working directory, and then `ln -s /mnt/c/Users/Public/odoo-dev ~/odoo-dev` creates the `~/odoo-dev` Linux directory, which is actually a link to the Windows directory. Now, you can run all commands on `~/odoo-dev`, such as the previous `git clone`, and the files are all also available in `C:\Users\Public\odoo-dev`.

The `-b 12.0` option in the Git command explicitly downloads the 12.0 branch of Odoo. At the time of writing, this is redundant since it is the default branch; however, this may change. The `--depth=1` option tells Git to download only the last revision, instead of the full change history, making the download significantly smaller and faster.

> To download the missing commit history later, you can run `git fetch --unshallow`.

Before we can run Odoo, we need to install the Python dependencies declared in the `requirements.txt` file:

```
$ pip3 install -r ~/odoo-dev/odoo/requirements.txt
```

Many of these dependencies have Debian packages available to install them, such as `python3-lxml`. A valid alternative is to install them using the `apt` package manager. This has the advantage of automatically installing the system dependencies when necessary. The list of dependencies used can be found in the `./odoo/debian/control` file.

A few additional Python packages, not included in `requirements.txt`, can be installed to suppress warning messages or enable additional features:

```
$ pip3 install num2words phonenumbers psycopg2-binary watchdog xlwt
```

The `pip3` utility can be installed in several different ways: the system package way and the native Python way. If a `pip3` command fails with an import error, reinstalling it in your system may solve the issue. The command for that is this: `sudo python3 -m pip uninstall pip && sudo apt install python3-pip --reinstall`.

Now, we can start the Odoo server instance by running the following:

```
$ ~/odoo-dev/odoo/odoo-bin
```

To stop the server and return to Command Prompt, press *Ctrl + C*.

Changed in Odoo 10
The script used to start Odoo is now `./odoo-bin`. In previous Odoo versions, it was `./odoo.py`.

By default, Odoo instances listen on port `8069`, so if we point a browser to `http://<server-address>:8069`, we will reach these instances.

As developers, we will need to work with several databases, so it's more convenient to create them from the command line, and we will learn how to do this. Now, press *Ctrl + C* in the terminal to stop the Odoo server and get back to Command Prompt.

Initializing a new Odoo database

To create and initialize an Odoo database with the Odoo data schema, we should run the Odoo server using the `-d` option:

```
$ ~/odoo-dev/odoo/odoo-bin -d testdb
```

This may take a minute to initialize the `testdb` database, and it will end with an INFO log message, **Modules loaded**. Note that it might not be the last log message, and it can be in the last three or four lines. With this, the server will be ready to listen to client requests.

Changed in Odoo 9
Since Odoo 9, the database is automatically created if it doesn't exist yet. In version 8, this was not so, and you needed to create the database manually, using the PostgreSQL `createdb` command.

By default, this will initialize the database with demonstration data, which is often useful for development databases. This is the equivalent to having the **Load demonstration data** checkbox ticked when creating a new database from the user interface.

To initialize a database without demonstration data, add the `--without-demo=all` option to the command.

At the time of writing, an issue with PostgreSQL specific to the Ubuntu WSL environment prevented the clean creation of new databases. The workaround for this is to manually create an empty database with the `createdb 12-library` command. This will show repeated messages saying `WARNING: could not flush dirty data: Function not implemented`. Despite the warning messages, the new database was correctly created. Press *Ctrl + C* to interrupt the warnings, and now you will be able to run the command to start Odoo and initialize the new database.

To be able to create a new database, your user must be a PostgreSQL superuser. The PostgreSQL setup script used in the *Installing Odoo from source* section takes care of that.

For a development environment, it is fine for the user running the Odoo instance to be a database superuser. However, for a production environment, Odoo security best practices recommend to never run a production instance with a database user that is a superuser.

Now that we have a running Odoo instance, we can access it by opening the `http://<server-name>:8069` URL with a web browser. This should present us with the Odoo login screen. If you don't know your server name, type the `hostname` command in the terminal in order to find it or use the `ifconfig` command to find the IP address.

The default administrator account is `admin`, with its password as `admin`. Upon logging in, you are presented with the **Apps** menu, displaying the available applications.

To stop the Odoo server instance and return to the command line, press *Ctrl + C* at the Terminal window running the server. Pressing the up arrow key will bring up the previous shell command, so it's a quick way to start Odoo again with the same options. The *Ctrl + C* keys followed by the up arrow key and *Enter* is a frequently used combination to restart the Odoo server during development.

Managing Odoo databases

We've seen how to create and initialize new Odoo databases from the command line. There are more commands worth knowing about for managing databases.

Although the Odoo server automatically takes care of managing databases, we can manually create PostgreSQL databases from the command line, using the following:

```
$ createdb MyDB
```

More interestingly, Odoo can also create a new database by copying an existing one, using the --template option. For this to work, the copied database can't have open connections to it, so make sure your Odoo instance is stopped and there is no other connection open for it. The command to use looks like this:

```
$ createdb --template=MyDB MyDB2
```

In fact, every time we create a database, a template is used. If none is specified, a predefined one called template1 is used.

To list the existing databases in your system, use the PostgreSQL psql utility with the -l option:

```
$ psql -l
```

Running the preceding command will list the databases we have created so far. If you followed the previous commands, you should see MyDB and MyDB2 listed . The list will also display the encoding used in each database. The default is **UTF-8**, which is the encoding needed for Odoo databases.

To remove a database you no longer need (or want to recreate), use the dropdb command:

```
$ dropdb MyDB2
```

Now, you know the basics to work with databases. To learn more about PostgreSQL, refer to the official documentation at http://www.postgresql.org/docs/.

Warning

The dropdb command will irrevocably destroy your data. Be careful when using it and always keep backups of important databases before using this command.

More server configuration options

The Odoo server supports quite a few other options. We can check all the available options with --help:

```
$ ~/odoo-dev/odoo/odoo-bin --help
```

We will review some of the most important options in the following sections. Let's start by looking at how the currently active options can be saved in a configuration file.

Odoo server configuration files

Most of the options can be saved in a configuration file. By default, Odoo will use the .odoorc file. In Linux systems, its default location is in the home directory ($HOME), and in the Windows distribution, it is in the same directory as the executable used to launch Odoo.

 In older Odoo/OpenERP versions, the name for the default configuration file was .openerp-serverrc. For backward compatibility, Odoo will still use this if it's present and no .odoorc file is found.

In a clean installation, the .odoorc configuration file is not automatically created. We should use the --save option to create the default configuration file, if it doesn't exist yet, and store the current instance configuration into it:

```
$ ~/odoo-dev/odoo/odoo-bin --save --stop-after-init
```

Here, we also used the --stop-after-init option to stop the server after it finishes its actions. This option is often used when running tests or asking to run a module upgrade to check whether it is installed correctly.

 Command options can be shortened as long as they remain unambiguous. For example, the --stop-after-init option can be shortened to --stop.

Now, we can inspect what was saved in this default configuration file:

```
$ more ~/.odoorc  # show the configuration file
```

This will show all the configuration options available with their default values. Editing them will be effective the next time you start an Odoo instance. Type q to quit and go back to the prompt.

We can also choose to use a specific configuration file, using the --conf=<filepath> option (or -c <filepath>). Configuration files don't need to have all the options you've just seen. Only the ones that actually change a default value need to be there.

Changing the listening port

The `--http-port=<port>` command option (or just `-p <port>`) allows us to change the listening port of a server instance from the default `8069`. This can be used to run more than one instance at the same time, on the same machine.

Changed in Odoo 11

The `--http-port` server option was introduced in Odoo 11 and replaces the old `--xmlrpc-port` option, used in previous versions.

Let's try this out. Open two terminal windows. On the first, run this:

```
$ ~/odoo-dev/odoo/odoo-bin --http-port=8070
```

Run the following command on the second terminal:

```
$ ~/odoo-dev/odoo/odoo-bin --http-port=8071
```

There you go, two Odoo instances on the same server listening on different ports! The two instances can use the same or different databases, depending on the configuration parameters used, and the two could be running the same or different versions of Odoo.

Different Odoo versions must work with different databases. Trying to use the same database with different Odoo versions won't work, since major versions have incompatible database schemas.

Database selection options

When developing with Odoo, it is common to work with several databases, and sometimes even with different Odoo versions. Stopping and starting different server instances on the same port, and switching between different databases, can cause web client sessions to behave improperly. This is because the browser stores session cookies.

Accessing our instance using a browser window running in private mode can help avoid some of these problems.

Another good practice is to enable a database filter on the server instance to ensure that it only allows requests for the database we want to work with, ignoring all others.

Changed in Odoo 11

Since Odoo 11, the `--database` (or `-d`) server option accepts a comma-separated list of database names, and setting the `--database` option automatically also sets the `--db-filter` option, so that only these databases can be used by that server instance. For versions before Odoo 11, we need to use `--db-filter` to limit the databases accessible through this server.

The `--db-filter` option limits the databases that an Odoo server instance can work with. It accepts a regular expression to be used as a filter for valid database names. To match an exact name, the expression should begin with ^ and end with $.

For example, to allow only the `testdb` database, we would use this command:

```
$ ~/odoo-dev/odoo/odoo-bin --db-filter=^testdb$
```

It is a good practice for the `--database` and `--db-filter` options to match the same database. In fact, since Odoo 11, this is the default, since setting `--database` by default sets the corresponding `--db-filter`.

Managing server log messages

The `--log-level` option allows us to set the log verbosity. This can be very useful to understand what is going on in the server. For example, to enable the debug log level, use the `--log-level=debug` option.

The following log levels can be particularly interesting:

- `debug_sql` to inspect SQL queries generated by the server
- `debug_rpc` to detail requests received by the server
- `debug_rpc_answer` to detail responses sent by the server

In fact, `--log-level` is a simplified way to set the Odoo logging verbosity. You might like to know that the more complete `--log-handler` option allows you to selectively turn on/off specific loggers.

By default, the log output is directed to standard output (your console screen), but it can be directed to a log file with the `--logfile=<filepath>` option.

Installing additional modules

Making new modules available in an Odoo instance so they can be installed is something that newcomers to Odoo frequently find confusing. But it doesn't have to be, so let's get familiar with that.

Finding community modules

There are many Odoo modules available on the internet. The Odoo app store at apps.odoo.com is a catalog of modules that can be downloaded and installed on your system. Another important resource is the **Odoo Community Association (OCA)** maintained modules, also available on GitHub at https://github.com/OCA/. The OCA is a non-profit organization created to coordinate community contributions, promoting software quality, development best practices, and open source values. You can learn more about the OCA at https://odoo-community.org/.

To add a module to an Odoo installation, we could just copy it into the addons directory alongside the official modules. In our case, the addons directory is at ~/odoo-dev/odoo/addons/. However, this is not a good idea. Our Odoo installation is a Git version-controlled code repository, and we want to keep it synchronized with the upstream GitHub repository. Polluting it with foreign modules will make it hard to manage.

Instead, we can select one or more additional locations for modules, which will also be used when the Odoo server looks for modules. Not only can we keep our custom modules in a different directory, without having them mixed with the official ones, we can also have them organized in several directories.

We can try this now by downloading the code from this book, available in GitHub, and making those add-on modules available in our Odoo installation. To get the source code from GitHub, run the following commands:

```
$ cd ~/odoo-dev
$ git clone
https://github.com/PacktPublishing/Odoo-12-Development-Essentials-Fourth-Ed
ition.git library
```

After this, we will have a new /library directory alongside the /odoo directory containing the modules. Now, we need to let Odoo know about this new module directory.

Configuring the add-ons path

The Odoo server has a configuration option called `addons_path` to set where the server should look for modules. By default, this points to the `/addons` directory, where the Odoo server is running. We can provide not only one, but a list of directories where modules can be found. This allows us to keep our custom modules in a different directory, without having them mixed with the official add-ons.

Let's start the server with an add-ons path that includes our new module directory:

```
$ cd ~/odoo-dev/odoo
$ ./odoo-bin -d 12-library --addons-path="../library,./addons"
```

If you look closer at the server log, you will notice a line reporting the add-ons path in use: `INFO ? odoo: addons paths: [...]`. Confirm that it contains our `library/` directory.

Installing Odoo in a Python virtual environment

It is a common case among Odoo developers to maintain code for several Odoo versions. Some organizational effort is needed to keep these projects alongside each other and working on the same development machine. And, there is some context switching needed when changing from one version to another. For example, the Odoo start executable is now `odoo-bin`, but in older versions it was `odoo.py`, and you need to remember that. With the move to Python 3, this can be even more confusing; you need to choose whether to use `python` / `pip` or `python3` / `pip3`, depending on the Odoo server version you are working on at that moment.

Python includes `virtualenv`, a tool to manage independent Python environments on the same machine. Each environment has its own Python executable and installed libraries. You just need to activate the environment you want to work with; from that point on, the `python` and `pip` commands will run the executable from that environment, and the Python libraries installed in it.

To ensure that `virtualenv` is available in our Debian/Ubuntu, run the following command:

```
$ sudo apt install virtualenv
```

Suppose we are working in the ~/odoo-dev directory, and we have Odoo 12 source code cloned at ~/odoo-dev/odoo. We will now create an virtual environment for our Odoo 12 project:

```
$ virtualenv -p python3 ~/odoo-dev/odoo12env
$ source ~/odoo-dev/odoo12env/bin/activate
```

The first command creates the odoo12env virtual environment, which uses Python 3. The corresponding directory is created, to store the corresponding files. The environment directory has a bin/ subdirectory including, among other things, the scripts to activate and deactivate this environment.

The second command uses the source Linux command to execute the environment's activate script. This will change the current context, so that the commands available from the environment's bin/ subdirectory are used first. It also changes Command Prompt, so that it shows the current activated environment. At this point, your terminal session should look like this:

```
(odoo12denv) $ python --version
Python 3.5.2
(odoo12denv) $ which python
/home/daniel/odoo-dev/odoo12env/bin/python
```

Once we have a virtual environment activated, we can install Odoo in it. This can be done using pip with the Odoo source code:

```
(odoo12denv) $ pip install -e ~/odoo-dev/odoo
```

The preceding command will install the Odoo source code at ~/odoo-dev/odoo, and the corresponding dependencies, in this virtual environment.

The -e option is important; it makes it an **editable** installation. Instead of copying a snapshot of the Odoo code into the virtual environment, it just keeps a reference to the original location of the Odoo code. Since the original source code is being used, we see in this environment the effect of changes in the source code.

The Odoo Python dependencies are automatically installed, so there is no need to manually install the packages in the requirements.txt file.

And, we can use pip to install any additional Python libraries we might need:

```
(odoo12denv) $ pip install phonenumbers num2words psycopg2-binary watchdog
xlwt
```

Notice that we don't need to remember whether we are working with Python 2 or Python 3. In a virtual environment, the `pip` command will always point to the correct version.

Next, we can run Odoo. The `pip` installation creates a `bin/odoo` command, which can be executed from anywhere, without the need to reference the directory where the source code is.

 If you decide to use virtual environments, whenever you come across a command using `odoo-bin` to run Odoo commands, you can replace it with just `odoo`.

The following command will start and stop your installed version of Odoo, printing a few log messages that can be useful to confirm things such as the Odoo version and the add-ons paths being used:

```
(odoo12denv) $ odoo --stop-after-init
```

A good practice is to keep the configuration files for your projects inside the virtual directory environment. This will initialize a `12-library` database for our project and create the corresponding `12-library.conf` file:

```
(odoo12denv) $ odoo -c ~/odoo-dev/odoo12-env/12-library.conf \
-d 12-library --addons-path=~/odoo-dev/library --save --stop
```

From now on, to start an Odoo server for our Library project, we use the following:

```
(odoo12denv) $ odoo -c ~/odoo-dev/odoo12-env/12-library.conf
```

Finally, when we are done, we can deactivate the environment, running the corresponding command:

```
(odoo12denv) $ deactivate
```

Now, suppose we also want to work on an Odoo 10 project on the same machine, which uses Python 2.7. Let's create that environment and install Odoo 10 in it:

```
$ cd ~/odoo-dev
$ git clone https://github.com/odoo/odoo.git -b 10.0 --depth=1 odoo10
$ virtualenv odoo10env
$ source odoo10env/bin/activate
(odoo10env) $ pip install -e ./odoo10
(odoo10env) $ odoo --version
(odoo10env) $ deactivate  # To finish working with this env.
```

To make it easier to switch between Odoo versions, we make another clone of the Odoo source, for branch 10.0, in the ~/odoo-dev/odoo10 directory. We then create the virtual environment, activate it, and use pip to make an editable installation of Odoo 10. virtualenv was used with no specific Python version (-p option), and so it defaults to Python 2, the version needed for Odoo 10.

If Python 2 is not available in your system, which is the case for out-of-the-box Ubuntu 18.04, you should install it in order to be able to run older Odoo versions:

```
$ sudo apt install python-dev
```

Downloading and installing add-on modules from PyPI

Community-contributed Odoo add-ons can be packaged as Python libraries, published to **Python Package Index (PyPI)**, and installed using pip like other libraries. For this to work, Odoo automatically adds the Python site-packages/ directory, where libraries are installed, to the Odoo addons path configuration. This packaging can be done using the **setuptools-odoo** tool (https://pypi.org/project/setuptools-odoo).

This is used by the OCA projects (https://github.com/OCA) to package and publish add-on modules on PyPI . Since the same module can exist for different Odoo versions, a prefix with the Odoo version is added to the module name. For example, the odoo12-addon-partner-fax PyPI package is the partner_fax add-on module for Odoo 12, which simply adds a fax field to partner: https://pypi.org/project/odoo12-addon-partner-fax/.

To download this module (and dependencies) from PyPI, and then install it in the odoo12env environment, use the following:

```
$ source ~/odoo-dev/odoo12env/bin/activate
(odoo12denv) $ pip install odoo12-addon-partner-fax
(odoo12denv) $ odoo -c ~/odoo-dev/odoo12-env/12-library.conf \
-i partner_fax --stop
```

The server development mode

To make life easier for developers , Odoo has the additional `--dev=all` option to active a few developer-friendly features.

Changed in Odoo 10
The `--dev=...` option was introduced in Odoo 10. It replaces the simpler and less featured `--debug` option, available in versions before 10.

This enables a few handy features to speed up our development cycle. The most important are the following:

- Reload Python code automatically once a Python file is saved, avoiding a manual server restart
- Read view definitions directly from the XML files, avoiding manual module upgrades

The `--dev=all` option will bring up the Python debugger (`pdb`) when an exception is raised. It's useful for doing a postmortem analysis of a server error. Note that it doesn't have any effect on logger verbosity. More details on the Python debugger commands can be found at `https://docs.python.org/3/library/pdb.html#debugger-commands`.

The `--dev` option accepts a comma-separated list of options, although the `all` option will be suitable most of the time. By default, the Python debugger, `pdb`, is used. Some people might prefer to install and use alternative debuggers, for their improved features or usability. Odoo allows us to also specify a specific debugger to use. Some popular options are `ipdb` and `pudb`. In Chapter 8, *Business Logic – Supporting Business Processes*, we will address how to make use of debuggers in our Odoo development.

To be able to automatically detect the changes in code files, the server developer mode requires an additional dependency to be installed, `python3-watchdog`. Before you can use it in an Ubuntu/Debian system, you need to install it using the following command:

```
$ sudo apt-get install python3-watchdog
```

For versions before Odoo 11 running on Python 2, install `python-watchdog` instead. It can also be installed using `pip`, with the `pip install watchdog` command .

Summary

In this chapter, we learned how to set up an Ubuntu system to host Odoo and install it from the GitHub source code. We also learned how to create Odoo databases and run Odoo instances.

We should now have a functioning Odoo environment to work with and be comfortable with managing databases and instances.

With this in place, we're ready to go straight into action. In the next chapter, we will create our first Odoo module from scratch and understand the main elements it involves.

So, let's get started!

Your First Odoo Application 3

Developing in Odoo usually means creating our own modules. In this chapter, we will create our first Odoo application and learn the steps needed to make it available to Odoo and install it.

We will get started by learning the basics of the development workflow—we'll create and install a new module, and update it to apply the changes we make throughout the development iterations.

Odoo follows a **Model-View-Controller** (**MVC**)-like architecture, and we will go through the different layers to implement a library application.

In this chapter, we will cover the following topics:

- Creating a new module, where the features will be implemented
- Adding an app's characteristic features, the top menu item, and security groups
- Adding automated tests that will initially fail, but should run with success before we finish
- Implementing the model layer, defining the app's data structures, and corresponding access security definitions
- Implementing the backend view layer, describing the internal user interface
- Implementing the business logic layer, supporting data validation and automation
- Implementing the web layer, describing the user interface for visitors and external users

With this approach, you will be able to gradually learn about the basic building blocks that make up an application and experience the iterative process of building an Odoo module from scratch.

Technical requirements

This chapter requires you to have an Odoo server installed and be able to start it from the command line, to perform actions such as installing modules or running tests. If you don't know how to do this yet, `Chapter 2`, *Preparing the Development Environment,* can help you.

In this chapter, we will create our first Odoo application from a blank slate, so we won't need any additional code to get started.

The code for this chapter can be found in the book's GitHub repository, `https://github.com/PacktPublishing/Odoo-12-Development-Essentials-Fourth-Edition`, in the `library_app` directory.

Overview of the library project

To better explore the topics explained in this chapter, we will see them work in practice using a learning project. We will create a new Odoo app to manage a book library. This project will be used in every chapter, and each chapter will be an iteration, adding features to the app.

Here, we will create the first iteration of the library app; the first feature to implement will be a book catalogue.

Library books should have the following data:

- Title
- Author(s)
- Publishing company
- Date published
- Cover image
- ISBN, with a function to check whether it is a valid ISBN
- Active flag, used to identify the books that should be publicly available

The book catalogue should be editable by the library manager, and read-only for the library operators. The book catalogue should be available on a public web page, showing only active books.

This is a simple project, but provides a useful working feature, and will be enough for us to cover the main components involved in Odoo apps.

Creating a new addon module

An addon module is a directory containing the files that implement some Odoo features. It can add new features or modify existing ones.

The addon module directory must contain a manifest, or descriptor file, named __manifest__.py, plus the other module files.

Some module addons are featured as apps. These represent applications available for Odoo, and usually add their own top-level menu item. They provide the core elements for a functional area, such as CRM or HR. Because of this, they are highlighted in the Odoo Apps menu. On the other hand, non-app module addons are expected to add features to these apps.

If your module adds new or major functionality to Odoo, it probably should be an app. If the module just makes changes to the functionality of an existing app, it probably should be a regular addon module.

To create a new module, we will:

1. Ensure that the directory where we will work is in the Odoo server addons path
2. Create the module's directory, which contains the manifest file
3. Optionally add an icon to represent the module
4. Choose a license for the module, if we intend to distribute it

After this, we can install the modules, to confirm that the modules are visible to the Odoo server and that the server installs it correctly.

Preparing the addons path

An addons module is a directory that contains an Odoo manifest file, and provides a new app or an additional feature for an existing app. The addons module's path is a list of directories, where the Odoo server will look for available addons. By default, the addons path includes the official apps bundled with Odoo, in the odoo/addons directory, and the base module providing the core features, in the odoo/odoo/addons directory.

We should add our own modules in specific directories, whether created by us, or downloaded from the App Store or elsewhere. For the Odoo server to be able to discover them, we should add these directories to the Odoo addons paths.

Following the instructions in Chapter 2, *Preparing the Development Environment,* we should have the Odoo server code at ~/odoo-dev/odoo/. Best practices dictates that our code should be kept in its own directory, and never mixed up with Odoo's original code. So, to host our custom modules, we will use a new addons directory alongside Odoo, which should be included in the addons path: ~/odoo-dev/custom-addons.

To add the new addons directory to the Odoo server addons path, change the current directory, and start the server with the appropriate addons path configuration:

```
$ cd ~/odoo-dev
$ ./odoo/odoo-bin -d todo --addons-path="custom-addons,odoo/addons" --save
```

The --save option saves the options you used in a configuration file. This spares us from repeating them every time we restart the server; just run ./odoo-bin and the last saved option will be used. You can specify the configuration file and location to use (and save to) using the -c option.

Look closely at the server log. It should have an INFO ? odoo: addons paths:[...] line. It should include our custom-addons directory.

Remember to also include any other addons directories you might be using. For instance, if you have a ~/odoo-dev/extra directory that contains additional modules to be used, you might want to include them too, using the --addons-path option:

```
--addons-path="custom-addons,extra,odoo/addons"
```

Now we need the Odoo instance to acknowledge the new module we just added.

The paths used are relative to the current work directory. In configuration files, absolute paths should be used, and the --save option will do that conversion.

Creating the module directory and manifest

At this point, we should have the ~/odoo-dev/custom-addons directory prepared to receive our Odoo modules, and properly added to the addons path, so that the Odoo server will be able to find them.

Odoo includes a `scaffold` command to automatically create a new module directory, with a basic structure already in place. We won't use it here, as we will manually create our module structure. You can learn more about it with the following command:

```
$ ~/odoo-dev/odoo/odoo-bin scaffold --help
```

An Odoo `addon` module is a directory that contains a `__manifest__.py` descriptor file. It also needs to be Python importable, so it must also have a `__init__.py` file.

> In previous versions, this descriptor file was named `__openerp__.py` or `__odoo__.py`. These name are still supported but are deprecated.

The module's directory name is its technical name. We will use `library_app` for it. The technical name must be a valid Python identifier—it should begin with a letter and can only contain letters, numbers, and the underscore character.

Perform the following steps to initialize the new module:

1. If using the command line, we can initialize our module directory with an empty `__init__.py` file in it, with these commands:

```
$ mkdir -p ~/odoo-dev/custom-addons/library_app
$ touch ~/odoo-dev/custom-addons/library_app/__init__.py
```

2. Let's add the manifest file. It should contain only a Python dictionary, with about a dozen possible attributes. Of them, only the `name` attribute is required, but the `description` and `author` attributes are also highly advised. Create the `__manifest__.py` file, alongside the `__init__.py` file, with the following content:

```
{
    'name': 'Library Management',
    'description': 'Manage library book catalogue and
lending.',
    'author': 'Daniel Reis',
    'depends': ['base'],
    'application': True,
}
```

The `depends` attribute can have a list of other modules that are required. Odoo will install them automatically when this module is installed. It's not a mandatory attribute, but it's advised to always have it. If no particular dependencies are needed, we should depend on the core `base` module.

You should be careful to ensure all dependencies are explicitly set here; otherwise, the module may fail to install in a clean database (due to missing dependencies) or have loading errors if, by chance, the other required modules are loaded afterward.

For our application, we don't need any specific dependencies, so we depend on the `base` module only.

To be concise, we chose to use only some essential descriptor keys:

- `name`: A string with the `addon` module title.
- `description`: A long text with the description of the features, usually in RST format.
- `author`: The author's name. It is a string, but can contain a comma-separated list of names.
- `depends`: A list of the `addon` modules it depends on. They will be automatically installed before this module is.
- `application`: A Boolean flag, declaring whether the `addon` module should be featured as an app in the apps list.

Instead of the `description` key, we can use a `README.rst` or `README.md` file in the module's top directory. If both exist, then the `manifest` description is used.

In a real-world scenario, we recommend that you also use the additional keys, since they are relevant for the Odoo App Store:

- `summary`: A string displayed as a subtitle for the module.
- `version`: By default, 1.0. It should follow versioning rules (see `http://semver.org/` for details). It is good practice to use the Odoo version before our module version, for example, 12.0.1.0.
- `license`: By default considered to be LGPL-3.
- `website`: A URL to get more information about the module. This can help people find more documentation or the issue-tracker to file bugs and suggestions.
- `category`: A string with the functional category of the module, which defaults to **Uncategorized**. A list of existing categories can be found in the security **Groups** form (at **Settings | User | Groups**), in the **Application** field drop-down list.

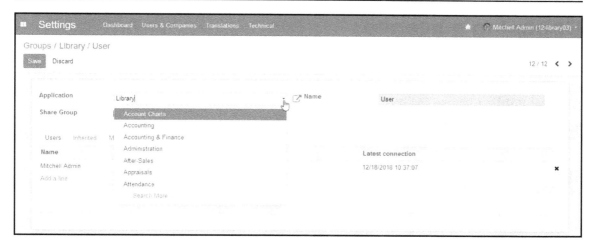

These other descriptor keys are also available:

- `installable`: By default, it's `True`, but can be set to `False` to disable a module.
- `auto_install`: If set to `True`, it will be automatically installed as soon as all its dependencies are already installed. It is used for *glue* modules, which connect two features together as soon as both are installed on the same instance.

Adding an icon

Modules can optionally have an icon representing them. In the case of modules creating a new app, this is particularly important, since the app is expected to have an icon in the apps menu.

To add an icon, to we need to add a `static/description/icon.png` file to the module, with the icon to be used.

To make it simpler, we will reuse the icon of the existing accounting application, copying the `odoo/addons/account/static/description/icon.png` file into the `custom-addons/library_app/static/description` directory.

In the command line, this can be done with the following code:

```
$ cd ~/odoo-dev
$ mkdir -p ./custom-addons/library_app/static/description
$ cp~/odoo-dev/odoo/addons/note/static/description/icon.png ./custom-
addons/library_app/static/description
```

Choosing a license

Choosing a license for your work is very important, and you should carefully consider which is the best choice for you, and its implications. The most-used licenses for Odoo modules are version 3 of the GNU **Lesser General Public License** (**LGPL**) and the **Affero General Public License** (**AGPL**).

The LGPL is more permissive and allows commercial modifications, without the need to share the corresponding source code.

The AGPL is a stronger open source license, and requires derivative work and service-hosting to share the source code.

You can learn more about the GNU licenses at https://www.gnu.org/licenses/.

Installing a new module

We now have a minimal addon module. It doesn't do anything yet, but we want to install it just to check that everything is working properly so far.

For this to be possible, the addons directory where our module is should be known to the Odoo server. We can confirm that by stopping and starting the Odoo server, and looking at the server log output—in the first log lines, we should find one with the odoo: addons paths: text, followed by the list of active addons paths being used. For more details on how to set the addons paths, refer to Chapter 2, *Preparing the Development Environment*.

To install a new module, we should start the server using both the -d and -i options. -d ensures that we are working with the correct Odoo database. And -i accepts a comma-separated list of modules to install.

Assuming that our development database is called dev12, the command to use is:

```
$ ./odoo-bin -d dev12 -i library_app
```

Pay close attention to the server log messages to confirm that the module was found and installed. You should be able to see this specific message in the log:
odoo.modules.registry: module library_app: creating or updating database tables.

Upgrading modules

Developing a module is an iterative process, and you will want changes made on source files to be applied to and made visible in Odoo. We can do this from the GUI, looking up the module in the **Apps** list and clicking on the **Upgrade** button.

However, when the changes are only in Python code, the upgrade may not have an effect. Instead of a module upgrade, an application server restart is needed. Since Odoo loads Python code only once, any later changes to code require a server restart to be applied.

In some cases, if the module changes were to both data files and Python code, you might need both operations. This is a common source of confusion for new Odoo developers.

But fortunately, there is a better way. The safest way to make all our changes to a module effective is to stop and restart the server instance, requesting that our modules are upgraded to our work database.

In the terminal where the server instance is running, use *Ctrl + C* to stop it. Then, start the server and upgrade the `library_app` module using the following command:

```
$ ./odoo-bin -d dev12 -u library_app
```

The `-u` option (or `--update` in the long form) requires the `-d` option and accepts a comma-separated list of modules to update. For example, we could use `-u library_app,mail`. When a module is updated, all other installed modules depending on it are also updated. This is essential to maintain the integrity of the inheritance mechanisms, used to extend features.

Changed in Odoo 11
Until Odoo 10.0, before a new addon module could be installed, the module list had to be manually updated from the **web client** menu option for it to be known to Odoo. Since 11.0, the list of modules available is automatically updated when a module is installed or updated.

Throughout this book, when you need to apply the changes made in the module code files:

- When adding model fields, an upgrade is needed. When changing Python code, including the manifest file, a restart is needed.
- When changing XML or CSV files, an upgrade is needed. When in doubt, do both: restart the server and upgrade the modules.

When in doubt, the safest way is to restart the Odoo instance with the -u <module> option. Pressing the up arrow key brings to you the previous command that was used. So, most of the time, when repeating this action, you will find yourself using the *Ctrl + C*, up, and *Enter* key combination.

Or, you can avoid these repeated start/stop actions using the dev=all option. It will automatically reload the changes made to your XML and Python files, as soon as they are saved. See Chapter 2, *Preparing the Development Environment,* for more details on this option.

Creating a new application

Some Odoo modules create new applications, and others add features or modify existing applications. While the technical components involved are about the same, an app is expected to include a few characteristic elements. Since we are creating a new library app, we should include them in our module.

An app should have:

- An icon, to be presented in the app list.
- A top-level menu item, under which all the app's menu items will be placed.
- Security groups for the app, so that it can be enabled only for users that need it, and where access security will be set.

To add an icon, we just need to place an icon.png file in the module's static/description/ subdirectory. This was done in the *Adding an icon* section.

Next, we will take care of the app's top-level menu.

Adding the app's top menu item

Since we are creating a new app, it should have a main menu item. On the CE, this is shown as a new entry in the top-left drop-down menu. On the EE, it is shown as an additional icon in the **App Switcher** main menu.

Menu items are view components added using XML data files. Create the
views/library_menu.xml file to define a menu item:

```
<?xml version="1.0"?>
<odoo>
  <!-- Library App Menu -->
  <menuitem id="menu_library"
            name="Library" />
</odoo>
```

The user interface, including menu options and actions, is stored in database tables. The
preceding code is an Odoo data file, describing a record to load into the Odoo database.
The <menuitem> element is an instruction to write a record on the ir.ui.menu model.

The id attribute is also called **XML ID**, and is used to uniquely identify each data element,
providing a way for other elements to reference it. For example, when adding library
submenu items, we will need to reference the XML ID of their parent menu item, which
should be menu_library. XML IDs are an important topic, and are discussed in greater
detail in Chapter 5, *Import, Export, and Module Data*.

The menu item added here is very simple, and the only attribute used is name. Other
frequently-used attributes are not used here. We didn't set a parent menu item, because
this is a top-level menu, and we didn't set action, because this menu item won't do
anything—it is only the top element where submenu items will later be placed.

Our module does not yet know about this new XML data file. For this to happen, it needs to
be declared in the __manifest__.py file, using the data attribute. It is a list of the data
files to be loaded by the module upon installation or upgrade. Add this attribute to the
manifest's dictionary:

```
'data': [
    'views/library_menu.xml',
],
```

To load these menu configurations into our Odoo database, we need to upgrade the
module. Doing that at this point won't have any visible effects. This menu item has no
actionable submenu yet, and so won't be shown. It will be visible later, once we add one,
and add the appropriate access-control permissions.

 Items in the menu tree are only shown if there are any visible submenu
items. The lower-level menu items, with Window Actions opening Views,
are only visible if the user has access to the underlying Model.

Adding security groups

Before features can be used by regular users, access must be granted for them. In Odoo, this is done using security groups—access privileges are granted to groups, and users are assigned security groups.

Odoo apps typically provide two groups, a user level, for use by regular users, and a manager level, with additional access to app configuration.

So, we will add these two security groups now. Access-security related files are usually kept in a /security module subdirectory, so we should create the security/library_security.xml file for these definitions. Security groups use categories to better organize related app. So, we will start by creating a category for our library app, in the ir.module.category model:

```xml
<?xml version="1.0" ?>
<odoo>

  <record id="module_library_category" model="ir.module.category">
    <field name="name">Library</field>
  </record>

</odoo>
```

Next, we will add the two security groups, starting with the user group. Add the following XML block inside the <odoo> element, just before the </odoo> closing tag:

```xml
<!-- Library User Group -->
<record id="library_group_user" model="res.groups">
  <field name="name">User</field>
  <field name="category_id"
         ref="module_library_category"/>
  <field name="implied_ids"
         eval="[(4, ref('base.group_user'))]"/>
</record>
```

The record is created in the res.groups model, and values are given for three fields:

- name is the group title.
- category_id is the related app. It is a relational field, so the ref attribute is used with an XML ID linking it to the category we've already created.

- `implied_ids` is a one-to-many relational field, and contains a list of groups that will also apply to users belonging to this group. It uses a special syntax that will be explained in `Chapter 5`, *Import, Export, and Module Data*. In this case, we are using code 4 to add a link to `base.group_user`, the basic internal user group.

Next, we will create the manager group. It should give us all the privileges granted to the user group, plus some additional access reserved for the app manager:

```xml
<!-- Library Manager Group -->
<record id="library_group_manager" model="res.groups">
  <field name="name">Manager</field>
  <field name="category_id"
         ref="module_library_category"/>
  <field name="implied_ids"
         eval="[(4, ref('library_group_user'))]"/>
  <field name="users"
         eval="[(4, ref('base.user_root')),
                (4, ref('base.user_admin'))]"/>
</record>
```

Here, we also see the `name`, `category_id`, and `implied_ids` fields, as before. `implied_ids` is set with a link to the library user group, to *inherit* its privileges.

We also set the value for the `users` field, so that the administrator and the internal root users are automatically app managers.

In previous Odoo versions, the `admin` administrator user was also the internal root user. In Odoo 12, we have a system root user, which is not shown in the user list, and is used internally by the framework when privilege-elevation is needed (`sudo`). The `admin` user can be used to log into the server and should have full access to all features, but can no longer bypass access security, as the system root user can.

We also need to add this new XML file to the module's `manifest` file:

```python
'data': [
    'security/library_security.xml',
    'views/library_menu.xml',
],
```

Notice that the `library_security.xml` file was added before `library_menu.xml`. The order in which data files are loaded is important, since you can only use identifier references that have already been defined. It is common for menu items to reference security groups, and so it is good practice to add security definitions before menu and view definitions.

Adding automated tests

Programming best practices include having automated tests for your code. This is even more important for dynamic languages such as Python—since there is no compilation step, you can't be sure there are no syntactic errors until the code is actually run by the interpreter. A good editor can help us spot these problems ahead of time, but can't help us ensure the code performs as intended, like automated tests can.

Changed in Odoo 12

In previous versions, Odoo also used tests described using YAML data files. YAML data-file support was removed in Odoo 12, so this type of test is not available anymore.

The **test-driven development (TDD)** method states that we should write tests up front, check that they fail, then develop the code that, in the end, should pass the tests. Inspired by this approach, we will add our module tests now, before we add the actual features:

1. The test code files should have a name starting with `test_` and should be imported from `tests/__init__.py`. But the `tests` directory (also a Python submodule) should not be imported from the module's top `__init__.py`, since it will be automatically discovered and loaded only when tests are executed.

2. Tests must be placed in the `tests/` subdirectory. Add a `tests/__init__.py` file with the following:

   ```
   from . import test_book
   ```

3. Add the actual test code, available in the `tests/test_book.py` file:

   ```
   from odoo.tests.common import TransactionCase

   class TestBook(TransactionCase):

       def setUp(self, *args, **kwargs):
           result = super().setUp(*args, **kwargs)
           self.Book = self.env['library.book']
           self.book_ode = self.Book.create({
               'name': 'Odoo Development Essentials',
               'isbn': '879-1-78439-279-6'})
           return result
       def test_create(self):
           "Test Books are active by default"
           self.assertEqual(self.book_ode.active, True)
   ```

This adds a simple test case that creates a new `Book` and verifies that the active field has the correct default value.

4. Run the tests by adding the `--test-enable` option while installing or upgrading the module:

```
$ ./odoo-bin -d dev12 -u library_app --test-enable
```

5. The Odoo server will look for a `tests/` subdirectory in the upgraded modules and will run them. At this point, the tests are expected to throw an error, so you should see `ERROR` messages related to the tests in the server log. This should change once we add the book model to the module.

Testing business logic

Now we should add tests for the business logic. Ideally, we want every line of code to be covered by at least one test case. In `tests/test_book.py`, add a few more lines of code after the `test_create()` method:

```
def test_check_isbn(self):
    "Check valid ISBN"
    self.assertTrue(self.book_ode._check_isbn)
```

It is recommended to, as much as possible, write a different test case for each action to check. This test case begins in a similar way to the previous one, creating a new `book`. This is needed because test cases are independent, and the data created or changed during one test case is rolled back when it ends. We then call the tested method on the created record and check whether the ISBN used is correctly validated.

If we now run the tests, they should fail, since the tested feature has not been implemented yet.

Testing access security

Access security can also be checked to confirm that users have the correct privileges granted.

By default, tests are executed with the Odoo internal user, __system__, which bypasses access security. So we need to change the user running the tests, to check whether the right access security has been given to them. This is done by modifying the execution environment, in `self.env`, by setting the `user` attribute to the user we want to run the tests with.

We can modify our tests to take this into account. Edit the `tests/test_book.py` file to add a `setUp` method:

```
def setUp(self, *args, **kwargs):
    result = super().setUp(*args, **kwargs)
    user_admin = self.env.ref('base.user_admin')
    self.env= self.env(user=user_admin)
    self.Book = self.env['library.book']
    self.book_ode = self.Book.create({
        'name': 'Odoo Development Essentials',
        'isbn': '879-1-78439-279-6'})
    return result
```

This first instruction calls the `setUp` code of the parent class. The next one changes the environment used to run the tests, `self.env`, to a new one that uses the `admin` user. No further changes are needed for the tests we already wrote.

The model layer

Now that Odoo knows about our new module, let's add a simple model to it.

Models describe business objects, such as an opportunity, sales order, or partner (customer, supplier, and so on). A model has a list of attributes and can also define its specific business logic.

Models are implemented using a Python class derived from an Odoo template class. They translate directly to database objects, and Odoo automatically takes care of that when installing or upgrading the module. The framework component responsible for this is **Object Relational Mapping (ORM)**.

Our module will be an application to manage a library, and the first feature we need is to manage the book catalogue, so at this point, this will be the only model we need to implement.

Creating the data model

The Odoo development guidelines state that the Python files for models should be placed inside a models subdirectory, and we should have one file for each model. So, we will create a models/library_book.py file in the main directory of the library_app module.

 The Odoo official coding guidelines can be found at http://www.odoo. com/documentation/12.0/reference/guidelines.html. Another relevant coding standards document is the Odoo Community Association coding guidelines: https://github.com/OCA/maintainer-tools/blob/master/ CONTRIBUTING.md.

Before that, we need to let Python know that the models directory should be used (*imported* in Python jargon). To do that, edit the module's main __init__.py file, like this:

```
from . import models
```

To import the Python code file to be used, we need to add a models/__init__.py file:

```
from . import library_book
```

Now we can create the models/library_book.py file with the following content:

```
from odoo import fields, models

class Book(models.Model):
    _name = 'library.book'
    _description = 'Book'
    name = fields.Char('Title', required=True)
    isbn = fields.Char('ISBN')
    active = fields.Boolean('Active?', default=True)
    date_published = fields.Date()
    image = fields.Binary('Cover')
    publisher_id = fields.Many2one('res.partner', string='Publisher')
    author_ids = fields.Many2many('res.partner', string='Authors')
```

The first line is a Python code import statement, making the models and fields objects from the Odoo core available.

The second line declares our new model. It's a Python class derived from models.Model.

The next line sets the _name attribute, defining the identifier that will be used throughout Odoo to refer to this model. Note that the actual Python class name, Book, is irrelevant for the Odoo framework. The _name value is what will be used as the model identifier.

Only `Model` names use dots (`.`) to separate keywords. Everything else uses underscores (_), addon modules, XML identifiers, table names, and so on.

Notice that this and the following lines are indented. If you're not familiar with Python, you should know that this is important—indentation defines a nested code block, so these four lines should all be equally indented.

Then we have the `_description` model attribute. It is not mandatory, but it provides a user-friendly name for the model records, which can be used for better user messages.

The remaining lines define the model's fields. It's worth noting that `name` and `active` are special field names. By default, Odoo will use the `name` field as the record's title when referencing it from other models.

The `active` field is used to activate records, and by default, only active records will be shown. This is useful for master date models, to hide away records that are no longer used in daily operations by users—for historical reasons, they need to be kept in the database. In our case, it will allow us to signal the books available in our library, and the ones no longer available.

We can see examples of other field types—`date_published` is a date field, for the book's publication date, and `image` is a binary field, to store the book's cover image.

We can see also examples of relation fields—the `publisher_id` field, which is a many-to-one relation for the publishing company, and `author_ids`, a many-to-many relation for the list of authors.

Both are relations between the book and the partner model. The partner model is built into the Odoo framework, and is where people, companies, and addresses should be stored. We are using it to store our list of publishers and authors.

That's it! For our Python code changes to take effect, the module needs to be upgraded, triggering the creation of the corresponding objects in the database.

We won't see any menu options to access this new model, since we haven't added them yet. Still, we can inspect the newly-created model using the **Technical** menu. In the **Settings** top menu, go to **Technical | Database Structure | Models**, search for the `library.book` model in the list, and click on it to see its definition:

If everything goes well, it will be confirmed that the model and fields were created. If you can't see them here, try a server restart with a module upgrade.

We can also see some additional fields that we didn't declare. These are reserved fields that Odoo automatically adds to every new model. They are as follows:

- id is a unique numeric identifier for each record in the model.
- create_date and create_uid specify when the record was created and who created it, respectively.
- display_name provides a textual representation for the record used, for example, when it is referenced in other records. It is computed and, by default, uses the text in the name field.
- write_date and write_uid confirm when the record was last modified and who modified it, respectively.
- __last_update is a helper that is not actually stored in the database. It is used for concurrency checks.

Setting up access security

You might have noticed that, upon loading, our module gets a warning message in the server log:

The model todo.task has no access rules, consider adding one.

The message is pretty clear—our new model has no access rules, so it can't be used by anyone yet. We already have the security groups for this app, and we now need to give them access to the app's models.

> Before Odoo 12, admin was a superuser that bypassed access security, and so had automatic access to all data models. In Odoo 12, this is no longer the case, and we need to set up ACLs on new models before the administrator user can see them.

Adding access control security

To get a picture of what information is needed to add access rules to a model, use the web client and go to **Settings | Technical | Security | Access Rights**:

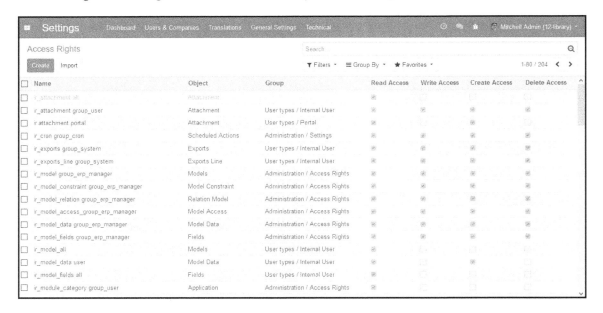

Here, we can see the ACL for some models. It indicates, per security group, what actions are allowed on records. This information has to be provided by the module using a data file to load the lines into the `ir.model.access` model. We will add full access to the employee group on the model. The internal user is the basic access group nearly everyone belongs to.

Changed in Odoo 12

The User form now has a user type section, only visible when the Developer Mode is enabled. It allows us to select between the mutually exclusive options—Internal user, portal (external users, such as customers), and public (website-anonymous visitors). This was changed to avoid misconfigurations where internal users are also included in portal or public groups, effectively reducing their access privileges.

This is done using a CSV file named `security/ir.model.access.csv`. Let's add it with the following content:

```
id,name,model_id:id,group_id:id,perm_read,perm_write,perm_create,perm_unlin
k access_book_user,BookUser,model_library_book,library_group_user,1,0,0,0
access_book_manager,BookManager,model_library_book,library_group_manager,1,
1,1,1
```

The filename must correspond to the model to load the data into, and the first line of the file has the column names. These are the columns provided in our CSV file:

- `id` is the record's external identifier (also known as XML ID). It should be unique in our module.
- `name` is a description title. It is only informative and it's best if it's kept unique.
- `model_id` is the external identifier for the model we are giving access to. Models have XML IDs automatically generated by the ORM; for `library.book`, the identifier is `model_library_book`.
- `group_id` identifies the security group to give permissions to. We grant access to the security groups created before: `library_group_user` and `library_group_manager`.
- The `perm_...` fields flag the access to grant `read`, `write`, `create`, or `unlink` (delete) access. We gave regular users read access and managers full access.

We must not forget to add the reference to this new file in the __manifest__.py descriptor's data attribute. It should look as shown in the following code:

```
'data': [
    'security/library_security.xml',
    'security/ir.model.access.csv',
    'views/library_menu.xml',
],
```

As before, upgrade the module for these additions to take effect. The warning message should be gone. And we can confirm that the permissions are OK by logging in with the admin user, since is was included in the Library Manager Group.

Row-level access rules

We know that, by default, records with the active flag set to False are not visible, but a user can access them if needed, using a filter. Suppose that we don't want the regular library users to be able to access inactive books at all. This can be done using record rules — defining filters limiting what particular records a security group can access.

We can find the **Record Rules** option in the **Technical** menu, alongside **Access Rights**.

Record rules are defined in the ir.rule model. As usual, we need to provide a distinctive name. We also need the model they operate on and the domain filter to use for the access restriction. The domain filter uses the usual list of tuples syntax used across Odoo. We will be explaining this domain expression syntax in Chapter 8, *Business Logic – Supporting Business Processes*.

Usually, rules apply to some particular security groups. In our case, we will make it apply to the employees group. If it applies to no security group in particular, it is considered global (the global field is automatically set to True). Global rules are different, because they impose restrictions that non-global rules can't override.

To add the record rule, we should edit the security/library_security.xml file to add the following XML section inside the <odoo> element:

```
<data noupdate="1">
  <record id="book_user_rule" model="ir.rule">
    <field name="name">Library Book User Access</field>
    <field name="model_id" ref="model_library_book"/>
    <field name="domain_force">
        [('active','=',True)]
    </field>
```

```
        <field name="groups" eval="[(4,ref('library_group_user'))]"/>
    </record>
</data>
```

The record rule is inside a `<data noupdate="1">` element, meaning that those records will be created on module install, but won't be rewritten on module updates. The point is to allow for these rules to be later customized without the risk of those customizations being lost when performing a module upgrade.

 While developing, `noupdate="1"` can be a nuisance, since, if you need to fix your rule, a module upgrade won't rewrite the data in the database. Because of this, you might want to temporarily have `noupdate="0"` during development, until you're happy with the data file.

In the `groups` field, you will also find a special expression. It's a one-to-many relational field, and has a special syntax to operate with. In this case, the `(4, x)` tuple indicates that x should be appended to the records, and here, x is a reference to the internal user group, identified by `base.group_user`. This special syntax to write on too many fields is discussed in more detail in `Chapter 6`, *Models – Structuring the Application Data*.

The view layer

The view layer describes the user interface. Views are defined using XML, which is used by the web client framework to generate data-aware HTML views.

We have menu items that can activate actions that can render views. For example, the **Users** menu item processes an action also called **Users**, which in turn renders a series of views. There are several view types available, such as the list (sometimes called **tree** for historical reasons) and **form** views, and the filter options made available in the top-right search box are also defined by a particular type of view, the search view.

The Odoo development guidelines state that the XML files defining the user interface should be placed inside a `views/` subdirectory.

Let's start creating the user interface for our to-do application.

In the next sections, we will make gradual improvements and frequent module upgrades to make those changes available. You might also want to try the `--dev=all` server option, which spares us from module upgrades while developing. Using it, the view definitions are read directly from the XML files so that your changes are immediately available to Odoo without the need for a module upgrade.

If an upgrade fails because of an XML error, don't panic! Read the error message in the server log carefully; it should point you to where the problem is. If you feel in trouble, just comment out the last edited XML portions or remove the XML file from __manifest__.py and repeat the upgrade. The server should start correctly.

Adding menu items

Now that we have the places to store our data, we want to have it available on the user interface. The first thing to do is add the corresponding menu options.

Edit the views/library_menu.xml file and, inside the <odoo> XML element, add the records that define a menu item and the action performed by it:

```xml
<!-- Action to open the Book list -->
<act_window id="action_library_book"
  name="Library Books"
  res_model="library.book"
  view_mode="tree,form"
/>
<!-- Menu item to open the Book list -->
<menuitem id="menu_library_book"
  name="Books"
  parent="library_menu"
  action="action_library_book"
/>
```

The user interface, including menu options and actions, is stored in database tables. The XML file is a data file used to load those definitions into the database when the addon module is installed or upgraded. The preceding code is an Odoo data file, describing two records to add to Odoo:

- The <act_window> element defines a client-side window action that will open the library.book model with the tree and form views enabled, in that order
- The <menuitem> defines a top menu item that calls the action_library_book action, which was defined before

We now need to upgrade the module again for these changes to take effect. Then, after a browser-page refresh, we should see the **Library** top menu, and it should have a submenu option available. Clicking on it displays a basic list view, and records can be edited using an automatically-generated form view. We can see it if we click on the **Create** button:

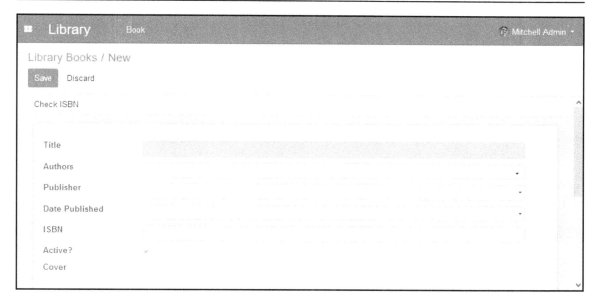

Even though we haven't defined our user interface view, the automatically-generated list and form views are functional, and allow us to start editing data right away.

Creating the form view

All views are stored in the database, in the `ir.ui.view` model. To add a view to a module, we declare a `<record>` element describing the view in an XML file, which is to be loaded into the database when the module is installed.

Add this new `views/book_view.xml` file to define the form view:

```xml
<?xml version="1.0"?>
<odoo>
  <record id="view_form_book" model="ir.ui.view">
    <field name="name">Book Form</field>
    <field name="model">library.book</field>
    <field name="arch" type="xml">
      <form string="Book">
        <group>
          <field name="name" />
          <field name="author_ids" widget="many2many_tags" />
          <field name="publisher_id" />
          <field name="date_published" />
          <field name="isbn" />
          <field name="active" />
```

```
            <field name="image" widget="image" />
          </group>
        </form>
      </field>
    </record>
  </odoo>
```

The `ir.ui.view` record has values for three fields: `name`, `model`, and `arch`. Another important element is the record `id`. It defines an XML ID identifier that can be used for other records to reference it.

The view is for the `library.book` model and is named `Book Form`. The name is just for information purpose; it does not have to be unique, but it should allow you to easily identify which record it refers to. In fact, the name can be entirely omitted; in that case, it will be automatically generated from the model name and the view type.

The most important field is `arch`, as it contains the view definition, highlighted in the previously listed XML code. The `<form>` tag defines the view type, and it contains the view structure.

In this case, it is the `<group>` element that contains the fields to be shown in the form. The fields automatically use an appropriate default widget, such as the date-selection widget for date fields. In some cases, we may want to use a different widget. That is the case for `author_ids`, which is using a widget to display the authors as a list of tags, and the `image` field, which is using a widget appropriate for handling images. A detailed explanation of view elements is provided in `Chapter 10`, *Backend Views – Design the User Interface*.

Remember to add this new file to the `data` key in the manifest file; otherwise, our module won't know about it and it won't be loaded:

```
'data': [
    'security/library_security.xml',
    'security/ir.model.access.csv',
    'views/library_menu.xml',
    'views/book_view.xml',
],
```

Remember that, for the changes to be loaded to our Odoo database, a module upgrade is needed. To see the changes in the web client, the form needs to be reloaded. Either click again on the menu option that opens it or reload the browser page (*F5* in most browsers).

Business document form views

The preceding section provided a basic form view, but we can make some improvements to it. For document models, Odoo has a presentation style that mimics a paper page. This form contains two elements: `<header>`, to contain action buttons, and `<sheet>`, to contain data fields.

We can now replace the basic `<form>` defined in the previous section with this one:

```
<form>
  <header>
    <!-- Buttons will go here -->
  </header>
  <sheet>
    <!-- Content goes here: -->
    <group>
      <field name="name" />
      <field name="author_ids" widget="many2many_tags" />
      <field name="publisher_id" />
      <field name="date_published" />
      <field name="isbn" />
      <field name="active" />
      <field name="image" widget="image" />
    </group>
  </sheet>
</form>
```

Adding action buttons

Forms can have buttons to perform actions. These buttons are able to run window actions such as opening another form or running Python functions defined in the model.

They can be placed anywhere inside a form, but for document-style forms, the recommended place for them is the `<header>` section.

For our application, we will add a field for the book ISBN, and have a button to check whether the ISBN is valid. The code for this will be in a method of the Book model. We will name it `button_check_isbn()`.

Even though we don't have the method created yet, we can already add the corresponding button to the form:

```
<header>
  <button name="button_check_isbn" type="object"
          string="Check ISBN" />
</header>
```

The basic attributes of a button consist of the following:

- The `string` with the text to display on the button
- The `type` of action it performs
- `name` is the identifier for that action
- `class` is an optional attribute to apply CSS styles, as in regular HTML

Using groups to organize forms

The `<group>` tag allows you to organize form content. Placing `<group>` elements inside a `<group>` element creates a two-column layout inside the outer group. It is advisable for group elements to have a `name` attribute so that it's easier for other modules to extend them.

We will use this to better organize our content. Let's change the `<sheet>` content of our form to match this:

```
<sheet>
  <group name="group_top">
    <group name="group_left">
      <field name="name" />
      <field name="author_ids" widget="many2many_tags" />
      <field name="publisher_id" />
      <field name="date_published" />
    </group>
    <group name="group_right">
      <field name="isbn" />
      <field name="active" />
      <field name="image" widget="image" />
    </group>
  </group>
</sheet>
```

The complete form view

At this point, our `library.book` form view should look like this:

```xml
<form>
  <header>
    <button name="check_isbn" type="object"
      string="Check ISBN" />
  </header>
  <sheet>
    <group name="group_top">
      <group name="group_left">
        <field name="name" />
        <field name="author_ids" widget="many2many_tags" />
        <field name="publisher_id" />
        <field name="date_published" />
      </group>
      <group name="group_right">
        <field name="isbn" />
        <field name="active" />
        <field name="image" widget="image" />
      </group>
    </group>
  </sheet>
</form>
```

The action buttons won't work yet, since we still need to add their business logic.

Adding list and search views

When viewing a model in list mode, a `<tree>` view is used. Tree views are capable of displaying lines organized in hierarchies, but most of the time, they are used to display plain lists.

We can add the following `<tree>` view definition to `book_view.xml`:

```xml
<record id="view_tree_book" model="ir.ui.view">
  <field name="name">Book List</field>
  <field name="model">library.book</field>
  <field name="arch" type="xml">
    <tree>
      <field name="name"/>
      <field name="author_ids" widget="many2many_tags" />
      <field name="publisher_id"/>
      <field name="date_published"/>
```

```
    </tree>
  </field>
</record>
```

This defines a list with four columns: `name`, `author_ids`, `publisher_id`, and `date_published`.

At the top-right corner of the list, Odoo displays a search box. The fields it searches in and the available filters are defined by a `<search>` view.

As before, we will add this to `book_view.xml`:

```xml
<record id="view_search_book" model="ir.ui.view">
  <field name="name">Book Filters</field>
  <field name="model">library.book</field>
  <field name="arch" type="xml">
    <search>
      <field name="publisher_id"/>
      <filter name="filter_inactive"
              string="Inactive"
              domain="[('active','=',True)]"/>
      <filter name="filter_active"
              string="Active"
              domain="[('active','=',False)]"/>
    </search>
  </field>
</record>
```

The `<field>` elements define fields that are also searched when typing in the search box. We added `publisher_id` to automatically suggest searching in the publisher field. The `<filter>` elements add predefined filter conditions, which can be toggled with a user click, are defined using a specific syntax. This will be addressed in more detail in `Chapter 10`, *Backend Views – Design the User Interface.*

Changed in Odoo 12
`<filter>` elements are now required to have a `name="..."` attribute, uniquely identifying each filter definition. If missing, the XML validation will fail and the module will not install or upgrade.

The business logic layer

The business logic layer encodes the application's business rules, such as validations and automatic computations. We will add the logic for our button now. This is done with Python code, using the methods in the Python class that represent the model.

Adding business logic

Previously, we added a button to the Book Form section to check whether the ISBN is valid. Modern ISBNs have 13 digits, where the last one is a check digit computed from the first 12.

There is little point getting into the details of the algorithm used, so here is a Python function that implements this validation. It should be added inside the class Book(...) object, before the name field:

```
@api.multi
def _check_isbn(self):
    self.ensure_one()
    digits = [int(x) for x in self.isbn if x.isdigit()]
    if len(digits) == 13:
        ponderations = [1, 3] * 6
        terms = [a * b for a, b in zip(digits[:12], ponderations)]
        remain = sum(terms) % 10
        check = 10 - remain if remain != 0 else 0
        return digits[-1] == check
```

The button_check_isbn() method of the Book model should use this function to validate the number in the ISBN field. If the validation fails, we should present the users with a warning message.

First, we need to import the Odoo API library, adding the corresponding import, as well as the Odoo Warning exception. To do this, we need to edit the library_book.py Python file so that these are the first lines of the file:

```
from odoo import api, fields, models
from odoo.exceptions import Warning
```

Next, still in the `models/library_book.py` file, add the following to the `Book` class:

```
@api.multi
def button_check_isbn(self):
    for book in self:
        if not book.isbn:
            raise Warning('Please provide an ISBN for %s' % book.name)
        if book.isbn and not book._check_isbn():
            raise Warning('%s is an invalid ISBN' % book.isbn)
    return True
```

For logic on records, we use the `@api.multi` decorator. Here, `self` will represent a recordset, and we should then loop through each record. In fact, this is the default for model methods, so the `@api.multi` decorator could be safely omitted here. We prefer to keep it for clarity.

The code loops through all the selected Book task records and, for each one, if the Book ISBN has a value, it checks whether it is a valid ISBN. If not, a warning message is raised for the user.

The Model method does not need to return anything, but we should have it at least return a `True` value. The reason is that not all client implementations of the XML-RPC protocol support None/Null values, and may raise errors when such a value is returned by a method.

This a good moment to upgrade the module and run the tests again, adding the `--test-enable` option to confirm that tests are now passing. You can also try it live, going into a Book Form and trying the button with both correct and incorrect ISBNs.

Web pages and controllers

Odoo also provides a web development framework, which can be used to develop website features closely integrated with our backend apps. We will take our first steps toward this by creating a simple web page to display the list of active books in our library. It will respond to web requests at the `http://my-server/library/books` address, so `/library/books` is the URL endpoint we want to implement.

We will just have a short taste of what web development with Odoo looks like. This topic is addressed in more depth in `Chapter 13`, *Creating Website Frontend Features*.

Web controllers are the components responsible for rendering web pages. Controllers are methods defined in an `http.Controller` class, and they are bound to URL endpoints. When that URL endpoint is accessed, the controller code executes, producing the HTML to be presented to the user. To help with rendering the HTML, we have the QWeb templating engine.

The convention is to place the code for controllers inside a `/controllers` subdirectory. First, edit `library_app/__init__.py` so that it also imports the `controllers` module directory:

```
from . import models
from . import controllers
```

We then need to add a `library_app/controllers/__init__.py` file so that the directory can be Python-imported, and add an import statement to it for the Python file we will add:

```
from . import main
```

Now add the actual file for the controller, `library_app/controllers/main.py`, with the following code:

```
from odoo import http

class Books(http.Controller):

    @http.route('/library/books', auth='user')
    def list(self, **kwargs):
        Book = http.request.env['library.book']
        books = Book.search([])
        return http.request.render(
            'library_app.book_list_template', {'books': books})
```

The `odoo.http` module, imported here, is the core component providing web-related features. The `http.Controller` object is the class controller it should derive from. We use it for the main controller class.

The particular name we choose for the class and for their methods is not relevant. The `@http.route` decorator is the important part, since it declares the URL endpoint that will be bound to the class method, `/books` in our case. By default, access to URL endpoints requires the user to be logged in. It is good practice to explicitly refer to the route's authorization mode, so we added the `auth='user'` argument. We can allow for anonymous access by adding the `auth='public'` parameter to `@http.route` instead.

If using `auth='public'`, the code in the controller should use `sudo()` to elevate permissions before trying to search Books. This will be further discussed in `Chapter 13`, *Creating Website Frontend Features*.

Inside the controller method, we access the environment using `http.request.env`. We use it to get a recordset with all active books in the catalogue.

The final step is to use `http.request.render()` to process the `library_app.index_template` QWeb template and generate the output HTML. We can make values available to the template through a dictionary, and this is used to pass the `books` recordset.

If we now restart the Odoo server, to reload the Python code, and try accessing the `/library/books` URL, we should get an error message in the server log: `ValueError: External ID not found in the system: library_app.book_list_template`. This is expected since we haven't defined that template yet. That should be our next step.

QWeb templates are a type of view, and should also go in the `/views` subdirectory. Let's create the `views/book_list_template.xml` file:

```xml
<?xml version="1.0" encoding="utf-8"?>
<odoo>

<template id="book_list_template" name="Book List">
  <div id="wrap" class="container">
    <h1>Books</h1>
      <t t-foreach="books" t-as="book">
        <div class="row">
          <span t-field="book.name" />,
          <span t-field="book.date_published" />,
          <span t-field="book.publisher_id" />
        </div>
      </t>
  </div>
</template>

</odoo>
```

The `<template>` element is used to declare a QWeb template. In fact, it is a shortcut for an `ir.ui.view` record, and this is the base model where templates are stored. The template contains the HTML to use, and makes use of QWeb-specific attributes. `t-foreach` is used to loop through each item of the `books` variable, made available by the controller's `http.request.render()` call. `t-field` takes care of properly rendering the content of a record field.

This is just a glimpse of the QWeb syntax. More details can be found in `Chapter 13`, *Creating Website Frontend Features*.

We still need to declare this file in the module manifest, like the other XML data files, so that it gets loaded and can be made available. After doing this and performing a module upgrade, our web page should be working. Open the `http://<my-server>:8069/library/books` URL and you should see a simple list of the available Books.

Summary

We created a new module from the start, covering the most frequently-used elements in a module—models, the three basic types of views (form, list, and search), business logic in model methods, and access security. We also learned about security access control, including record rules, and how to create web pages using web controllers and QWeb templates.

In the process, we got familiar with the module-development process, which involves module upgrades and application-server restarts to make the gradual changes effective in Odoo.

Always remember, when adding model fields, an upgrade is needed. When changing Python code, including the manifest file, a restart is needed. When changing XML or CSV files, an upgrade is needed; also, when in doubt, do both: restart the server and upgrade the modules.

We've gone through the essential elements and steps to create a new Odoo app. But in most cases, our modules will be extending existing apps to add features. This is what we will learn about in the next chapter.

Questions

1. Is `library-app` a correct module name?
2. Should a module define **access control lists** (**ACL**) for all Models defined in it?
3. Can we enforce some users to only access a subset of the records in a Model?
4. What is the difference between a relational field and other field types?
5. What are the main view components used in an Odoo app?
6. How are backend views defined?
7. Where should business logic be implemented in an Odoo app?
8. What is the web page templating engine used by Odoo?

Further Reading

All of the Odoo-specific topics presented here will be covered in more depth in the remaining chapters of this book.

The official documentation offers some relevant resources that make good complementary reading:

- The Building a Module tutorial: `https://www.odoo.com/documentation/12.0/howtos/backend.html`
- The Odoo Guidelines provide a list of code conventions and guidelines for module development: `https://www.odoo.com/documentation/12.0/reference/guidelines.html`
- The Odoo Community Association Guidelines provide a good resource for Odoo development best practices: `https://github.com/OCA/maintainer-tools/blob/master/CONTRIBUTING.md`

Learning Python is important for Odoo development. There are some good Python books from the *Packt* catalogue, such as *Learn Python Programming – Second Edition*: `https://www.packtpub.com/application-development/learn-python-programming-second-edition`.

Extending Modules

4

One of Odoo's most powerful features is its ability to add features without directly modifying the underlying objects.

This is achieved through inheritance mechanisms, which function as modification layers on top of existing objects. These modifications can happen at every level—Models, Views, and business logic. Instead of directly modifying an existing module, we create a new module so that we can add the intended modifications.

The previous chapter guided us through creating a new app from scratch. In this chapter, we will learn how to create modules that extend existing apps or modules by leveraging existing core or community features.

To achieve this, we will discuss the following topics:

- In-place Model extension, to add features to existing Models
- Modifying data records to extend Views, and adding features or modifying data to change data records that have been created by other modules
- More Model inheritance mechanisms, such as delegation inheritance and mixin classes
- Extending Python methods to add features to the app's business logic
- Extending Web Controllers and Templates to add features to web pages

Technical requirements

For this chapter, you will need an Odoo server that you can command from a terminal session.

The code in this chapter depends on the code that we created in Chapter 3, *Your First Odoo Application*. You should have your add-ons path and should install the library_app module. You can find the code in the ch04 directory of the GitHub repository at https://github.com/PacktPublishing/Odoo-12-Development-Essentials-Fourth-Edition.

Learning project – extending the Library app

In Chapter 3, *Your First Odoo Application*, we created the initial module for the Library app, providing a book catalogue. Now, we will create a module, library_member, that extends the Library app to add the ability for library members to borrow books.

It will extend the Book Model and add a flag, signaling if they are available to borrow a book. This information should be shown in the Book form and on the website catalogue page.

It should add the Library Member master data Model. Members should store personal data, such as name, address, and email, similarly to Partners, and have specific data, such as the library card number. The most efficient solution is to use Delegation inheritance, where a Library Member record will be automatically created and contain a related Partner record. This solution makes all Partner fields available for Members, without data structure duplication.

We would like to provide Members with the messaging and social features that are available on the borrowing form, including the planned activities widget, to allow for better collaboration.

We plan to introduce a feature that allows Members to borrow Books from the Library, but it will be out of scope for now.

The following is a summary of the changes to introduce:

- **Books**:
  - Add an Is Available? field. For now, it will be managed manually, but this should be automated later.
  - Extend the ISBN validation logic to also support 10-digit ISBNs.
  - Extend the web catalogue page to identify unavailable books and to allow the user to filter through only books that are available.

- **Members**:
  - Add a new Model to store the person's Name, Card Number, and contact information, such as Email, and Address.
  - Add the social discussion features and the planned Activities features.

To start working on this extension module, we should create the `library_member` directory alongside the `library_app`, and add two files—an empty `__init__.py` file, and a `__manifest__.py` file with the following content:

```
{
    'name': 'Library Members',
    'description': 'Manage people who will be able to borrow books.',
    'author': 'Daniel Reis',
    'depends': ['library_app'],
    'application': False,
}
```

Now, we are ready to start working on the module's features.

In-place Model extension

Our first task is to add the `is_available` Boolean field to the Book Model. For this, we will use the classic, in-place, Model extension. The value for this field could be automatically computed, based on the book borrow and return transactions, but for now, we will keep it as a simple field.

To extend an existing Model, we will use a Python class with an `_inherit` attribute, thus identifying the Model to be extended. The new class inherits all of the features of the parent Odoo Model, and we only need to declare the modifications we want to introduce. These modifications will also be available everywhere else this Model is used. We can think of this type of inheritance as getting a reference for the existing Model and making in-place changes to it.

Adding fields to a Model

New Models are defined through Python classes. Extending Models is also done through Python classes, with help from an Odoo-specific inheritance mechanism, that is, the _inherit class attribute. This _inherit class attribute identifies the Model to be extended. The new class inherits all of the features of the parent Odoo Model, and we only need to declare the modifications to introduce.

The coding style guidelines recommend having a Python file for each Model, so we will add a `library_member/models/library_book.py` file, extending the original Model. Let's start by adding the __init__.py code files needed for that file to be actually included in the module:

1. Add the `library_member/__init__.py` file, making it known the code that's in the `models` subdirectory:

```
from . import models
```

2. Add the `library_member/models/__init__.py` file, importing the used code files inside that subdirectory:

```
from . import library_book
```

3. Create the `library_member/models/library_book.py` file, extending the `library.book` Model:

```
from odoo import fields, models

class Book(models.Model):
    _inherit = 'library.book'
    is_available = fields.Boolean('Is Available?')
```

We used the _inherit class attribute to declare the Model to extend. Notice that we didn't use any other class attributes, not even _name. This is not needed, unless we want to make changes to any of them.

> The _name is the Model identifier; what happens if we try to change it? In fact, you can, and if you do, it creates a new Model that is a copy of the inherited one. This is called **prototype inheritance**, and will be discussed later in this chapter.

You can think of this as getting a reference to a Model definition living in a central registry, and making in-place changes to it. These can be adding fields, modifying existing fields, modifying Model class attributes, or even methods with business logic.

To have the new Model fields added to the database tables, we will now install the add-on module. If everything goes as expected, the newly added fields should be seen when inspecting the `library.book` Model, in the **Technical** | **Database Structure** | **Models** menu option.

Modifying existing fields

As seen in the previous section, adding new fields to an existing Model is quite straightforward. Sometimes, we want to modify an existing field. This is also simple to do.

When extending a Model, existing fields can be modified incrementally. This means that we just need to define the field attributes to change or add.

We will make two simple changes to the Book fields that were originally created in the `library_app` module:

- Add a help tooltip to the `isbn` field, explaining that we now also support 10-digit ISBNs (we will implement this later in the chapter)
- Add a database index on the `publisher_id` field to make searches on it more efficient

We should edit the `library_member/models/library_book.py` file, and add the following lines to the `library.book` Model:

```
# class Book(models.Model):
    # ...
    isbn = fields.Char(help="Use a valid ISBN-13 or ISBN-10.")
    publisher_id = fields.Many2one(index=True)
```

This modifies the fields with the specified attributes, leaving all the other attributes that were not explicitly mentioned unmodified.

After this, when we upgrade the module, if we go to a Book form and hover the mouse pointer over the ISBN field, we will see the tooltip message added there. The effect of `index=True` is harder to notice, but it can be seen in the Field definition, which is accessible from the **Settings** | **Technical** | **Database Structure** | **Models** menu.

Modifying Views and data

Views and other data components of a module can also be modified by an extension module. In the case of Views, we will usually want to add features. The presentation structure for a View is defined in the `arch` field, which contains XML data. This XML data can be extended by locating the place where we want the modification, and then declaring the action to perform, such as appending some more XML elements there.

For the remaining data elements, they represent records that were written to the database, and extension modules can perform write operations on them to change some values.

Extending Views

Forms, lists, and search Views are defined using the arch XML structures. To extend Views, we need a way to modify this XML. This means locating XML elements and then introducing modifications at those points.

The XML record for View inheritance is just like the one for regular Views, but also using the `inherit_id` attribute, with a reference to the View to be extended.

We will use this to extend the Book View to add the `is_available` field.

The first thing we need to do is find the XML ID for the View to be extended. We can find that by looking up the View in the Settings app and the **Technical** | **User Interface** | **Views** menu. The XML ID for the Book form is `library_app.view_form_book`. While there, we should also find the XML element where we want to insert our changes. We will be adding the `Is Available?` field after the **ISBN** field. We usually identify the element to use by its `name` attribute. In this case, we have `<field name="isbn" />`.

We will add an XML file for the extensions made to the Partner Views, `views/book_view.xml`, with the following content:

```xml
<?xml version="1.0"?>
<odoo>
  <record id="view_form_book_extend" model="ir.ui.view">
    <field name="name">Book: add Is Available? field</field>
```

```xml
            <field name="model">library.book</field>
            <field name="inherit_id" ref="library_app.view_form_book"/>
            <field name="arch" type="xml">

               <field name="isbn" position="after">
                 <field name="is_available" />
               </field>

            </field>
         </record>
      </odoo>
```

In the preceding code, we highlighted the inheritance-specific element. The `inherit_id` record field identifies the View to be extended by referring to its external identifier using the special `ref` attribute. External identifiers will be discussed in more detail in `Chapter 5`, *Import, Export, and Module Data*.

Views are defined using XML, and are stored in the architecture field, `arch`. To extend a View, we locate the node where the extension will take place, and then perform the intended change, such as adding XML elements.

The simplest way to locate a node is to use an element with a distinctive attribute, usually, name. We then add the `position` attribute, declaring the type of change to make.

In the example in the previous section, the extension node was the `<field>` element with `name="isbn"`, and the change made was to append additional XML content after the selected element:

```xml
            <field name="isbn" position="after">
              <!-- Changed content goes here -->
            </field>
```

Any XML element and attribute can be used to select the node to use as the extension point, except for `string` attributes. The value of string attributes is translated to the user's active language, so it can't be used as a node selector.

> Before version 9.0, the string attribute (for the displayed label text) could also be used as an extension locator. Since 9.0, this is not allowed anymore. This limitation is related to the language translation mechanism operating on those strings.

Once an XML node has been selected as an extension point, we need to indicate the extension operation to perform. This is done using the `position` attribute:

- `inside` (the default): Appends the content inside the selected node, which should be a container, such as `<group>` or `<page>`.
- `after`: Adds the content to the parent element, after the selected node.
- `before`: Adds the content to the parent element, before the selected node.
- `replace`: Replaces the selected node. If used with empty content, it deletes the element. Since Odoo 10, it also allows you to wrap an element with other markup by using `$0` in the content to represent the element being replaced.
- `attributes`: Modifies attribute values for the matched element. The content should have one or more `<attribute name="`**attr-name**`">`**value**`<attribute>` elements, such as `<attribute name="invisible">True></attribute>`. If used with no body, as in `<attribute name="invisible"/>`, the attribute is removed from the selected element.

> While `position="replace"` allows us to delete XML elements, this should be avoided: it can break depending modules that may be depending on the deleted node as a placeholder to add other elements. As an alternative, consider making the element invisible.

Except for the `attributes` position, the preceding locators can be combined with a child element with `position="move"`. The effect is to move the child locator target node to the parent locator's target position.

> **Changes in Odoo 12**:
> The `position="move"` child locator is new in Odoo 12, and is not available in previous versions.

For example:

```
<field name="target_field" position="after">
    <field name="my_field" position="move"/>
</field>
```

The other View types, such as list and search Views, also have an `arch` field, and can be extended in the same way as form Views can.

Selecting extension points with XPath

In some cases, we may not have an attribute with a unique value to use as the XML node selector. This can happen when the element to select does not have a `name` attribute, as is the case for the `<group>`, `<notebook>`, or `<page>` View elements. Another frequent case is when there are several elements with the same `name` attribute, as in the case of Kanban QWeb Views, where the same field can be included more than once in the same XML template.

For these cases, we need a more sophisticated way to locate the XML element to extend. Being XML, the natural way to locate elements in XML is to use XPath expressions.

For example, taking the Book form View defined in the previous chapter, an XPath expression to locate the `<field name="isbn">` element is `//field[@name]='isbn'`. This expression finds `<field>` elements with a `name` attribute equal to `isbn`.

The XPath equivalent to the Book form View extension made in the previous section would be as follows:

```
<expr="//field[@name='isbn']" position="after">
 <field name="is_available" />
</xpath>
```

More information on the supported XPath syntax can be found in the official Python documentation: `https://docs.python.org/3/library/xml.etree.elementtree.html#supported-xpath-syntax`.

If an XPath expression matches multiple elements, only the first one will be selected as the target for extension. Therefore, they should be made as specific as possible, using unique attributes. Using the `name` attribute is the easiest way to ensure that we find the exact elements we want to use as an extension point. Thus, it is important to have these unique identifiers in the XML elements of the Views we create.

Modifying data

Unlike Views, regular data records don't have an XML `arch` structure and can't be extended using XPath expressions. However, they can still be modified by replacing the values in their fields.

The `<record id="x" model="y">` data loading elements actually perform an insert or update operation on Model `y`: If record `x` does not exist, it is created; otherwise, it is updated/written over.

Since records in other modules can be accessed using a `<module>.<identifier>` global identifier, it's possible for our module to overwrite something that was written before by another module.

 Note that since the dot is reserved to separate the module name from the object identifier, it can't be used in identifier names. Instead, you should use the underscore character.

As an example, we will change the name of the **User** security group to **Librarian**. We will modify the `library_app.library_group_user` record.

For this, we will add the `library_member/security/library_security.xml` file, along with the following code:

```
<odoo>
  <!-- Modify Group name -->
  <record id="library_app.library_group_user" model="res.groups">
    <field name="name">Librarian</field>
  </record>
</odoo>
```

Note that we used a `<record>` element, writing only to the `name` field. You can think of this as a write operation on the selected fields.

 When using a `<record>` element, we can select the fields we want to write on, but the same is not true for shortcut elements, such as `<menuitem>` and `<act_window>`. These need all of the attributes to be provided, and missing any of them will set the corresponding field to an empty value. However, you can use `<record>` to set a value on a field that was originally created through a shortcut element.

Before upgrading the module to see the effect of this change, don't forget to add the `library_member/security/library_security.xml` file to the `data` key in the manifest file.

More Model inheritance mechanisms

Previously, we saw the basic extension of Models, called **classic inheritance**, in the official documentation. This is the most frequent use of inheritance, and the easiest way to think about it is as an **in-place extension**. You take a Model and extend it. As you add new features, they are added to the existing Model. A new Model isn't created.

We can also inherit from multiple parent Models, setting a list of values to the _inherit attribute. Most of the time, this is done with **mixin classes.** Mixin classes are Models that implement generic features to be reused. They are not expected to be used on their own, like regular Models, and are like a container of features, ready to be added to other Models.

If, along with _inherit, we also use the _name attribute with a value different from the parent Model, we get a new Model by reusing the features from the inherited one, with its own database table and data. The official documentation calls this **prototype inheritance**. Here, you take a Model and create a brand new one that is a copy of the original one. As you add new features to it, they will be added only to the new Model, and the original Model will be left unchanged.

We also have the **delegation inheritance** method, which is available by using the _inherits attribute (notice the s on the end). It allows us to create a new Model that contains and extends an existing Model. When a new record is created for the new Model, a new record in the original Model is also created and linked, using a many-to-one field. Observers of the new Model see all of the fields, both from the original and new Models, although, behind the scenes, each Model handles its own data.

Let's explore these possibilities in more detail.

Copying features with prototype inheritance

The method we used to extend the Model used only the _inherit attribute. We defined a class by inheriting the library.book Model and added some features to it. The class attribute _name was not explicitly set; implicitly, it was library.book.

However, if we set a different value on the _name attribute, it will create a new Model by copying features from the inherited ones.

In practice, this type of inheritance is usually used with abstract mixin classes. It is rarely, if ever, used to inherit from regular Models, since that would create duplicate data structures.

Odoo also has a delegation inheritance mechanism that avoids this data structure duplication, so it is usually preferred when inheriting from regular Models. Let's look at it in more detail.

Embedding Models using delegation inheritance

Delegation inheritance allows us to reuse data structures, without actually duplicating them in the database. This is done by embedding a Model inside another. UML terms this is a composition relationship: the child cannot exist without the parent, but the parent can exist without the child.

For example, for the core User Model, each record contains a Partner record, and so has all of the fields you find on a Partner available, plus a few fields that are specific to Users.

For the Library project, we want to add a `Library Members` Model. Members will be able to borrow books, and have a library card that can be used when borrowing books. We want to record the card number, and we also want to be able to store personal information, such as email and address. The Partner Model already supports contact and address information, so it's best to reuse it, instead of creating duplicate data structures.

We will create a `library_member/models/library_member.py` file for this new Member Model with the following code:

```
from odoo import fields, models

class Member(models.Model):
    _name = 'library.member'
    _description = 'Library Member'
    card_number = fields.Char()
    partner_id = fields.Many2one(
        'res.partner',
        delegate=True,
        ondelete='cascade',
        required=True)
```

With delegation inheritance, the `library.member` Model embeds the inherited Model, `res.partner`, so that when a new Member record is created, a related Partner is automatically created and referenced in the `partner_id` field.

Changes in Odoo 8:

The `delegate=True` field attribute was introduced with the new API. Before that, delegation inheritance was defined using a Model attribute, like this: `_inherits = {'res.partner': 'partner_id'}`. This is still supported, and is described in the official documentation, but the `delegate=True` field attribute has the same effect and is simpler to use.

Through the delegation mechanism, all fields of the embedded Model are automatically made available as if they were fields of the parent Model fields. In this case, the Member Card Model has all of the Partner fields available for use, such as name, address, and email, plus the ones specific to members, such as card_number. Behind the scenes, the Partner fields are stored in the linked Partner record, and no data structure duplication occurs.

Note that the same is not true for Model methods:
the methods from the Partner Model are not made available in the Member Model.

The advantage of this, compared to prototype inheritance, is that there is no need to repeat data structures, such as addresses, across several tables. Any new Model that needs to include an address can delegate that to an embedded partner Model. If modifications are introduced in partner address fields, these are immediately available to all of the Models that are embedding them.

It may be useful to note that the delegation could be replaced by a combination of the following:

- A many-to-one filed to the parent record
- An override to the create() method, to automatically create and set the parent record
- The related fields to the parent fields, for the specific fields we want to expose

Sometimes, this is more appropriate than a full-fledged delegation inheritance. For instance, res.company does not inherit res.partner, but uses a res.partner record to store several of its fields.

We should not forget to add this code file to library_member/model/__init__.py. It should look like this:

```
from . import library_book
from . import library_member
```

To be able to try the Member Model we created, there are some additional steps we need to work on:

- Adding the security ACLs
- Adding the Menu item

- Adding the Form and List Views
- Updating the manifest file so that we can declare these new data files

It's a good exercise to try to add these by yourself now. Anyway, here is a detailed implementation of the steps to do so :

To add the security ACLs, create the `library_member/security/ir.model.access.csv` file with the following code:

```
id,name,model_id:id,group_id:id,perm_read,perm_write,perm_create,perm_unlin
k
access_member_user,Member User
Access,model_library_member,library_app.library_group_user,1,1,1,0
access_member_manager,Member Manager
Access,model_library_member,library_app.library_group_manager,1,1,1,1
```

To add the menu item, create the `library_member/views/library_menu.xml` file with the following code:

```xml
<?xml version="1.0"?>
<odoo>
    <act_window id="action_library_member"
      name="Library Members"
      res_model="library.member"
      view_mode="tree,form" />
    <menuitem id="menu_library_member"
      name="Members"
      action="action_library_member"
      parent="library_app.library_menu" />
</odoo>
```

To add the Views, create the `library_member/views/member_view.xml` file with the following code:

```xml
<?xml version="1.0"?>
<odoo>
  <record id="view_form_member" model="ir.ui.view">
    <field name="name">Library Member Form View</field>
    <field name="model">library.member</field>
    <field name="arch" type="xml">
      <form>
        <group>
          <field name="name" />
          <field name="email" />
          <field name="card_number" />
        </group>
      </form>
```

```
      </field>
    </record>

    <record id="view_tree_member" model="ir.ui.view">
      <field name="name">Library Member List View</field>
      <field name="model">library.member</field>
      <field name="arch" type="xml">
        <tree>
            <field name="name" />
            <field name="card_number" />
        </tree>
      </field>
    </record>
  </odoo>
```

Finally, we should edit the manifest to declare these three new files:

```
'data': [
  'views/book_view.xml',
  'security/library_security.xml',
  'security/ir.model.access.csv',
  'views/member_view.xml',
  'views/library_menu.xml',
],
```

If everything was entered correctly, after a module upgrade, we should be able to work with the new Library Member Model.

Extending Models using mixin classes

The main use for prototype inheritance is to support mixin classes. Mixins are abstract Models, based on `models.Abstract` (instead of `models.Model`) that have no actual representation in the database. Instead, they provide a set of features that can be reused by (mixed in) other Models.

The Odoo add-ons offer several mixins, but the two most widely used ones are provided by the Discuss app (`mail` add-on module):

- The `mail.thread` Model provides features for a message board, found at the bottom or right-hand side of many document forms, as well as the logic regarding messages and notifications. This is something we will often want to add to our Models, so let's learn how to do that.
- The `mail.activity.mixin` Model provides the planning of to-do tasks.

Changes in Odoo 11

The `mail` module now provides the Activities task management features through the `mail.activity.mixin` abstract Model. This feature was introduced in version 11, and is not available in earlier versions.

We will add both mixins to the Members Model.

The social network messaging features are provided by the `mail.thread` Model of the `mail` module. To add it to a custom Model, we need to do the following:

1. Add a dependency on the add-on module by providing the mixin Models: `mail`
2. Have the class inherit the `mail.thread` and `mail.activity.mixin` mixin classes
3. Add the data fields provided by the `message_follower_ids`, `message_ids` ,and `activity_ids` mixins to the form View

Regarding the first step, our extension module will need the additional `mail` dependency on the module's `__manifest__.py` file:

```
'depends': ['library_app', 'mail'],
```

Regarding the second step, the inheritance from the mixin classes is done using the `_inherit` attribute. We should edit the `library_member/models/library_member.py` file and add the following:

```
class Member(models.Model):
    _name = 'library.member'
    _description = 'Library Member'
    _inherit = ['mail.thread', 'mail.activity.mixin']
```

With this single extra line of code, our Model will include all additional fields and methods provided by these mixins.

The third step is to add the relevant fields to our form View. Edit the `library_member/views/member_view.xml` file to add these fields at the bottom of the form:

```
<record id="view_form_member" model="ir.ui.view">
  <field name="name">Library Member Form View</field>
  <field name="model">library.member</field>
  <field name="arch" type="xml">
    <form>
      <group>
        <field name="name" />
        <field name="email" />
```

```
                <field name="card_number" />
        </group>
        <!-- mail mixin fields -->
        <div class="oe_chatter">
            <field name="message_follower_ids" widget="mail_followers"/>
            <field name="activity_ids" widget="mail_activity"/>
            <field name="message_ids" widget="mail_thread"/>
        </div>
    </form>
  </field>
</record>
```

The `mail` module also provides specific web widgets to present these fields. We use them in the preceding code.

After we upgrade the module, to install these changes, our Members form will look like this:

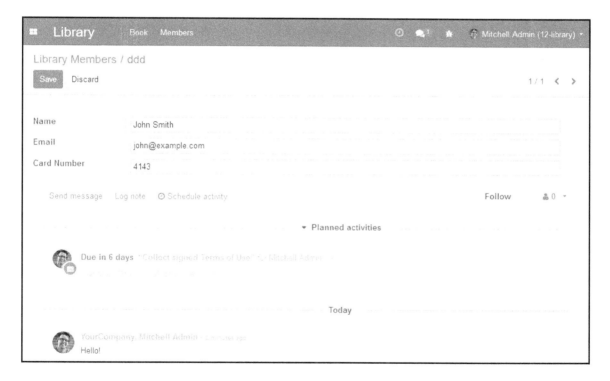

In some cases, regular users will only have access to the records they are following. In these cases, we should create an addition access Record Rule to ensure that Users can see the records they follow. For our example project, this is not a relevant feature, but it could be added using a Domain such as `[('message_partner_ids', 'in', [user.partner_id.id])]`.

Extending Python methods

The business logic that's coded into Python methods can also be extended. For this, Odoo borrows the mechanism that Python already provides for inherited objects to extend their parent class behavior.

As a practical example, we will extend the Library Book ISBN validation logic. The logic provided by the base Library app only validates modern 13-digit ISBNs, but some older titles might have a 10-digit ISBN. We will extend the `_check_isbn()` method to also validate these cases.

Add this additional method in the `library_member/models/library_book.py` file:

```python
from odoo import api, fields, models


class Book(models.Model):
    _inherit = 'library.book'
    is_available = fields.Boolean('Is Available?', readonly=False)

    @api.multi
    def _check_isbn(self):
        self.ensure_one()
        digits = [int(x) for x in self.isbn if x.isdigit()]
        if len(digits) == 10:
            ponderators = [1, 2, 3, 4, 5, 6, 7, 8, 9]
            total = sum(a * b for a, b in zip(digits[:9], ponderators))
            check = total % 11
            return digits[-1] == check
        else:
            return super()._check_isbn()
```

To extend a method, we define it again, and at some point, can use `super()` to call the method's existing implementation. In our method, we check whether it is a 10-digit ISBN, and in that case, perform the missing validation logic. Otherwise, we fall back to the original ISBN checking logic that can handle the 13-digit case.

If you want to try it, or even better, write a test case, here is an example of a 10-digit ISBN: 0-571-05686-5. It is the original ISBN of William Golding's *Lord of the Flies*.

Changes in Odoo 11
Since Odoo 11, the main Python version that's supported is Python 3 (Python 3.5 in Odoo 12). For previous Odoo versions, using Python 2, super() needed two arguments, passing the class name and self. In that case, the last statement would use super(Book, self)._check_isbn().

Extending web controllers and templates

Extensibility is something we expect in all features of Odoo, and web features are no exception, so existing controllers and templates can be extended.

As an example, we will extend our Book catalogue web page to leverage the book availability information we just added:

- On the Controller side, we will add support to a query string parameter, to filter only the available books: /library/books?available=1
- On the Template side, we will add an indication on the books that are not available

Extending Web Controllers

Web Controllers should not have actual business logic, and focus on presentation logic. We might want to add support for additional URL parameters or even routes, which are used to change the presentation of the web page.

We will extend the /library/books endpoint to support a query string parameter, available=1, filtering the catalogue of book to only the available titles.

To extend an existing Controller, we need to import the corresponding Object, and then implement the method with the additional logic.

Let's add a new `library_member/controllers/main.py` file with the following code:

```
from odoo import http
from odoo.addons.library_app.controllers.main import Books

class BooksExtended(Books):
    @http.route()
    def list(self, **kwargs):
        response = super().list(**kwargs)
        if kwargs.get('available'):
            Book = http.request.env['library.book']
            books = Book.search([('is_available', '=', True)])
            response.qcontext['books'] = books
        return response
```

The controller to extend, `Books`, was defined in the `library_app/controllers/main.py` file. Therefore, we will import it from `odoo.addons.library_app.controllers.main`. This is different from Models, where we use a central registry, which is accessible through the `env` object, to reference any Model class, without knowing the particular file implementing it. With controllers, we don't have that, and we need to know the module and file implementing the controller to extend.

We then declare a class, `BooksExtended`, based on the original one, `Books`. The identifier name used for this class is not relevant. We just use it to inherit and extend the methods defined in the original class.

Next, we (re)define the controller method to be extended, `list()`. It needs to be decorated with at least the simple `@http.route()` for its route to be kept active. If used like this, with no arguments, it will preserve the routes defined by the parent class. But we could also add parameters to this `@http.route()` decorator so that we can redefine and replace the class routes.

In the extended `hello()` method, we start by using `super()` to run the existing code. This returns a Response object resulting from that processing. The Response has attributes with the template to render, `template`, and the context to use when rendering, `qcontext`. But the HTML is yet to be generated. That will only happen when the controller finishes running. This gives us the opportunity to change the Response attributes before the final rendering is done.

The `list()` method has a `**kwargs` argument, capturing all parameters given into a `kwargs` dictionary. These are the parameters given in the URL, such as `?available=1`. The method checks the `kwargs` for an `available` key with a value, and if so, changes the `qcontext` to have a books recordset with only the available books.

We should not forget to make this new Python file known to our module. We can do this by adding the controllers subdirectory to the `library_member/__init__.py` file:

```
from . import models
from . import controllers
```

And the `library_member/controllers/__init__.py` file with this line of code:

```
from . import main
```

After this, accessing `http://localhost:8069/library/books?available=1` should show us only the books with the `Is Available?` field checked.

Extending QWeb Templates

To modify the actual presentation of the web page, we need to extend the QWeb template being used.

We will be extending the `library_app.book_list_template` to show additional information on the books that are not available.

Add the `library_member/views/book_list_template.xml` file by using the following code:

```
<odoo>
  <template id="book_list_extended"
            name="Extended Book List"
            inherit_id="library_app.book_list_template">

    <xpath expr="//span[@t-field='book.publisher_id']" position="after">
      <t t-if="not book.is_available">
        <b>(Not Available)</b>
      </t>
    </xpath>

  </template>
</odoo>
```

Web page templates are XML documents, just like the other Odoo View types, and we can use `xpath` to locate elements and then manipulate them, just like we could with the other View types. The inherited template is identified in the `<template>` element by the `inherit_id` attribute.

> **TIP**
>
> In the preceding example, we used the more versatile `xpath` notation, but in this case, we could have used the equivalent simplified notation: `<span t-field="book.publisher_id" position=after>`.

We should not forget to declare this additional data file in our add-on manifest, `library_member/__manifest__.py`:

```
'data': [
    'views/book_view.xml',
    'security/library_security.xml',
    'security/ir.model.access.csv',
    'views/member_view.xml',
    'views/library_menu.xml',
    'views/book_list_template.xml',
],
```

After this, accessing `http://localhost:8069/library/books` should show the additional (**Not Available**) information on the books that are not available.

Summary

Extensibility is a key feature of the Odoo framework. We can build add-on modules that change or add features to other existing add-ons at the several layers needed to implement features in Odoo.

At the Model layer, we use the `_inherit` Model attribute to get a reference to an existing Model and then perform in-place modifications on it. The field objects inside the Model also support incremental definitions so that we can *re-declare* an existing field, providing only the attributes to change.

Additional Model inheritance mechanisms allow you to reuse data structures and business logic. The Delegation inheritance, activated with a `delegate=True` attribute on a many-to-one relation field (or the old style `inherits` Model attribute), makes all the fields from the related Model available, and reuses its data structure. The Prototype inheritance, using `_inherit` with additional Models, allows you to copy features (data structure definition and methods) from other Models, and enable the use of abstract mixin classes, providing a set of reusable features, such as document discussion messages and followers.

At the View layer, the View structures are defined using XML, and extensions can be made by locating an XML element (using XPath or the Odoo simplified syntax) and providing the XML fragment to add. Other data records created by a module can also be modified by extension modules by simply referencing the corresponding complete XML ID and performing a write operation on the intended fields.

At the Business Logic layer, extensions can be made with the same mechanism that's used for Model extension, and re-declaring the methods to extend. Inside them, the `super()` Python function is used to call the code of the inherited method, and our additional code can run before or after that.

For the frontend web pages, the presentation logic in Controllers can be extended in a similar way to Model methods, and the web templates are also Views with an XML structure, so these can be extended in the same way as the other View types.

In the next chapter, we will go deeper into Models, and explore everything they can offer us.

Questions

1. How can we extend an existing Model to add a mixin, such as `mail.thread`?
2. What changes are needed to also have the Phone field available in the Member form View?
3. What happens if you create a Model class with a name attribute that's different from the inherit attribute (for example, `_name='y'` and `_inherit='x'`)?
4. Can XPath be used to modify data records from other modules?
5. When inheriting a Model to extend it, can we extend a method and not use `super()` to call the original code being inherited?
6. How can we extend the Book catalogue web page to add the ISBN field at the end of the line, without referencing any particular field name?

Further reading

The following are some additional references to the official documentation, which can provide useful information regarding module extensions and inheritance mechanisms:

- **Model inheritance**: `https://www.odoo.com/documentation/12.0/reference/orm.html#inheritance-and-extension`
- **View inheritance**: `https://www.odoo.com/documentation/12.0/reference/views.html#inheritance`
- **Web Controllers**: `https://www.odoo.com/documentation/12.0/reference/http.html#controllers`

Import, Export, and Module Data

5

Most Odoo module definitions, such as user interfaces and security rules, are actually data records that are stored in specific database tables. The XML and CSV files found in modules are not used by Odoo applications at runtime. They are a means of loading those definitions into database tables.

Because of this, an important part of Odoo modules is representing data in files so that it can be loaded into a database upon module installation.

Modules can also have initial data and demonstration data. Data files allow us to add that to our modules. Additionally, understanding Odoo data representation formats is important in order to export and import business data within the context of a project's implementation.

The following topics will be covered in this chapter:

- Understanding the external identifier concept
- Exporting and importing data files
- Using CSV files
- Adding module data
- Using XML data files

Technical requirements

This chapter requires you to have an Odoo server running, with the library app base module installed.

The module's code can be found in this book's GitHub repository, `https://github.com/PacktPublishing/Odoo-12-Development-Essentials-Fourth-Edition`, in the `ch03/` directory. You may have also installed the `library_member` module that we created in `Chapter 4`, *Extending Modules,* but it is not needed to follow this chapter.

The code for this chapter can be found in the same GitHub repository, `https://github.com/PacktPublishing/Odoo-12-Development-Essentials-Fourth-Edition`, in the `ch05/` directory. It contains a copy of the original `library_app` that we created in `Chapter 3`, *Your First Odoo Application,* with additional files that have been added for this chapter.

Understanding the external identifier concept

An **external identifier**, also called **XML ID**, is a human-readable string identifier that uniquely identifies a particular record in Odoo. They are important when loading data into Odoo, allowing us to modify an existing data record, or to reference it in other data records.

We will first introduce how external identifiers work and how we can inspect them.

Then, we will learn how to use the web client to find the external identifiers for particular data records, since this is frequently needed when creating add-on modules, thus extending existing features.

How external identifiers work

The actual database identifier for a record is an automatically assigned sequential number, and there is no way to know ahead of time what ID will be assigned to each record during module installation. External identifiers provide a way to reference a related record without the need to know the actual database ID assigned to it. The XML ID provides a convenient alias for the database ID so that we can use it whenever we need to reference a particular record.

Records defined in Odoo module data files use XML IDs. One reason for this is to avoid creating duplicate records when upgrading a module. The module upgrade will load the data files into the database again. We want it to detect pre-existing records in order for them to be updated, instead of creating duplicate records.

Another reason to use XML IDs is to support interrelated data: data records that need to reference other data records. Since we can't know the actual database ID, we can use the XML ID, so the translation will be transparently handled by the Odoo framework.

Odoo takes care of translating the external identifier names into the actual database IDs that have been assigned to them. The mechanism behind this is quite simple: Odoo keeps a table with the mapping between the named external identifiers and their corresponding numeric database IDs: the `ir.model.data` model.

We must have **Developer mode** enabled to have the menu option available. Check whether you have the **Developer mode** bug icon in the upper-right, next to the user avatar icon. If not, you should enable it now in the **Settings** top menu. You can refer to `Chapter 1`, *Quick Start Using the Developer Mode* , for more details.

We can inspect the existing mappings using the **Settings** | **Technical** | **Sequences & Identifiers** | **External Identifiers** menu item. For example, if we visit the external identifiers list and filter it by the `library_app` **Module**, we will see the external identifiers generated by the module we created:

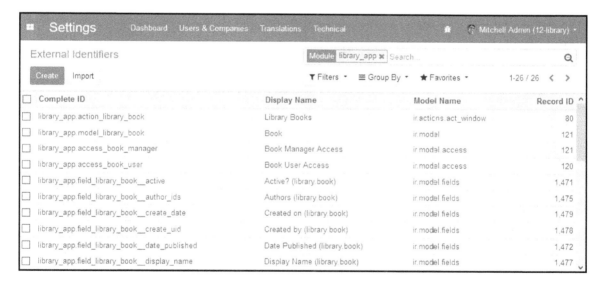

We can see that the external identifiers have **Complete ID** labels. Notice how they are composed of the module name and the identifier name, joined with a dot, for example, `library_app.action_library_book`.

External identifiers only need to be unique inside an Odoo module so that there is no risk of two modules conflicting because of accidentally choosing the same identifier name. The global unique identifier is built by joining the module name with the actual external identifier name. This is what you can see in the **Complete ID** field.

When using an external identifier in a data file, we can choose to use either the complete identifier or just the external identifier name. Usually, it's simpler to just use the external identifier name, but the complete identifier enables us to reference data records from other modules. When doing so, make sure that those modules are included in the module dependencies to ensure that those records are loaded before ours.

> There are some cases where the complete ID is needed, even if referring to an XML ID from the same module.

At the top of the list, we can see the `library_app.action_library_book` complete identifier. This is the menu action we created for the module, which is also referenced in the corresponding menu item. By clicking on it, we go to the form view with its details. There, we can see that the `action_library_book` external identifier in the `library_app` module maps to a specific record ID in the `ir.actions.act_window` model, which is 80, in our case:

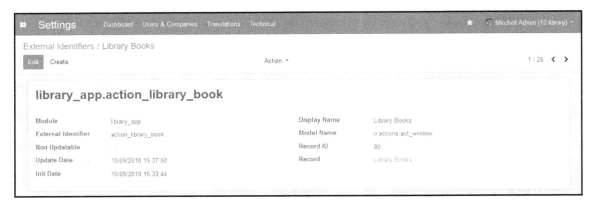

Besides providing a way for records to easily reference other records, external identifiers also allow you to avoid data duplication on repeated imports. If the external identifier is already present, the existing record will be updated, avoiding the creation of a new, duplicate record.

Finding external identifiers

When writing data records for our modules, we frequently need to look up the existing external identifiers to use for our reference.

One way to do this is to use the **Settings** | **Technical** | **Sequences & Identifiers** | **External Identifiers** menu, which was shown earlier. We can also use the **Developer** menu for this. As you may recall from Chapter 1, *Quick Start Using the Developer Mode and Concepts*, the **Developer** menu is activated in the **Settings** dashboard, in an option at the bottom-right.

To find the external identifier for a data record, we should open the corresponding form view, select the **Developer** menu, and then choose the **View Metadata** option. This displays a dialog with the record's database ID and external identifier (also known as the XML ID).

For example, to look up the demo user ID, we should navigate to the users form view, and at **Settings** | **Users**, select the **View Metadata** option from the Developer Tools menu. From the following example, we can see that the XML ID is base.user_demo and that the database ID is 6:

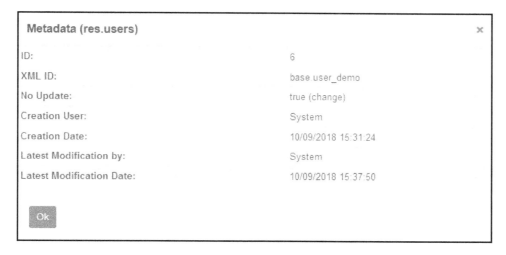

To find the external identifier for view elements, such as form, tree, search, or action, the **Developer** menu is also a good source of help. For this, we can use the appropriate **Edit View** option to open a form with the details for the corresponding view. There, we will find an **External ID** field, providing the information we are looking for.

For example, in the following screenshot, we can see that the **External ID** for the library `Book Form` view is `library_app.view_form_book`:

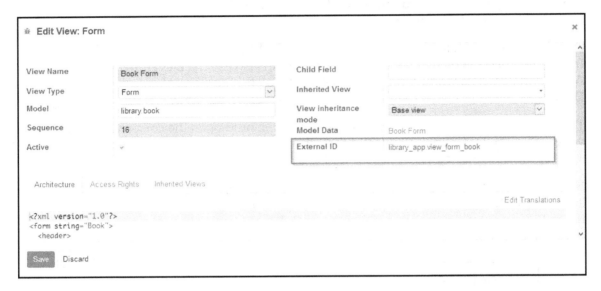

Exporting and importing CSV data files

An easy way to generate data files and get an insight on what structure the files should have is to use the built-in export feature.

With generated CSV files, we can learn about the format that's needed to import data manually into the system, or edit them to perform mass updates, or even use them to produce demo data for our add-on modules.

Here, we will learn about the basics of exporting and importing data from Odoo's user interface.

Exporting data

Data exporting is a standard feature that's available in any list view. To use it, we must first pick the rows to export by selecting the corresponding checkboxes, on the far left, and then selecting the **Export** option from the **Action** button at the top of the list.

First, we should add a couple of Odoo books to the Library app, with their publishers and authors. For the following example, we created `Odoo Development Essentials 11` and `Odoo 11 Development Cookbook`.

We also need to have the Contacts app installed so that we can see a Partner list view and are able to export those records from there. Notice that the default view is `Kanban` with the contact cards, so you need to switch to the `list` view:

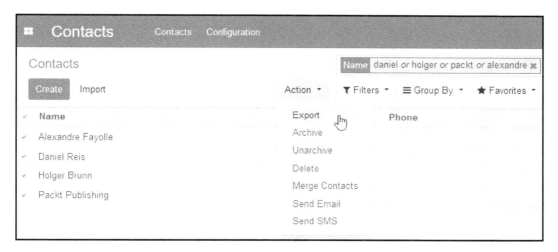

We can also tick the checkbox in the header of the column to select all of the available records that match the current search criteria.

Changes in Odoo 9

In previous Odoo versions, only the records seen on the screen (the current page) would actually be exported. In Odoo 9, this was changed, so that a ticked checkbox in the header would export all of records that matched the current filter, not just the ones currently being displayed. This is very useful for exporting large sets of records that do not fit on the screen.

The **Export** option takes us to the **Export Data** dialog form, where we can choose what and how to export. We are concerned with exporting in a way that allows us to later import that file, either manually or as part of an add-on module:

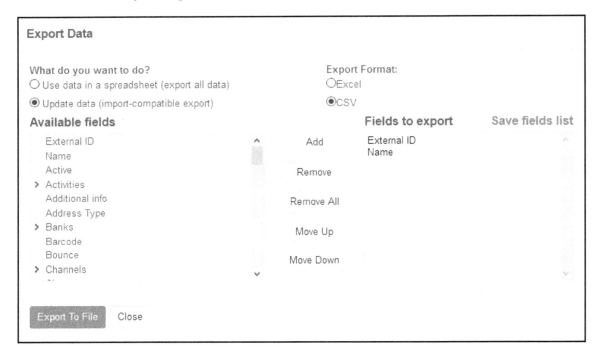

At the top of the dialog form, we have two selections available:

- **What do you want do do?** (**Export type** in previous versions): Choose the **Import-Compatible Export** option so that the data is exported in a format-friendly manner to a later import.
- **Export formats**: We can choose between CSV or Excel. We will choose a CSV file to get a better understanding of the raw export format, which is still understood by any spreadsheet application.

Next, we pick the columns we want to export. In this example, we did a very simple export, and chose **External ID** and **Name**. If we then click on the **Export To File** button, we will start the download of a file with the exported data. We should end up with a CSV text file similar to this:

```
"id","name"
"__export__.res_partner_43_f82d2ecc","Alexandre Fayolle"
"__export__.res_partner_41_30a5bc3c","Daniel Reis"
"__export__.res_partner_44_6be5a130","Holger Brunn"
"__export__.res_partner_42_38b48275","Packt Publishing"
```

The first row contains the field names, which will be used during the import to automatically map the columns to their destination.

As expected, we can see two columns:

- `id`, with the external ID assigned to each record. If none exist yet, a new one is automatically generated using the `__export__` prefix in place of an actual module name.
- `name`, with the Contact / Partner name.

Having the External ID enables us to edit the exported data and later re-import it, thus updating those records with the changes made.

> Because of the automatically generated record identifiers, the export or import features can be used to mass edit Odoo data: export the data to CSV, use a spreadsheet software to mass edit it, and then import it back to Odoo.

Importing data

First, we have to make sure that the import feature is enabled. It should be enabled by default. If not, the option is available in the **Settings** app, in the **General Settings** menu item. Under the **Users** section, the **Import & Export** option should be checked.

With this option enabled, list views show an **Import** option next to the **Create** button at the top of the list.

> The **Import & Export** setting installs the `base_import` module, which is responsible for providing this feature.

Let's try a bulk edit on our Contact or Partner data. Open the CSV file we just downloaded in a spreadsheet or a text editor and change a few values. We can also add some new rows, leaving the id column blank for them.

As mentioned previously, the first column, id, provides a unique identifier for each row. This allows pre-existing records to be updated instead of us needing to duplicate them when we import the data back to Odoo. If we edit any of the names in the exported file, the corresponding record will be updated when we import the file.

For the new rows that have been added to the CSV file, we can choose to either provide an external identifier of our choice or we can leave the id column blank. Either way, a new record will be created for them. As an example, we added a line with no id and the name Phillip K. Dick to be created in the database.

After saving the changes to the CSV file, click on the **Import** option (next to the **Create** button), and we will be presented with the import assistant:

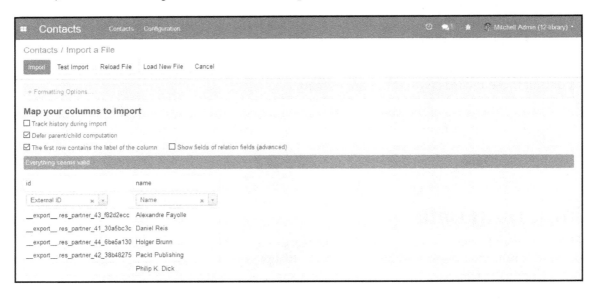

There, we should select the CSV file's location on the disk and then click on the **Test Import** button, at the top right, to check it for correctness.

Since the file to import is based on an Odoo export, there is a good chance that it will be valid, and the columns will be automatically mapped to their proper destination in the database. Depending on the application used to edit the data file, you may have to play with the separator and encoding options to get the best results.

Now, we can click on **Import**, and there you go, our modifications and new records should have been loaded into Odoo.

Related records in CSV data files

The examples in the previous section were quite simple, but the data files can become more complex once we start using relational fields, linking records from several tables.

We handled Partner records used in Books. We will now look at how we can represent the reference for these Partners in a CSV file for Book data. In particular, we have a many-to-one (or a foreign key) relation for the Publisher (`publisher_id` field) and a many-to-many relation for the Authors (`author_ids` field).

In the CSV file header line, relation columns should have `/id` appended to their name. It will reference the related records using external identifiers. In our example, we will load the book publisher in a `publisher_id/id` field, using the external ID for the related partner as values.

> It is possible to use `/.id` instead so that we can use the actual database IDs (the real numeric identifier assigned), but this is rarely what we need. Unless you have good reason to do otherwise, always use external IDs instead of database IDs. Also, remember that database IDs are specific to a particular Odoo database, and so, most of the time, it won't work correctly if imported into a database other than the original one.

Many-to-many fields can also be imported through CSV data files. It's as easy as providing a comma-separated list of external IDs, surrounded by double quotes. For example, to load the book authors, we would have an `author_ids/id` column, where we would use a comma-separated list of the External IDS of the Partners to link as values:

```
id, name, author_ids/id
book_odc11, "Odoo 11 Development Cookbook",
"__export__.res_partner_43_f82d2ecc,__export__.res_partner_44_6be5a130"
```

One-to-many fields often represent header or lines, or parent or child relations, and there is special support to import these types of relations: for the same parent record, we can have several related lines.

Here, we have an example of a one-to-many field in the partners model: a company partner can have several child contacts. If we export the data from the **Partner** model, and include the **Contacts/Name** field, we will see the structure that can be used to import this type of data:

id	name	child_ids/id	child_ids/name
base.res_partner_12	Azure Interior	base.res_partner_address_15	Brandon Freeman
		base.res_partner_address_28	Colleen Diaz
		base.res_partner_address_16	Nicole Ford

The `id` and `name` columns are for the parent records, and the `child_ids` columns are for the child records. Notice how the parent record columns are left blank for child records after the first one.

The preceding table, represented as a CSV file, looks as follows:

```
"id","name","child_ids/id","child_ids/name"
"base.res_partner_12","Azure
Interior","base.res_partner_address_15","Brandon Freeman"
"","","base.res_partner_address_28","Colleen Diaz"
"","","base.res_partner_address_16","Nicole Ford"
```

We can see that the first two columns, `id` and `name`, have values in the first line and are empty in the next two lines. They have data for the parent record, which is the Contact's Company.

The other two columns are both prefixed with `child_ids/` and have values on all three lines. They have data for the contacts related to the parent company. The first line has data for both the company and the first contact, and the lines that follow have data for the columns of the child contacts.

Adding module data

Modules use data files to load their default data, demonstration data, user interface definitions, and other configurations into the database. For this, we can use both CSV and XML files.

Changes in Odoo12
The YAML file format was also supported until Odoo 11, and was removed in Odoo 12. Still, for a usage example, you can look at the l10n_be official module in Odoo 11, and for information on the YAML format, you can visit http://yaml.org/.

CSV files used by modules are exactly the same as those we have seen and used for the import feature. When using them in modules, the filename must match the name of the model to which the data will be loaded. For example, a CSV file loading data into the library.book model must be named library.book.csv.

A common usage of data CSV files is for accessing security definitions that have been loaded into the ir.model.access model. They usually use CSV files in a security/ subdirectory, named ir.model.access.csv.

Demonstration data

Odoo add-on modules may install demonstration data, and it is considered good practice to do so. This is useful for providing usage examples for a module and the datasets to be used in tests. Demonstration data for a module is declared using the demo attribute of the __manifest__.py manifest file. Just like the data attribute, it is a list of filenames with the corresponding relative paths inside the module.

We should add some demonstration data to our library.book module. An easy way to do this is to export some data from the development database with the module installed.

The convention is to place data files in a data/ subdirectory. We should save these data files in the library_app add-on module as data/library.book.csv. Since this data will be owned by our module, we should edit the id values to remove the __export__ prefix in the identifiers generated by the export feature.

As an example, our res.partner.csv data file might look as follows:

```
id,name
res_partner_alexandre,"Alexandre Fayolle"
res_partner_daniel,"Daniel Reis"
res_partner_holger,"Holger Brunn"
res_partner_packt,"Packt Publishing"
```

And the `library.book.csv` data file with the Book demo data as follows:

```
"id","name","date_published","publisher_id/id","author_ids/id"
library_book_ode11,"Odoo Development Essentials
11","2018-03-01",res_partner_packt,res_partner_daniel

library_book_odc11,"Odoo 11 Development
Cookbook","2018-01-01",res_partner_packt,"res_partner_alexandre,res_partner
_holger"
```

Note that we added an extra line break for clarity, but it should not be in the `module` file.

We must not forget to add these data files to the `__manifest__.py` manifest's `demo` attribute:

```
'demo': [
    'data/res.partner.csv',
    'data/library.book.csv',
],
```

The files are loaded in the order they are declared. This is important, since records in a file cannot reference other records that haven't yet been created.

Next time we update the module, as long as it is installed with demo data enabled, the content of the file will be imported.

 While data files are also re-imported on module upgrades, this is not the case for the demo data files: these are only imported upon module installation.

Of course, XML files can also be used to load or initialize data, leveraging the additional features they provide, when compared to plain CSV files.

Using XML data files

While CSV files provide a simple and compact format to represent data, XML files are more powerful and give more control over the loading process. For example, their filenames are not required to match the model to be loaded. This is because the XML format is much richer and more information regarding what to load can be provided through the XML elements inside the file.

We already used XML data files in the previous chapters. The user interface components, such as views and menu items, are, in fact, records that are stored in system models. The XML files in the modules are the means used to load these records into the instance database.

To showcase this, we will add a second data file to the `library_app` module, `data/book_demo.xml`, with the following content:

```xml
<?xml version="1.0"?>
<odoo noupdate="1">
  <!-- Data to load -->
  <record model="res.partner" id="res_partner_huxley">
    <field name="name">Aldous Huxley</field>
  </record>
  <record model="library.book" id="library_book_bnw">
    <field name="name">Brave New World</field>
    <field name="author_ids"
           eval="[(4, ref('res_partner_huxley'))]" />
    <field name="date_published">1932-01-01</field>
  </record>
</odoo>
```

As usual, the new data file must be declared in the `__manifest__.py` file:

```python
'demo': [
    'data/res.partner.csv',
    'data/library.book.csv',
    'data/book_demo.xml',
],
```

Similar to the CSV data file we saw in the previous section, this file also loads data into the Library Books Model.

XML data files have an `<odoo>` top element, inside of which we can have several `<record>` elements that correspond to the CSV data rows.

The `<odoo>` top element in data files was introduced in version 9.0 and replaces the former `<openerp>` tag. A `<data>` section inside the top element is still supported, but it's now optional. In fact, now, `<odoo>` and `<data>` are equivalent, so we could use either one as top elements for our XML data files.

A `<record>` element has two mandatory attributes, `model` and `id`, for the external identifier for the record, and contains a `<field>` tag for each field to write on.

Note that the slash notation in the field names is not available here; we can't use `<field name="publisher_id/id">`. Instead, the `ref` special attribute is used to reference external identifiers. We'll discuss the values of the relational to-many fields in a moment.

You may have noticed the `noupdate="1"` attribute in the top `<odoo>` element. This prevents the data records from being loaded on module upgrades so that any later edits to them are not lost.

The noupdate data attribute

When a module is upgraded, the data file loading is repeated, and the module's records are rewritten. It is important to keep in mind that this means that upgrading a module will overwrite any manual changes that might have been made to the module's data.

Notably, if views were manually modified to add customization, these changes will be lost with the next module upgrade. To avoid this, the correct approach is to instead create inherited views with the changes we want to introduce.

This rewrite behavior is the default, but it can be changed so that some of the data is only imported at install time, and is ignored in later module upgrades. This is done using the `noupdate="1"` attribute in the `<odoo>` or `<data>` elements.

This is useful for data that is to be used as initial configuration but is expected to be customized later, because these manually made customizations will be safe from module upgrades. For example, it is frequently used for record access rules, allowing them to be adapted to implementation-specific needs.

It is possible to have more than one `<data>` section in the same XML file. We can take advantage of this to separate data to import only once, with `noupdate="1"`, and data that can be re-imported on each upgrade, with `noupdate="0"`. `noupdate="0"` is the default, so we can just omit it if we prefer. Note that we need to have a top-level XML element, so in this case, we will use two `<data>` sections. They must be inside a top level `<odoo>` or `<data>` element.

The `noupdate` attribute can be tricky when developing modules, because changes made to the data later will be ignored. One solution is to, instead of upgrading the module with the `-u` option, re-install it using the `-i` option. Reinstalling from the command line using the `-i` option ignores the `noupdate` flags on data records.

The `noupdate` flag is stored in the **External Identifier** information for each record. It's possible to manually edit it directly using the **External Identifier** form, which is available in the **Technical** menu, by using the **Non Updatable** checkbox.

Changes in Odoo 12
In the **Developer Menu**, when accessing **View Metadata**, the dialog box now also shows the value for the **No Update** flag, along with the record's **XML ID**. Furthermore, the No Update flag can be changed there by clicking on it.

Defining records in XML

In an XML data file, each `<record>` element has two basic attributes, `id` and `model`, and contains `<field>` elements that assign values to each column. The `id` attribute corresponds to the record's external identifier and the `model` attribute corresponds to the target model. The `<field>` elements have a few different ways to assign values. Let's look at them in detail.

Setting field values directly

The `name` attribute of a `<field>` element identifies the field to write on.

The value to write is the element content: the text between the field's opening and closing tag. For dates and date-times, `eval` attributes with expressions returning `date` or `datetime` objects will work. Returning strings with `"YYYY-mm-dd"` and `"YYYY-mm-dd HH:MM:SS"` will be properly converted. For boolean fields, the `"0"` and `"False"` values are converted to `False`, and any other non-empty values will be converted to `True`.

Changes in Odoo 10
The way Boolean `False` values are read from data files is improved in Odoo 10. In previous versions, any non-empty values, including `"0"` and `"False"`, were converted to `True`. Until Odoo 9, Boolean values should be set using the `eval` attribute, such as `eval="False"`.

Setting values using expressions

A more elaborate alternative for setting a field value is the `eval` attribute. It evaluates a Python expression and assigns the result to the field.

The expression is evaluated in a context that, besides Python built-ins, also has some additional identifiers that are available to build the expression to evaluate.

To handle dates, the following Python modules are available: `time`, `datetime`, `timedelta`, and `relativedelta`. They allow you to calculate date values, something that is frequently used in demonstration and test data, so that the dates used are close to the module installation date. For more information about these Python modules, see the documentation at https://docs.python.org/3/library/datatypes.html.

For example, to set a value to yesterday, we will use the following code:

```
<field name="date_published"
       eval="(datetime.now() + timedelta(-1))" />
```

Also available in the evaluation context is the `ref()` function, which is used to translate an external identifier into the corresponding database ID. This can be used to set values for relational fields. As an example, we can use it to set the value for `publisher_id`:

```
<field name="publisher_id" eval="ref('res_partner_packt')" />
```

Setting values on many-to-one relation fields

For many-to-one relation fields, the value to write is the database ID for the linked record. In XML files, we usually know the XML ID for the record, and we need to have it translated into the actual database ID.

One way is to use the `eval` attribute with a `ref()` function, like we just did in the previous section.

A simpler alternative is to use the `ref` attribute, which is available for `<field>` elements. Using it to set the value for the `publisher_id` many-to-one field, we would write the following:

```
<field name="publisher_id" ref="res_partner_packt" />
```

Setting values on to-many relation fields

For one-to-many and many-to-many fields, instead of a single ID, a list of related IDs is expected. Furthermore, several operations can be performed—we may want to replace the current list of related records with a new one, or append a few records to it, or even unlink some records.

To support write operations on to-many fields, we use a special syntax in the `eval` attribute. To write to a to-many field, we use a list of triples. Each triple is a `write` command that does different things according to the code used in the first element.

To overwrite the list of authors of a book, we would use the following code:

```
<field name="author_ids"
       eval="[(6, 0,
              [ref('res_partner_alexandre'),
               ref('res_partner_holger')]
              )]"
/>
```

To append a linked record to the current list of the authors of a book, we would use the following code:

```
<field name="author_ids"
       eval="[(4, ref('res_partner_daniel'))]"
/>
```

The preceding examples are the most common. In both cases, we used just one command, but we could chain several commands in the outer list. The `append (4)` and `replace (6)` commands are the most used. In the case of the `append (4)`, the last value of the tripled is not used and is not needed, so it can be omitted, as we did in the preceding code sample.

The complete list of available commands is as follows:

- `(0, _ , {'field': value})` creates a new record and links it to this one.
- `(1, id, {'field': value})` updates the values on an already linked record.
- `(2, id, _)` removes the link to and deletes the `id` related record.
- `(3, id, _)` removes the link to, but does not delete, the `id` related record. This is usually what you will use to delete related records on many-to-many fields.
- `(4, id, _)` links an already existing record. This can only be used for many-to-many fields.
- `(5, _, _)` removes all the links, without deleting the linked records.
- `(6, _, [ids])` replaces the list of linked records with the provided list.

The _ underscore symbol used in the preceding list represents irrelevant values, usually filled with 0 or `False`.

The trailing irrelevant values can be safely omitted. For example, (4, id, _) can be used as (4, id).

Shortcuts for frequently used models

If we go back to Chapter 3, *Your First Odoo Application*, we will find elements other than `<record>` in the XML files, such as `<act_window>` and `<menuitem>`.

These are convenient shortcuts for frequently used models, with a more compact notation compared to the regular `<record>` elements. They are used to load data into base models, supporting the user interface, and will be explored in more detail later, in Chapter 10, *Backend Views – Designing the User Interface*.

For reference, these are the shortcut elements available, along with the corresponding models they load data into:

- `<act_window>` is for the window action model, `ir.actions.act_window`
- `<menuitem>` is for the menu items model, `ir.ui.menu`
- `<report>` is for the report action model, `ir.actions.report.xml`
- `<template>` is for QWeb templates stored in the `ir.ui.view` model

Changes in Odoo 11
The `<url>` tag was deprecated and removed. In previous versions, it was used to load records for the URL action model, `ir.actions.act_url`.

It is important to note that, when used to modify existing records, the shortcut elements overwrite all the fields. This differs from the `<record>` basic element, which only writes to the fields provided. So, for cases where we need to modify just a particular field of a user interface element, we should do it using a `<record>` element instead.

Other actions in XML data files

So far, we have seen how to add or update data using XML files. But XML files also allow you to delete data and execute arbitrary model methods. This can be useful for more complex date setups.

Deleting records

To delete a data record, we can use the `<delete>` element, providing it with either an ID or a search domain to find the target records.

For example, using a search domain to find the record to delete looks as follows:

```
<delete
  model="res.partner"
  search="[('id','=',ref('library_app.res_partner_daniel'))]"
/>
```

If we know the specific ID to delete, we can use it with the `id` attribute instead. This was the case for the previous example, so it could also be written like this, for the same effect:

```
<delete model="res.partner" id="library_app.res_partner_daniel" />
```

Calling model methods

An XML file can also execute arbitrary methods during its load process through the `<function>` element. This can be used to set up demo and test data.

For example, the Notes app, which is bundled with Odoo, uses it to set up demonstration data:

```
<data noupdate="1">
<function
    model="res.users"
    name="_init_data_user_note_stages"
    eval="[]" />
</data>
```

This calls the `_init_data_user_note_stages` method of the `res.users` Model, passing no arguments. The argument list is provided by the `eval` attribute, which is an empty list in this case.

Summary

In this chapter, we learned how to represent data in text files. These can be used to manually import data into Odoo, or to include in add-on modules as default or demonstration data.

At this point, we should be able to export and import CSV data files from the web interface, and leverage external IDs to detect and update records that already exist in the database. This can also be used to perform a mass edit on data, by editing and reimporting a CSV file that has been exported from Odoo.

We also learned about how the XML data files are structured, and all the features they provide, in more detail. These were not only set values on fields, but also performing actions such as deleting records and calling model methods.

In the next chapter, we will focus on how to use records to work with the data contained in models. This will give us the necessary tools to then implement our application's business logic and rules.

Questions

1. What is the difference between an XML ID and an external ID?
2. What type of data files can be used for addon modules?
3. What is wrong in the following XML fragment?
   ```
   <field name="user_id">[(4, 0, [ref(base.user_demo)])]</field>?
   ```
4. Can a data file in one addon module overwrite a record created in another module?
5. When an addon module is upgraded, are all of its data records rewritten to the module's default values?

Further reading

The Odoo official documentation provides additional resources on data files: https://www.odoo.com/documentation/12.0/reference/data.html#.

Models – Structuring the Application Data

6

In `Chapter 3`, *Your First Odoo Application*, we saw an overview of all the main components involved in building an application for Odoo. In this and the next chapters, we will go into detail on each of the layers that make up an application: models, views, and business logic.

In this chapter, we will learn more about the model layer, and how to use models to design the data structures that support applications. We will explore the capabilities of models and fields, including defining model relations, adding computed fields, and creating data constraints.

The following topics will be covered in this chapter:

- Learning project—improving the Library app
- Creating models
- Creating fields
- Relationships between models
- Computed fields
- Model constraints
- About the Odoo base models

Technical requirements

The code in this chapter is based on the code created in `Chapter 3`, *Your First Odoo Application*. The necessary code can be found in the `ch03/` directory of the Git repository at `https://github.com/PacktPublishing/Odoo-12-Development-Essentials-Fourth-Edition`. The code of this chapter can be found at `https://github.com/PacktPublishing/Odoo-12-Development-Essentials-Fourth-Edition/tree/master/ch05/library_app`.

You should have it in your add-ons path and install the `library_app` module. The examples in this chapter will modify and add code in that add-on module.

Learning project – improving the Library app

In `Chapter 3`, *Your First Odoo Application*, we created the `library_app` add-on module, implementing a simple `library.book` model to represent the book catalog. In this chapter, we will revisit that module to enrich the data we can store regarding each book.

We will add a category hierarchy, to use for book categorization, with the following:

- **Name**: The category title
- **Parent**: The Parent category it belongs to
- **Subcategories**: The categories that have this one as parent
- **Featured book or author**: A selected book or author that represents this category

The book model already has fields for essential information, and we will add a few more to showcase the several data types available in Odoo.

We will also add some constraints to the Books Model:

- The title and publication date should be unique
- ISBNs entered should be valid

Creating models

Models are at the heart of the Odoo framework. They describe the application's data structure, and are the bridge between the application server and the database storage. Business logic can be implemented around models to provide the application's features, and user interfaces are created on top of them.

Next, we will learn about a model's generic attributes, used to influence their behavior, and the several model types we have available to use—regular, transient, and abstract.

Model attributes

Model classes can use additional attributes that control some of their behaviors. These are the most commonly used attributes:

- _name is the internal identifier for the Odoo model we are creating. This is mandatory when creating a new model.
- _description is a user-friendly title for the model's records, shown when the model is viewed in the user interface. This is optional but recommended.
- _order sets the default order to use when the model's records are browsed, or shown in a list view. It is a text string to be used as the SQL order by clause, so it can be anything you could use there, although it has smart behavior and supports translatable and many-to-one field names.

Our book model is already using the _name and _description attributes. We can add it in the _order to have it ordered by default by book title, and then by reverse order of publication date (from newest to oldest):

```
class Book(models.Model):
    _name = 'library.book'
    _description = 'Book'
    _order = 'name, date_published desc'
```

There are a few more attributes that can be used in advanced cases:

- _rec_name indicates the field to use as the record description when referenced from related fields, such as a many-to-one relationship. By default, it uses the name field, which is a common field in models, but this attribute allows us to use any other field for that purpose.
- _table is the name of the database table supporting the model. Usually, it is left to be automatically defined by the ORM, using the model name with the dots replaced by underscores. But, it's possible to set it to indicate a specific table name.
- _log_access=False can be specified to prevent the automatic creation of the audit tracking fields: create_uid, create_date, write_uid, and write_date.
- _auto=False can be specified to prevent the automatic creation of the underlying database table. If needed, the init() class method should be overridden to create the supporting database object, a table or a view.

We can also have the _inherit and _inherits attributes, used to extend modules. We will look closer at them later in this chapter.

Models and Python classes

Odoo models are represented by Python classes. In the preceding code, we have a Python class, `Book`, based on the `models.Model` class, which defines a new Odoo model called `library.book`.

Odoo models are kept in a central registry, available in the `env` environment object (referred to as a `pool` in the old API). It is a dictionary that keeps references to all the model classes available in the database, and its entries can be referenced by a model name. Specifically, the code in a model method can use `self.env['library.book']` to retrieve the model class representing the `library.book` model.

You can see that model names are important since they are the keys used to access the registry. The convention for model names is to use a list of lowercase words joined with dots, such as `library.book` or `library.book.category`. Other examples from the core modules are `project.project`, `project.task`, and `project.task.type`.

We should use the singular form for model names: `library.book` rather than `library.books`.

For historical reasons, it is possible to find some core models that don't follow this, such as `res.users`, but this is not the rule.

Model names must be globally unique. Because of this, the first word should correspond to the main application the module relates to. For our Library app features, we will prefix all models with `library`. Other examples from the core modules are `project`, `crm`, and `sale`.

Python classes, on the other hand, are local to the Python file where they are declared. The identifier used for them is only significant for the code in that file, and is rarely relevant. Since there is no risk of collision with classes in other modules, there is no need for class identifiers to be prefixed by the main application they relate to.

The convention for class identifiers is to use `CamelCase`. This follows the Python standard defined by the PEP8 coding conventions.

Transient and abstract models

In the preceding code, and in most Odoo models, classes are based on the `models.Model` class. These types of model have permanent database persistence: database tables are created for them and their records are stored until explicitly deleted.

However, Odoo also provides two other model types to be used: transient and abstract models.

Transient models are based on the `models.TransientModel` class and are used for wizard-style user interaction. Their data is still stored in the database, but it is expected to be temporary. A vacuum job periodically clears old data from these tables. For example, the **Load a Language** dialog window, found in the **Settings | Translations** menu, uses a Transient model to store user selections and implement wizard logic. An example of using a Transient model is discussed in `Chapter 8`, *Business Logic – Supporting Business Processes*.

Abstract models are based on the `models.AbstractModel` class and have no data storage attached to them. They can be used as reusable feature sets, to be mixed in with other models using Odoo's inheritance capabilities. For example, `mail.thread` is an abstract model provided by the Discuss app, used to add message and follower features to other models.

Inspecting existing models

The models and fields created through the Python classes have their metadata available through the user interface. With the **Developer Mode** enabled, in the **Settings** top menu, navigate to the **Technical | Database Structure | Models** menu item. Here, you will find the list of all the models available in the database.

Clicking on a model in the list will open a form with its details:

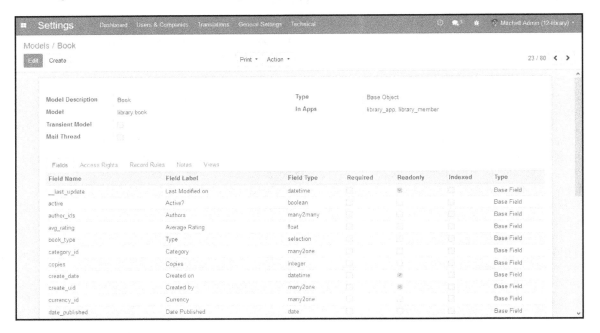

This is a good tool for inspecting the structure of a model, since, in one place, you can see the results of all the customization of different modules. In this case, as you can see near the top right of the form, in the **In Apps** field, the library.book definitions for this model come from both the library_app and library_member modules.

In the lower area, we have some tabs available with additional information:

- **Fields** with a quick reference for the model's fields
- **Access Rights** with the access control rules granted to security groups
- **Views** with the list of views available for this model

We can find the model's **External Identifier** here using the **Developer menu**, with the **View Metadata** option. The model's external identifiers, or XML IDs, are automatically generated by the ORM but are fairly predictable—for the library.book model, the external identifier is model_library_book. These XML IDs are frequently used in the CSV files defining the security ACLs.

As we have seen in `Chapter 1`, *Quick Start Using the Developer Mode*, the **Models** form is editable! It's possible to create and modify models, fields, and views from here. You can use this to build prototypes that would later be implemented as add-on modules.

Creating fields

After creating a new model, the next step is to add fields to it. Odoo supports all the basic data types expected, such as text strings, integers, floating point numbers, Booleans, dates, date-times, and image or binary data.

Let's explore the several types of field available in Odoo.

Basic field types

We will revisit the book model to present the several field types available. We should edit the `library_app/models/library_book.py` file and edit the `Book` class to look like this:

```
# class Book(models.Model):
    # ...

    # String fields: name = fields.Char('Title')
    isbn = fields.Char('ISBN')
    book_type = fields.Selection(
        [('paper','Paperback'),
         ('hard','Hardcover'),
         ('electronic','Electronic'),
         ('other', 'Other')],
        'Type')
    notes = fields.Text('Internal Notes')
    descr = fields.Html('Description')

    # Numeric fields:
    copies = fields.Integer(default=1)
    avg_rating = fields.Float('Average Rating', (3, 2))
    price = fields.Monetary('Price', 'currency_id')
    currency_id = fields.Many2one('res.currency')  # price helper

    # Date and time fields:
    date_published = fields.Date()
    last_borrow_date = fields.Datetime(
        'Last Borrowed On',
        default=lambda self: fields.Datetime.now())
```

```
# Other fields:
active = fields.Boolean('Active?')
image = fields.Binary('Cover')

# Relational Fields
# ...to be added...
```

Here, we have a sample of the non-relational field types available in Odoo with the positional arguments expected by each one.

 Python allows for two types of arguments: positional and keyword. Positional arguments are expected to be used in a specific order. For example, `f(x, y)` should be called with something like `f(1, 2)`. Keyword arguments are passed with the name of the argument. For the same example, we could use `f(x=1, y=2)`, or even mix both style with `f(1, y=2)`. More information on keyword arguments can be found in the Python official documentation at `https://docs.python.org/3/tutorial/controlflow.html#keyword-arguments`.

For most non-relational fields, the first argument is the field title, corresponding to the `string` field argument. It is used as the default text for the user interface labels. It's optional and, if not provided, a title string will be automatically generated from the field name, replacing underscores with spaces and capitalizing the first letter in each word.

These are the non-relational field types available, along with the positional arguments expected by each:

- `Char(string)` is a single line of text. The only positional argument expected is the string field label.
- `Text(string)` is a multiline text. The only positional argument is the string the field label.
- `Selection(selection, string)` is a drop-down selection list. The selection positional arguments is a `[('value', 'Title'),]` list of tuples. The first tuple element is the value stored in the database. The second tuple element is the description presented in the user interface. This list can be extended by other modules using the `selection_add` keyword argument.
- `Html(string)` is stored as a text field, but has specific handling of the user interface for HTML content presentation. For security reasons, it is sanitized by default, but this behavior can be overridden.
- `Integer(string)` just expects a string argument for the field title.

- `Float(string, digits)` has a second optional argument digits, an (x, y) tuple with the field's precision. x is the total number of digits; of those, y are decimal digits.
- `Monetary(string, currency_field)` is similar to a float field, but has specific handling for currency. The `currency_field` second argument is used to set the field storing the currency being used. By default, it is expected to be the `currency_id` field.
- `Date(string)` and `Datetime(string)` fields expect only the string text as a positional argument.
- `Boolean(string)` holds True or False values, as you might expect, and only has one positional argument for the string text.
- `Binary(string)` stores file-like binary data, and also expects only the string argument. It can be handled by Python code using `base64` encoded strings.

Changed in Odoo 12

The `Date` and `Datetime` fields are now handled in the ORM as date objects. In previous versions, they were handled as text string representations, and, to be manipulated, needed explicit conversion to and from Python date objects.

`Text` fields, `Char`, `Text`, and `Html`, have a few specific attributes:

- `size` (*Char* fields only) sets a maximum size allowed. It's recommended to not use it unless there is a good reason for it, for example, a social security number with a maximum length allowed.
- `translate` makes the field contents translatable, holding different values for different languages.
- `trim`, set to True by default, activates automatic trimming of surrounding white space, performed by the web client. This can be explicitly disabled by setting `trim=false`.

Changed in Odoo 12

The trim field attribute was introduced in Odoo 12. In previous versions, text fields saved surrounding white space.

Other than these, we also have the relational fields, which will be introduced later in this chapter. However, before that, there is still more to know about the attributes of the field types.

Common field attributes

Fields have additional attributes available for us to define their behavior.

These are the generally available attributes, usually used as keyword arguments:

- `string` is the field's default label, to be used in the user interface. Except for `Selection` and `Relational` fields, it is the first positional argument, so most of the time it is not used as a keyword argument. If not provided, it is automatically generated from the field name.
- `default` sets a default value for the field. It can be a specific value (such as the `default=True` in the `active` field), or a callable reference, either a named function or an anonymous function.
- `help` provides the text for tool tips displayed to users when they hover their mouse over the field in the UI.
- `readonly=True` makes the field not editable in the user interface by default. This is not enforced at the API level; code in model methods will still be capable of writing to it. It is only a user interface setting.
- `required=True` makes the field mandatory in the user interface by default. This is enforced at the database level by adding a `NOT NULL` constraint on the column.
- `index=True` adds a database index on the field, for faster search operations at the expense of slightly slower write operations.
- `copy=False` has the field ignored when using the duplicate record feature, the `copy()` ORM method. Field values are copied by default, except for to-many relational fields, that are not copied by default.
- `groups` allows limiting the field's access and visibility to only some groups. It expects a comma-separated list of XML IDs for security groups, such as `groups='base.group_user,base.group_system'`.
- `states` expects dictionary mapping values for UI attributes depending on values of the `state` field. The attributes that can be used are `readonly`, `required`, and `invisible`, for example, `states={'done':[('readonly',True)]}`.

Note that the `states` field attribute is equivalent to the `attrs` attribute in views. Also, note that views support a `states` attribute, but it has a different use: it accepts a comma-separated list of states to control when the element should be visible.

Here is an example of the use of keyword arguments for field attributes:

```
name = fields.Char(
    'Title',
    default=None,
    index=True,
    help='Book cover title.',
    readonly=False,
    required=True,
    translate=False,
)
```

As mentioned before, the default attribute can have a fixed value, or a reference to a function to dynamically compute the default value. For trivial computations, we can use a `lambda` function to avoid the overhead of creating a named function or method. Here is a common example, computing a default value with the current date and time:

```
last_borrow_date = fields.Datetime(
    'Last Borrowed On',
    default=lambda self: fields.Datetime.now(),
)
```

The `default` value can also be a function reference, or a string with the name of a yet to be declared function:

```
last_borrow_date = fields.Datetime(
    'Last Borrowed On',
    default='_default_last_borrow_date',
)

def _default_last_borrow_date(self):
    return fields.Datetime.now()
```

These two attributes can be helpful when the module data structure changes between versions:

- `deprecated=True` logs a warning whenever the field is being used.
- `oldname='field'` is used when a field is renamed in a newer version, enabling the data in the old field to be automatically copied into the new field, upon the next module upgrade.

Special field names

Some field names are special, either because they are reserved by the ORM for special purposes, or because some built-in features make use of some default field names.

The id field is reserved to be used as an automatic number uniquely identifying each record and the database primary key. It's automatically added to every model.

The following fields are automatically created on new models, unless the _log_access=False model attribute is set:

- create_uid is for the user that created the record.
- create_date is for the date and time when the record is created.
- write_uid is for the last user to modify the record.
- write_date is for the last date and time when the record was modified.

The information in these fields is available in the web client, for any record, in the **Developer Mode** menu, with the **View Metadata** option.

Some built-in API features expect specific field names by default. Our lives would be easier if we could avoid using these field names for purposes other than the intended ones. Some of them are actually reserved and can't be used for other purposes at all:

- name (usually a Char) is used by default as the display name for the record. Usually, it is a Char, but can also be a Text or a Many2one field type. The field used for the display name can be changed with the _rec_name Model attribute.
- active (type Boolean) allows us to deactivate records. Records with active=False will automatically be excluded from queries. This automatic filter can be disabled by adding {'active_test': False} to the current context. It can be used as a record *archive* or *soft delete* feature.
- state (type Selection) represents the basic states of the record's life cycle. It allows using the states field attribute to have different UI behavior depending on record state. Dynamically modify the view: fields can be made readonly, required, or invisible in specific record states.
- parent_id and parent_path (type Integer and Char) have special meaning for parent or child hierarchical relations. We will discuss them in detail later in this chapter.

 Changed in Odoo 12
Hierarchical relations now use the parent_path field, which replaces the parent_left and parent_right fields (of type Integer) used in previous versions, now deprecated.

So far, we've discussed non-relational fields. But a good part of an application data structure is about describing the relationships between entities. Let's look at that now.

Relationships between models

Non-trivial business application have a structured data model, and need to relate the data from the different entities involved. To do this, we need to use relational fields.

Looking again at our Library app, in the book model we can see the following relationships:

- Each book can have one publisher. This is a **many-to-one relationship**, implemented in the database engine as a foreign key. The inverse is a **one-to-many relationship**, meaning that each publisher can have many books.
- Each book can have many authors. That's a **many-to-many** relationship. The inverse relationship is also a many-to-many, since each author can have many books.

We will explore each of these relationships in the next sections.

A particular case is hierarchical relationships, where records in a Model are related to other records in the same Model. We will introduce a book category model to explain that case.

Finally, the Odoo framework also supports flexible relationships, where a field is able to point to records in different tables. These are called `Reference` fields.

Many-to-one relationships

A many-to-one relationship is a reference to a record in another model. For example, in the library book model, the `publisher_id` field represents the book publisher, and is a reference to a record in the partner model:

```
publisher_id = fields.Many2one(
    'res.partner', string='Publisher')
```

The `Many2one` fields, first positional argument is the related model (the `comodel` keyword argument), as is the case for all relational fields.

The second positional argument is the field label (the `string` keyword argument), but this is not the case for the other relational fields, so the preferred option is to always use `string` as a keyword argument, as we did in the previous code.

A many-to-one Model field creates a field in the database table, with a foreign key to the related table, and holding the database ID of the related record.

The following keyword arguments specific to many-to-one fields can also be used:

- `ondelete` defines what happens when the related record is deleted:
  - `set null` (the default): an empty value is set when the related record is deleted
  - `restricted` raises an error preventing the deletion
  - `cascade` will also delete this record when the related record is deleted
- `context` is a dictionary of data, meaningful for the web client views, to carry information when navigating through the relationship, for example, to set default values. It will be better explained in `Chapter 8`, *Business Logic - Supporting Business Processes*.
- `domain` is a domain expression: a list of tuples used to filter the records made available for selection on the relation field. See `Chapter 8`, *Business Logic - Supporting Business Processes*, for more details.
- `auto_join=True` allows the ORM to use SQL joins when doing searches using this relationship. If used, the access security rules will be bypassed, and the user could have access to related records the security rules wouldn't allow, but the SQL queries will be more efficient and run faster.
- `delegate=True` creates a delegation inheritance with the related Model. When used, you must also set `required=True` and `ondelete='cascade'`. See `Chapter 4`, *Extending Modules*, for more information on delegation inheritance.

One-to-many inverse relationships

A one-to-many relationship is the inverse of the many-to-one. It lists the records of the related Model that have a reference to this record.

For example, in the library book model, the `publisher_id` field is a many-to-one relationship with the partner model. This means that the partner model can have a one-to-many inverse relation with the book model, listing the books published by each partner.

To have that relationship available, we can add it in the partner model. Add the `library_app/models/res_partner.py` file with this:

```
from odoo import fields, models

class Partner(models.Model):
    _inherit = 'res.partner'
    published_book_ids = fields.One2many(
        'library.book',   # related model
        'publisher_id',   # field for "this" on related model
        string='Published Books')
```

Since we are adding a new code file to the module, we must not forget to also import it in the `library_app/models/__init__.py` file:

```
from . import library_book
from . import res_partner
```

The `One2many` fields accept three positional arguments:

- The related model (`comodel_name` keyword argument).
- The field in that model referring to this record (`inverse_name` keyword argument).
- The field label (`string` keyword argument).

The additional keyword arguments available are the same as for many-to-one fields: `context`, `domain`, and `ondelete` (here acting on the **many** side of the relationship).

Many-to-many relationships

A many-to-many relationship is used when we have a to-many relationship on both sides. Taking our library books example again, we can find a many-to-many relationship between books and authors: each book can have many authors, and each author can have many books.

On the books side, we have on the `library.book` model:

```
class Book(models.Model)
    _name = 'library.book'
    author_ids = fields.Many2many(
        'res.partner', string='Authors')
```

On the authors side, we can add the inverse relation to the res.partner model:

```
class Partner(models.Model):
    _inherit = 'res.partner'
    book_ids = fields.Many2many(
        'library.book', string='Authored Books')
```

The Many2many minimal signature accepts one positional argument for the related model (the comodel_name keyword argument), and it is strongly recommended to also provide the string argument with the field label.

At the database level, many-to-many relationships don't add any columns to the existing tables. Instead, a special relationship table is automatically created, to store the relations between records. This special table has only two ID fields, with foreign keys for each of the two related tables.

By default, the relationship table name is the two table names joined with an underscore and _rel appended at the end. In the case of our books or authors relationship, it should be named library_book_res_partner_rel.

On some occasions, we may need to override these automatic defaults. One such case is when the related models have long names, and the name for the automatically generated relationship table is too long, exceeding the 63-character PostgreSQL limit. In these cases, we need to manually choose a name for the relationship table to conform to the table name size limit.

Another case is when we need a second many-to-many relationship between the same models. In these cases, we need to manually provide a name for the relationship table so that it doesn't collide with the table name already being used for the first relationship.

There are two alternatives to manually override these values: either using positional arguments or keyword arguments.

Using positional arguments for the field definition, we have the following:

```
# Book <-> Authors relation (using positional args)
author_ids = fields.Many2many(
    'res.partner',          # related model (required)
    'library_book_res_partner_rel',  # relation table name to use
    'a_id',                 # rel table field for "this" record
    'p_id',                 # rel table field for "other" record
    'Authors')              # string label text
```

We can instead use keyword arguments, which may be preferred for readability:

```
# Book <-> Authors relation (using keyword args)
author_ids = fields.Many2many(
    comodel_name='res.partner', # related model (required)
    relation='library_book_res_partner_rel', # relation table name
    column1='a_id', # rel table field for "this" record
    column2='p_id', # rel table field for "other" record
    string='Authors') # string label text
```

Similarly to one-to-many relational fields, many-to-many fields can also use the keyword arguments `context`, `domain`, and `auto_join`.

When creating abstract models, don't use the many-to-many field's `column1` and `column2` attributes . There is a limitation in the ORM design regarding abstract models, and when you force the names of the relationship columns, they cannot be cleanly inherited anymore.

Hierarchical relationships

Parent-child tree relationships are represented using a many-to-one relationship with the same model, used for each record to references its parent. The inverse one-to-many relation corresponds to the record's direct children.

Odoo provides improved support for these hierarchical data structures, with the additional `child_of` and `parent_of` operators available in domain expressions. These operators are available as long as the model has a `parent_id` field (or has a `_parent_name` valid Model definition).

We can enable faster querying on the hierarchy tree by setting the `_parent_store=True` Model attribute and adding the `parent_path` helper field. This fields stores additional information about the hierarchy tree structure that is leveraged for faster queries.

Changed on Odoo 12

The `parent_path` helper field was introduced in Odoo 12. Previous versions used the `parent_left` and `parent_right` integer fields for the same purpose. These are deprecated as of Odoo 12.

Be aware that these additional operations come with storage and execution time penalties, so they are best used when you expect to read more frequently than write, such as in the case of category trees. This is only necessary when optimizing deep hierarchies with many nodes, and can be misused for small or shallow hierarchies.

To showcase hierarchical structures, we will add a Category tree to the Library app, to be used to categorize our Books. For this, we will add the `library_app/models/library_book_category.py` file with this code:

```python
from odoo import api, fields, models

class BookCategory(models.Model):
    _name = 'library.book.category'
    _description = 'Book Category'
    _parent_store = True

    name = fields.Char(translate=True, required=True)
    # Hierarchy fields
    parent_id = fields.Many2one(
        'library.book.category',
        'Parent Category',
        ondelete='restrict')
    parent_path = fields.Char(index=True)

    # Optional but good to have:
    child_ids = fields.One2many(
        'library.book.category',
        'parent_id',
        'Subcategories')
```

Here, we have a basic model with a `parent_id` field to reference the parent record.

To enable the indexing of the hierarchy, for faster tree search, we add the `_parent_store=True` model attribute. When doing so, the `parent_path` field must also be added, and it must be indexed. The field used to refer to the parent is expected to be named `parent_id`, but any other field name can be used as long as we declare that in the `_parent_name` optional model attribute.

It is often convenient to add a field to list the direct children. This is the one-to-many inverse relation seen in the previous code.

For the previous code to be used by our module, remember to add a reference to its file in `library_app/models/__init__.py`:

```python
from . import library_book_category
from . import library_book
from . import res_partner
```

Flexible relationships using Reference fields

Regular relational fields reference one fixed co-model. The `Reference` field type does not have this limitation and supports flexible relationships, so that the same field is not restricted to always be pointing to the same destination model.

As an example, we will use it in our book category model to add a reference to a highlighted book or author. So, the field could refer to either a book or a partner:

```
# class BookCategory(models.Model):
    highlighted_id = fields.Reference(
        [('library.book', 'Book'), ('res.partner', 'Author')],
        'Category Highlight',
    )
```

The field definition is similar to a `selection` field, but here the selection list holds the models available to be used on the field. In the user interface, the user will first pick a model from the available list, and then pick a specific record from that model.

Changed in Odoo 12

The referenceable models configuration table was removed. In previous Odoo versions, it could be used to configure the models that can be used in `Reference fields`. It was available in the **Settings | Technical | Database Structure** menu. These configuration could be leveraged in `Reference field` using the `odoo.addons.res.res_request.referenceable_models` function in place of the model selection list.

Here are a few additional technical details about reference fields that can be useful:

- Reference fields are stored in the database as a `model,id` string
- the `read()` method, meant for use from external applications, returns them formatted as a `('model_name', id)` tuple, instead of the usual `(id, 'display_name')` pair for many-to-one fields

Computed fields

Fields can have their values automatically calculated by a function, instead of simply reading a database stored value. A computed field is declared just like a regular field, but has the additional `compute` argument to define the function used for its computation.

In most cases, computed fields involve writing some business logic. So, to take full advantage of this feature, we need to learn the topics explained in Chapter 8, *Business Logic - Supporting Business Processes*. We can still explain computed fields here, but will keep the business logic as simple as possible.

Let's work on an example. Books have a publisher. We would like to have the the publisher's country in book form.

For this, we will use a computed field, based on the publisher_id, which will take its value from the publisher's country_id field.

We should edit the book model in the library_app/models/library_book.py file to add the following:

```
# class Book(models.Model):
    publisher_country_id = fields.Many2one(
        'res.country', string='Publisher Country',
        compute='_compute_publisher_country',
    )

    @api.depends('publisher_id.country_id')
    def _compute_publisher_country(self):
        for book in self:
            book.publisher_country_id = book.publisher_id.country_id
```

The preceding code adds the publisher_country_id field, and the _compute_publisher_country method used to compute it. The function name was passed to the field as a string argument, but it may also be passed a callable reference (the function identifier, without the surrounding quotes). In that case, we need to make sure the function is defined in the Python file before the field is.

The @api.depends decorator is needed when the computation depends on other fields, as it usually does. It lets the server know when to recompute stored or cached values. One or more field names are accepted as arguments and dot-notation can be used to follow field relationships. In our case, our field should be recomputed whenever the country_id of the book's publisher_id is changed.

As usual, the self argument is the recordset object to work with. So, we need to iterate over it to act on each individual record. The computed value is set using the usual assignment (write) operation. In our case, the computation is quite simple, we assign it to the current book's publisher_id.country_id value.

The same computation method can be used for more than one field. In that case, the same method is used on several `compute` field arguments, and the computation method should assign values to all the computed fields.

 The computation function must assign a value to the field, or fields, to compute. If your computation method has `if` conditions, make sure that all run paths assign values to the computed field(s). Otherwise, the computation will error in cases where it fails to assign a value to the computed field(s).

We won't be working on the views for this module yet, but you can make a quick edit on the task form to confirm the computed field is working as expected by using the **Developer Mode**, picking the **Edit View** option, and adding the field directly in the form XML. Don't worry, it will be replaced by the clean module view on the next upgrade.

Searching and writing to computed fields

The computed field we just created can be read, but it can't be searched or written to. By default, computed field values are written on the fly, and are not stored in the database. That's why we can't search them like we can regular fields.

We can enable these search and write operations by implementing specialized functions for them. Along with the `compute` function, we can also set a `search` function to implement the search logic, and the `inverse` function to implement the write logic.

Using these, our computed field declaration looks as follows:

```
# class Book(models.Model):
    publisher_country_id = fields.Many2one(
        'res.country', string='Publisher Country',
        compute='_compute_publisher_country',
        # store = False,  # Default is not to store in db
        inverse='_inverse_publisher_country',
        search='_search_publisher_country',
    )
```

Writing in a computed field is the *inverse* logic of computation. So, the function in charge of handling the write operation is called the **inverse**. In our case, the inverse function is simple. The computation just copied the `book.publisher_id.country_id` value to `book.publisher_country_id`. The inverse operation is to copy the value written in `book.publisher_country_id` to the `book.publisher_id.country_id` field:

```
def _inverse_publisher_country(self):
    for book in self:
        book.publisher_id.country_id = book.publisher_country_id
```

Notice that this modifies data in the publisher's partner record, and so will also change the value seen in all books with the same publisher. Regular access controls apply to these write operations, so this action will only be successful if the current user also has write access to the partner model.

To enable search operations on a computed field, we need to implement its **search** function. For this, we need to be able to convert a search domain on the computed field to a search domain using regular stored fields. In our case, the actual search should be done on the `country_id` field of the linked `publisher_id` Partner record:

```
def _search_publisher_country(self, operator, value):
    return [('publisher_id.country_id', operator, value)]
```

When we perform a search on a Model, a domain expression is used as an argument with the filter to apply. Domain expressions are explained in more detail in Chapter 8, *Business Logic - Supporting Business Processes*, but, for now, you should know that they are a list of (`field`, `operator`, `value`) conditions.

The `search` function is called whenever this computed field is found in conditions of a domain expression. It receives the `operator` and `value` for the search and is expected to translate the original search element into an alternative domain search expression. The `country_id` field is stored in the related partner model, so our search implementation just alters the original search expression to use the `publisher_id.country_id` field instead.

Storing computed fields

Computed field values can also be stored in the database, by setting `store = True` in their definition. They will be recomputed when any of their dependencies change. Since the values are now stored, they can be searched just like regular fields, and a search function is not needed.

Related fields

The computed field we implemented in the previous section just copies a value from a related record into a model's own field. This is a common use case that can be automatically handled by Odoo using the **related field** feature.

Related fields make available, directly in a model, fields that belong to a related model and are accessible using a dot notation chain. This makes them available in situations where dot notation can't be used, such as UI form views.

To create a related field, we declare a field of the required type, just like with regular computed fields, but instead of `compute` we use the `related` attribute, setting it with the dot notation field chain to reach the desired field.

We can use a reference field to get the exact same effect as the previous example, the `publisher_country_id` computed field:

```
# class Book(models.Model):
    publisher_country_related = fields.Many2one(
        'res.country', string='Publisher Country (related)',
        related='publisher_id.country_id',
    )
```

Behind the scenes, related fields are just computed fields that conveniently implement `search` and `inverse` methods. This means that we can search for and write to them out of the box, without having to write any additional code. By default, related fields are read only, so the inverse write operation won't be available. To enable it, set the `readonly=False` field attribute.

Changed in Odoo 12

The `related` fields are now read only by default: `readonly=True`. In previous Odoo versions, they were writable by default, but it was proven to be a dangerous default, since it could allow changes to setup or master data in cases where it was not expected to be allowed.

It's also worth noting that these Related fields can also be stored in a database using `store=True`, just like any other computed field.

Model constraints

Often, applications need to ensure data integrity, and enforce some validations to ensure that data is complete and correct.

The PostgreSQL database manager supports many useful validations, such as avoiding duplicates, or checking that values meet certain simple conditions. Model can declare and use PostgreSQL constraints for this.

Some checks require more sophisticated logic, and are better implemented as Python code. For these cases, we can use specific model methods implementing Python constraint logic.

SQL model constraints

SQL constraints are added to the database table definition and are enforced directly by PostgreSQL. They are defined using the `_sql_constraints` class attribute.

It is a list of tuples, and each tuple has the format `(name, code, error)`:

- **name** is the constraint identifier name
- **code** is the PostgreSQL syntax for the constraint
- **error** is the error message to present to users when the constraint is not verified

We will add two SQL constraints to the Book Model. One is a unique constraint ensuring that we don't have repeated books with the same title and publication date; the other is to check that the publication date is not in the future:

```
# class Book(models.Model):
    _sql_constraints = [
        ('library_book_name_date_uq',  # Constraint unique identifier
         'UNIQUE (name, date_published)',  # Constraint SQL syntax
         'Book title and publication date must be unique.'),  # Message
        ('library_book_check_date',
         'CHECK (date_published <= current_date)',
         'Publication date must not be in the future.'),
    ]
```

For more information on the PostgreSQL constraint syntax, see the official documentation at `https://www.postgresql.org/docs/10/static/ddl-constraints.html`.

Python model constraints

Python constraints can use a piece of arbitrary code to check the conditions. The checking function should be decorated with `@api.constrains` and an indication of the list of fields involved in the check. The validation is triggered when any of them is modified and will raise an exception if the condition fails.

In the case of the Library app, an obvious example is to prevent inserting incorrect ISBN numbers. We already have the logic to check that an ISBN is correct, in the `_check_isbn()` method. We can use it now in a model constrain to prevent saving incorrect data:

```
from odoo.exceptions import ValidationError

# class Book(models.Model):
    @api.constrains('isbn')
    def _constrain_isbn_valid(self):
        for book in self:
            if book.isbn and not book._check_isbn():
                raise ValidationError(
                    '%s is an invalid ISBN' % book.isbn)
```

About the Odoo base Models

In the previous chapters, we had the chance to create new Models, such as the Book model, but we also made use of the already existing Models, such as the Partner Model, provided by Odoo out of the box. We will have here a basic introduction to these built-in models.

At the core of Odoo, we have the `base` add-on module. It provides the essential features needed for Odoo apps. Then, we have a set of built-in add-on modules, providing the official apps and features made available with the standard product.

The base module provides two kinds of Models:

- Information Repository, `ir.*` models
- Resources, `res.*` models

The **Information Repository** is used to store data needed by Odoo to know how to work as an application, such as Menus, Views, Models, Actions, and so on. The data we find in the **Technical** menu is usually stored in information repository models. Some relevant examples are these:

- `ir.actions.act_window` for Windows Actions
- `ir.ui.menu` for Menu Items
- `ir.ui.view` for Views
- `ir.model` for Models
- `ir.model.fields` for Model Fields
- `ir.model.data` for XML IDs

The resources contain basic data about the world, which can be useful for applications in general. These are the more important resource models:

- `res.partner` for business partners, such as customers, suppliers, and so on, and addresses
- `res.company` for company data
- `res.currency` for currencies
- `res.country` for countries
- `res.users` for application users
- `res.groups` for application security groups

This should provide you with useful context to better understand where the models come from whenever you come across them in the future.

Summary

As we approach the end of this chapter, we should now be familiar with all the possibilities models give us to structure data models.

We have seen that models are usually based on the `models.Model` class, but we can also use `models.Abstract` for reusable mixin models and `models.Transient` for wizards or advanced user interaction dialogs. We have seen the general model attributes available, such as `_order` for default sort order, and `_rec_name` for the default field to use for record representation.

The fields in a model define all the data they will store. We have also seen the non-relational field types available, and the attributes they support. We also learned about the several types of relational fields, many-to-one, one-to-many, and many-to-many, and how they define relationships between models, including hierarchical parent/child relationships.

Most fields store user input in the database, but fields can have values automatically computed by Python code. We have seen how to implement computed fields, and some advanced possibilities we have, such as making them writable and searchable.

Also part of model definitions are constraints, enforcing data consistency and validation. These can be implemented either using PostgreSQL or Python code.

Once we have created the data model, we should populate it with some default and demonstration data. In the next chapter, we will learn how to use data files to export, import, and load data using our system.

Recordsets – Working with Model Data

7

In the previous chapters, we gave an overview of model creation and how to load and export data from models. Now that we have our data model and some data to work with, it's time to learn more about how we can programmatically interact with them.

The **Object-Relational Mapping** (**ORM**) supporting our models provides a few methods for this interaction, called the **Application Programming Interface** (**API**). These start with the basic **Create, Read, Update, Delete** (**CRUD**) operations, but also include other operations, such as data export and import, or utility functions to aid the user interface and experience. It also provides some decorators that we already saw in the previous chapters. These allow us, when adding new methods, to let the ORM know how they should be handled.

In this chapter, we'll cover the following topics:

- Using the shell command to interactively explore the ORM API
- Understanding the execution environment and context
- Querying data using recordsets and domains
- Accessing data in recordsets
- Writing on records
- Composing recordsets
- Using low-level SQL and database transactions

Technical requirements

The code examples in this chapter will be executed in an interactive shell and do not require any code from previous chapters.

Using the shell command

Python has a command-line interface that is a great way to explore its syntax. Similarly, Odoo also has an equivalent feature, where we can interactively try commands to see how they work. This the `shell` command.

To use it, run Odoo with the `shell` command and the database to be used, as shown here:

```
$ ./odoo-bin shell -d 12-library
```

You should see the usual server start up sequence in the terminal until it stops on a >>> Python prompt waiting for your input.

Changed in Odoo 9
The shell feature was added in version 9.0. For version 8.0, there is a community back-ported module to add it. Once downloaded and included in the addons path, no further installation is necessary. It can be downloaded from `https://www.odoo.com/apps/modules/8.0/shell/`.

Here, `self` will represent the record for the `Administrator` user, as you can confirm by typing the following:

```
>>> self
res.users(1,)
>>> self._name
'res.users'
>>> self.name
'OdooBot'
>>> self.login
'__system__'
```

In the shell session here, we inspected our environment:

- The `self` command represents a `res.users` recordset containing only the record with the 1 ID.
- The recordset model name, inspecting `self._name`, is `'res.users'`, as expected.

- The value for the record **name** field is `OdooBot`.
- The value for the record **login** field is `__system__`.

 Changed in Odoo 12
The user with ID 1 superuser has changed from admin to the internal system user that does not have its own login. The admin is now the user with ID 2 and is not a superuser, but by default apps include it in all security groups. The main reason for this is to avoid having users perform day-to-day activities with the superuser account. Doing so is dangerous because it bypasses all access rules and allows mixing inconsistent data, such as cross-company relationships. It's now meant to be used only for troubleshooting or very specific cross-company operations.

As with Python, you can exit the prompt using *Ctrl + D*. This will also close the server process and return you to the system shell prompt.

The execution environment

The server shell provides a `self` reference similar to what you would find inside a method of the `res.users` user model.

As we have seen, `self` is a recordset. **Recordsets** carry with them environment information, including the user browsing the data and additional context information, such as the language and the time zone.

In the following sections, we will learn about the attributes made available in the execution environment, the usefulness of the environment context, and how to modify this context.

Environment attributes

We can inspect the current environment with the following code:

```
>>> self.env
<openerp.api.Environment object at 0xb3f4f52c>
```

The execution environment in `self.env` has the following attributes available:

- `env.cr` is the database cursor being used.
- `env.user` is the record for the current user.
- `env.uid` is the ID for the session user. It's the same as `env.user.id`.
- `env.context` is an immutable dictionary with a session context.

The environment also provides access to the registry where all of the installed models are available. For example, `self.env['res.partner']` returns a reference to the partner model. We can then use `search()` or `browse()` on it to retrieve recordsets:

```
>>> self.env['res.partner'].search([('name', 'like', 'Ad')])
res.partner(10, 35, 3)
```

In this example, the returned recordset for the `res.partner` model contains three records, with IDs 10, 35, and 3. The recordset is not ordered by ID, because the default order for the corresponding model was used. In the case of the partner model, the default `_order` is `display_name`.

The environment context

The **context** is dictionary carrying session data that can be used on both the client-side user interface and the server-side ORM and business logic.

On the client side, it can carry information from one view to the next, such as the ID of the record active on the previous view, after following a link or a button, or it can provide default values to be used in the next view.

On the server side, some recordset field values can depend on the locale settings provided by the context. In particular, the `lang` key affects the value of translatable fields. Context can also provide signals for server-side code.

For example, the `active_test` key, when set to `False`, changes the behavior of the ORM's `search()` method, ignoring the `active` flag on records, so that the inactive (soft deleted) records are also returned.

An initial context from the web client looks like this:

```
{'lang': 'en_US', 'tz': 'Europe/Brussels', 'uid': 2}
```

You can see the `lang` key with the user language, `tz`, the time zone information, and `uid` with the current user ID.

The content in records might be different depending on the current context:

- translated fields can have different values depending on the active lang language
- datetime fields can show different times depending on the active tz timezone

When opening a form from a link or a button in a previous view, an active_id key is added to the context, with the ID of the record we were positioned at, in the origin form. In the particular case of list views, we have an active_ids context key containing a list of the record IDs selected in the previous list.

On the client side, the context can be used to set default values or activate default filters on the target view, using keys with the default_ or default_search_ prefixes.

Here are some examples:

- To set the current user as a default value of the user_id field, we use { 'default_user_id': uid}
- To have a filter_my_books filter activated by default on the target view, we use { 'default_search_filter_my_tasks': 1}

Modifying the recordset execution environment

The recordset execution environment is immutable, and so it can't be modified. But we can create a modified environment and then run actions using it.

To do so, we can make use of the following methods:

- env.sudo(user) is provided with a user record and returns an environment with that user. If no user is provided, the __system__ root superuser will be used, which allows for running specific operations, bypassing security rules.
- env.with_context(<dictionary>) replaces the context with a new one.
- env.with_context(key=value,...) modifies the current context, setting values for some of its keys.

Additionally, we have the env.ref() function, taking a string with an external identifier and returning a record for it, as shown here:

```
>>> self.env.ref('base.user_root')
res.users(1,)
```

Querying data with recordsets and domains

Inside a method or a shell session, `self` represents the current model, and we can only access that model's records. To access other models, we should use `self.env`. For example, `self.env['res.partner']` returns a reference to the Partner model (which is also an empty recordset).

We can then use `search()` or `browse()` on it to retrieve recordsets, and the `search()` methods use a domain expression to define for the record selection criteria.

Creating recordsets

The `search()` method takes a domain expression and returns a recordset with the records matching those conditions. An empty domain `[]` will return all records.

 If the model has the `active` special field, by default only the records with `active=True` will be considered.

The following keyword arguments can also be used:

- `order` is a string to be used as the `ORDER BY` clause in the database query. This is usually a comma-separated list of field names. Each field name may be followed by the `DESC` keyword, to indicate a descending order.
- `limit` sets a maximum number of records to retrieve.
- `offset` ignores the first n results; it can be used with `limit` to query blocks of records at a time.

Sometimes, we just need to know the number of records meeting certain conditions. For that we can use `search_count()`, which returns the record count instead of a recordset. It saves the cost of retrieving a list of records just to count them, so it is much more efficient when we don't have a recordset yet and just want to count the number of records.

The `browse()` method takes a list of IDs or a single ID and returns a recordset with those records. This can be convenient in cases where we already know the IDs of the records we want.

Some usage examples of this are shown here:

```
>>> self.env['res.partner'].search([('name', 'like', 'Ag')])
res.partner(9, 31)
>>> self.env['res.partner'].browse([9, 31])
res.partner(9, 31)
```

Domain expressions

The **domain** is used to filter data records. They use a specific syntax that the Odoo ORM parses to produce the SQL WHERE expressions that will query the database.

A domain expression is a list of conditions. Each condition is a ('<field_name>', '<operator>', <value>') tuple. For example, this is a valid domain expression, with only one condition: [('is_done','=',False)].

The following is an explanation of each of these elements:

- <field_name> is the field being filtered and can use dot-notation for fields in related models.
- <value> is evaluated as a Python expression. It can use literal values, such as numbers, Booleans, strings, or lists, and can use fields and identifiers available in the evaluation context. There are actually two possible evaluation contexts for domains:
  - When used on the client side, such as in window actions or field attributes, the raw field values used to render the current view are available, but we can't use dot-notation on them
  - When used on the server side, such as in security record rules and in server Python code, dot-notation can be used on fields, since the current record is an object
- The <operator> can be one of the following:
  - The usual comparison operators are <, >, <= , >=, =, and !=.
  - '=like' and '=ilike' matches against a pattern, where the underscore symbol, _, matches any single character and the percentage symbol, %, matches any sequence of characters.
  - 'like' matches against a '%value%' pattern. 'ilike' is similar but case insensitive. The 'not like' and 'not ilike' operators are also available.
  - 'child of' finds the children values in a hierarchical relation for the models configured to support hierarchical relations.

- `'in'` and `'not in'` are used to check for inclusion in a given list, so the value should be a list of values. When used on a **to-many** relation field, the `in` operator behaves like a `contains` operator.
- `'not in'` is the opposite of `in` and is used to check that the value is not contained in a list of values.

A domain expression is a list of items and can contain several condition tuples. By default, these conditions will implicitly be combined using the AND logical operator. This means that it will only return records meeting all of the conditions.

Explicit logic operators can also be used—the ampersand symbol, `'&'`, for AND operations (the default), and the pipe symbol, `'|'`, for OR operations. These will operate on the next two items, working in a recursive way. We'll look at this in more detail in a moment.

 For a slightly more formal definition, a domain expression uses prefix notation, also known as Polish notation, where operators precede operands. The AND and OR operators are binary operators, while NOT is a unary operator.

The exclamation point, `'!'`, represents the NOT operator and is available and operates on the next item. So it should be placed before the item to be negated. For example, the `['!', ('is_done', '=', True)]` expression will filter all not-done records.

The **next item** can also be an operator item acting on its next items, defining nested conditions. An example may help us to better understand this.

In server-side record rules, we can find domain expressions similar to this one:

```
['|',
    ('message_follower_ids', 'in', [user.partner_id.id]),
    '|',
        ('user_id', '=', user.id),
        ('user_id', '=', False)
]
```

This domain filters all of the records where the current user is in the follower list and is the responsible user, or does not have a responsible user set.

The first `'|'` **OR** operator acts on the follower's condition plus the result of the next condition. The next condition is again the union of two other conditions—records where either the user ID is the current session user or it is not set.

The following diagram illustrates the abstract syntax tree representation of the previous example domain expression:

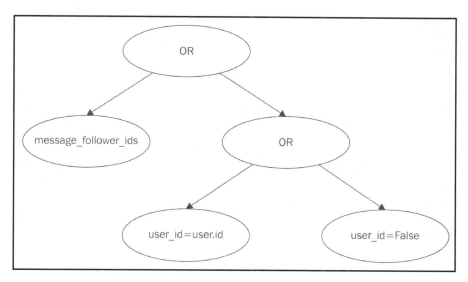

Accessing data on recordsets

Once we have a recordset, we want to inspect the data contained in it. In the following sections, we will explore how to access data in recordsets.

We can get field values for individual records, called singletons. Relational fields have special properties, and we can use dot-notation to navigate through linked records. Finally, we have some considerations on handling date and time records and converting them between different formats.

Accessing data on records

The special case of a recordset with only one record is called a **singleton**. Singletons are still a recordset and can be used wherever a recordset is expected.

But unlike multi-element recordsets, singletons can access their fields using the dot-notation, like this:

```
>>> print(self.name)
OdooBot
```

In the next example, we can see the same `self` singleton recordset also behaves as a recordset, and we can iterate it. It has only one record, so only one name is printed out:

```
>>> for rec in self:
        print(rec.name)
OdooBot
```

Trying to access field values on recordsets with more than one record will result in an error, so this can be an issue in the cases where we are not sure if we are working with a singleton recordset. For methods designed to work only with a singleton, we can check this using `self.ensure_one()` at the beginning. It will raise an error if `self` is not a singleton.

 An empty record is also a singleton. This is convenient since accessing field values will return a `None` value, instead of raising an error. This is also true for relational fields, and accessing related records using dot notation won't raise errors.

Accessing relational fields

As we saw earlier, models can have relational fields—**many-to-one**, **one-to-many**, and **many-to-many**. These field types have recordsets as values.

In the case of many-to-one, the value can be a singleton or an empty recordset. In both cases, we can directly access their field values. As an example, the following instructions are correct and safe:

```
>>> self.company_id
res.company(1,)
>>> self.company_id.name
'YourCompany'
>>> self.company_id.currency_id
res.currency(1,)
>>> self.company_id.currency_id.name
'EUR'
```

Conveniently, an empty recordset also behaves like singleton, and accessing its fields doesn't return an error but just returns `False`. Because of this, we can traverse records using dot-notation without worrying about errors from empty values, as shown here:

```
>>> self.company_id.parent_id
res.company()
>>> self.company_id.parent_id.name
False
```

Accessing date and time values

In recordsets, `date` and `datetime` values are represented as native Python objects. For example, when we look up the last `admin` login date:

```
>>> self.browse(2).login_date
datetime.datetime(2018, 11, 2, 16, 47, 57, 327756)
```

Since the date and datetime values are Python objects, they have all of the manipulation features available for these objects.

Changed in Odoo 12

The `date` and `datetime` field values are represented as Python objects, unlike previous Odoo versions, where `date` and `datetime` values were represented as text strings. These field type values can still be set using text representations, like in previous Odoo versions.

Dates and times are stored in the database in a naive **Coordinated Universal Time (UTC)** format, not time zone aware. The `datetime` values seen on recordsets are also in UTC. When presented to the user in the web client, the `datetime` values are converted into the user's timezone, according to the current session's time zone setting, stored in the context `tz` key, such as `{'tz': 'Europe/Brussels'}`. This conversion is a web client responsibility, as it isn't done by the server.

For example, a 12:00 AM datetime entered by a Brussels (UTC+1) user is stored in the database as 10:00 AM UTC, and will be seen by a New York (UTC-4) user as 06:00 AM.

The Odoo server log message timestamps use UTC time and not the local server time.

The opposite conversion, from session timezone to UTC, also needs to be done by the web client, when sending the `datetime` user input back to the server .

Date objects can be compared and can be subtracted to find the time elapsed between both dates. This time elapsed is a `timedelta` object. And `timedelta` objects can be added or subtracted to `date` and `datetime` objects, performing `date` arithmetic.

These objects are provided by the Python standard library `datetime` module. Here is a sample of the essential operations we can do with it:

```
>>> from datetime import date
>>> date.today()
datetime.date(2018, 11, 3)
>>> from datetime import timedelta
>>> timedelta(days=7)
datetime.timedelta(7)
>>> date.today() + timedelta(days=7)
datetime.date(2018, 11, 10)
```

A full reference for the `date`, `datetime`, and `timedelta` data types can be found at : `https://docs.python.org/3.6/library/datetime.html`.

Odoo also provides a few additional convenience functions in the `odoo.tools.date_utils` module. These functions are as follows:

- `start_of(value, granularity)` is the start of a time period with the specified granularity—`year`, `quarter`, `month`, `week`, `day`, or `hour`.
- `end_of(value, granularity)` is the end of a time period for the given granularity.
- `add(value, **kwargs)` adds a time interval to the given value. The `**kwargs` arguments are to be used by a `relativedelta` object to define the time interval. These arguments can be `years`, `months`, `weeks`, `days`, `hours`, `minutes`, and so on.
- `subtract(value, **kwargs)` subtracts a time interval to the given value.

The `relativedelta` object is from the `dateutil` library and can perform `date` arithmetic using `months` or `years` (the Python `timedelta` standard library only supports `days`). The documentation for it can be found at: `https://dateutil.readthedocs.io`.

The following are a few examples of the usage of the previous functions:

```
>>> from odoo.tools import date_utils
>>> from datetime import datetime
>>> date_utils.start_of(datetime.now(), 'week')
datetime.datetime(2018, 10, 29, 0, 0)
>>> date_utils.end_of(datetime.now(), 'week')
datetime.datetime(2018, 11, 4, 23, 59, 59, 999999)
>>> from datetime import date
>>> date_utils.add(date.today(), months=2)
datetime.date(2019, 1, 3)
>>> date_utils.subtract(date.today(), months=2)
datetime.date(2018, 9, 3)
```

These utility functions are also exposed in both the `odoo.fields.Date` and the `odoo.fields.Datetime` objects, along with these:

- `fields.Date.today()` returns a string with the current date in the format expected by the server and using UTC as a reference. This is adequate to compute default values. In this case, we should use only the function name without the parenthesis.

- `fields.Datetime.now()` returns a string with the current `datetime` in the format expected by the server using UTC as a reference. This is adequate to compute default values.

- `fields.Date.context_today(record, timestamp=None)` returns a string with the current `date` in the session's context. The time zone value is taken from the record's context. The optional `timestamp` parameter is a `datetime` object and will be used instead of the current time, if provided.

- `fields.Datetime.context_timestamp(record, timestamp)` converts a naive `datetime` value (without time zone) into a time zone aware `datetime`. The time zone is extracted from the record's context, hence the name of the function.

Converting text-represented dates and times

Prior to Odoo 12, we needed to convert text representations for `date` and `datetimes` before we could do any arithmetic with them. Some tools are provided to help with this conversion from text into native data types and then back into text.

These are useful when working with previous Odoo versions and are still relevant for Odoo 12; for this case, we need to work with a date that arrives to us formatted as text.

To facilitate conversion between formats, both `fields.Date` and `fields.Datetime` objects provide these functions:

- `to_date` converts a string into a `date` object.
- `to_datetime(value)` converts a string into a `datetime` object.
- `to_string(value)` converts a `date` or `datetime` object into a string in the format expected by the Odoo server, up to version 11.

The text formats used by both functions are the Odoo predefined defaults, defined in the following:

- `odoo.tools.DEFAULT_SERVER_DATE_FORMAT`
- `odoo.tools.DEFAULT_SERVER_DATETIME_FORMAT`

They map to `%Y-%m-%d` and `%Y-%m-%d %H:%M:%S`, respectively.

An example of a usage of `from_string` is as follows:

```
>>> from odoo import fields
>>> fields.Datetime.to_datetime('2018-11-21 23:11:55')
datetime.datetime(2018, 11, 21, 23, 11, 55)
```

For other date and time formats, the `strptime` method from the `datetime` object can be used:

```
>>> from datetime import datetime
>>> datetime.strptime('03/11/2018', '%d/%m/%Y')
datetime.datetime(2018, 11, 3, 0, 0)
```

Writing on records

We have two different ways to write on records—using object-style direct assignment and using the `write()` method. The first one is simpler to use but only works with one record at a time and can be less efficient. Since each assignment performs a `write` operation, redundant recomputations may happen. The latter requires special syntax to write on relation fields, but a single command can write on several fields and records, and more efficient field recomputations.

Writing with object-style value assignment

Recordsets implement the active record pattern. This means that we can assign values to them, and these changes will be made persistent in the database. This is an intuitive and convenient way to manipulate data, but only works with one field and one record at a time.

Here is an example:

```
>>> root = self.env['res.users'].browse(1)
>>> print(root.name)
OdooBot
>>> root.name = 'Superuser'
>>> print(root.name)
Superuser
```

While using the active record pattern, the value of relational fields can be set by assigning a recordset.

For many-to-one fields, the value assigned must be a single record (a singleton recordset).

For to-many fields, the value can also be assigned with a recordset, replacing the list of linked records, if any, with a new one. Here, a recordset with any size is allowed.

Writing with the write() method

We can also use the `write()` method to update several fields of several records at the same time, using a single database instruction. So its usage should be preferred in cases where efficiency is important.

The `write()` method takes a dictionary to map fields to values. These are updated on all elements of the recordset and nothing is returned, as shown here:

```
>>> recs = Partner.search( [('name', 'ilike', 'Azure')] )
>>> recs.write({'comment': 'Hello!'})
True
```

Unlike object-style assignment, when using the `write()` method, we can't assign recordset objects to relational fields directly. Instead, we need to use the record IDs that need to be extracted from the recordset.

When writing on a many-to-one field, the value to write must be the related record's ID. For example, instead of `self.write({'user_id': self.env.user})`, we should rather use `self.write({'user_id': self.env.user.id})`.

When writing on a to-many field, the value to write must be the same special syntax used in XML data files, described in `Chapter 5`, *Import, Export, and Module Data*.

For example, let's set a book authors' list to `author1` and `author2`, which are two Partner records. The | pipe operator can join records to create a recordset, so using object-style assignment, we could write the following:

```
publisher.child_ids = author1 | author2
```

Using the `write()` method, the same operation looks like this:

```
book.write( { 'child_ids': [(6, 0, [author1.id, author2.id])] } )
```

Recalling the write syntax explained in `Chapter 5`, *Import, Export, and Module Data*, the most common commands are as follows:

- `(4, id, _)` to add a record
- `(6, _, [ids])` to replace the list of linked records with the list provided

Writing date and time values

Since Odoo 12, date and time fields can be written using values in Python native data types, both using direct assignment and using `write()`.

We can still write date and time using text-represented values:

```
>> demo = self.search([('login', '=', 'demo')])
>>> demo.login_date
False
>>> demo.login_date = '2018-01-01 09:00:00'
>>> demo.login_date
datetime.datetime(2018, 1, 1, 9, 0)
```

Creating and deleting records

The `write()` method is used to write dates on existing records. But we also need to create and delete records. This is done using the `create()` and `unlink()` model methods.

The `create()` method takes a dictionary with the fields and values for the record to be created, using the same syntax as `write()`. Default values are automatically applied as expected, which is shown here:

```
>>> Partner = self.env['res.partner']
>>> new = Partner.create({'name': 'ACME', 'is_company': True})
>>> print(new)
res.partner(59,)
>>> print(new.customer)   # customer flag is True by default
True
```

The `unlink()` method deletes the records in the recordset, as shown here:

```
>>> rec = Partner.search([('name', '=', 'ACME')])
>>> rec.unlink()
2018-11-02 17:01:01,433 18380 INFO 12-library odoo.models.unlink: User #1
deleted mail.message records with IDs: [27]
2018-11-02 17:01:01,458 18380 INFO 12-library odoo.models.unlink: User #1
deleted ir.attachment records with IDs: [385,
384, 383]
2018-11-02 17:01:01,466 18380 INFO 12-library odoo.models.unlink: User #1
deleted res.partner records with IDs: [46]
2018-11-02 17:01:01,474 18380 INFO 12-library odoo.models.unlink: User #1
deleted mail.followers records with IDs: [6]
True
```

Previously, we saw several log messages for other records being deleted. These are delete cascades of records related to the partner being removed.

We also have available the `copy()` model method, useful to duplicate an existing record. It accepts an optional argument with the values to change on the new record, for example, to create a `new` user copying from the `demo` user:

```
>>> demo = self.env.ref('base.user_demo')
>>> new = demo.copy({'name': 'Daniel', 'login': 'daniel', 'email':''})
```

Fields with the `copy=False` attribute won't be automatically copied. To-many relational fields have this flag disabled by default and so won't be copied.

Composing recordsets

Recordsets support some additional operations. We can check whether a record is included or not in a recordset. If x is a singleton recordset and `my_recordset` is a recordset containing many records, we can use the following:

- `x in my_recordset`
- `x not in my_recordset`

The following operations are also available:

- `recordset.ids` returns the list with the IDs of the recordset elements.
- `recordset.ensure_one()` checks whether it's a single record (singleton); if it's not, a `ValueError` exception is raised.
- `recordset.filtered(func)` returns a filtered recordset, and `func` can be a function or a dot-separated expression representing a path of fields to follow, as shown in the examples that follow.
- `recordset.mapped(func)` returns a list of mapped values. Instead of a function, a string of text can be used for the name of the field to map.
- `recordset.sorted(func)` returns an ordered recordset. Instead of a function, a string of text can be used for the name of the field to sort by. An optional `reverse=True` argument is also available.

Here are some usage examples for these functions:

```
>>> rs0 = self.env['res.partner'].search([])
>>> len(rs0)  # how many records?
40
>>> starts_A = lambda r: r.name.startswith('A')
>>> rs1 = rs0.filtered(starts_A)
>>> print(rs1)
res.partner(41, 14, 35)
>> rs1.sorted(key=lambda r: r.id, reverse=True)
res.partner(41, 35, 14)
>>> rs2 = rs1.filtered('is_company')
>>> print(rs2)
res.partner(14,)
>>> rs2.mapped('name')
['Azure Interior']
>>> rs2.mapped(lambda r: (r.id, r.name))
[(14, 'Azure Interior')]
```

We'll surely want to add, remove, or replace the elements in these related fields, and so this leads to the question—how can recordsets be manipulated?

Recordsets are immutable, meaning that their values can't be directly modified. Instead, modifying a recordset means composing a new recordset based on existing ones.

One way to do this is using the supported set operations:

- `rs1 | rs2` is the **union** set operation and results in a recordset with all elements from both recordsets.
- `rs1 + rs2` is the **addition** set operation to concatenate both recordsets into one. It may result in a set with duplicate records.
- `rs1 & rs2` is the **intersection** set operation and results in a recordset with only the elements present in both recordsets.
- `rs1 - rs2` is the **difference** set operation and results in a recordset with the `rs1` elements not present in `rs2`.

The slice-notation can also be used, as shown in these examples:

- `rs[0]` and `rs[-1]` retrieve the first element and the last element, respectively.
- `rs[1:]` results in a copy of the recordset without the first element. This yields the same records as `rs - rs[0]` but preserves their order.

Changed in Odoo 10

Since Odoo 10, recordset manipulation has preserved order. This is unlike previous Odoo versions, where recordset manipulation was not guaranteed to preserve the order, although addition and slicing were known to maintain record order.

We can use these operations to change a recordset by removing or adding elements. Here are some examples:

- `self.author_ids |= author1` adds the `author1` record, if not in the recordset
- `self.author_ids -= author1` removes the specific record `author1` if present in the recordset
- `self.author_ids = self.author_ids[:-1]` removes the last record

The relational fields contain recordset values. Many-to-one fields can contain a singleton recordset, and to-many fields contain recordsets with any number of records.

Low-level SQL and database transactions

Database-writing operations are executed in the context of a database transaction. Usually, we don't have to worry about this as the server takes care of that while running model methods.

But, in some cases, we may need finer control over the transaction. This can be done through the `self.env.cr` database cursor, as shown here:

- `self.env.cr.commit()` commits the transaction's buffered `write` operations.
- `self.env.cr.rollback()` cancels the transaction's `write` operations since the last commit or all if no commit was done.

In a shell session, your data manipulation won't be made effective in the database until you use `self.env.cr.commit()`.

With the cursor `execute()` method, we can run SQL directly in the database. It takes a string with the SQL statement to run and a second optional argument with a tuple or list of values to use as parameters for the SQL. These values will be used where the `%s` placeholders are found.

Caution!

With `cr.execute()` we should not directly compose the SQL query concatenating parameters. Doing so is a well-known security risk that can be exploited through SQL injection attacks. Always use the `%s` placeholders and the second parameter to pass values.

If you're using a `SELECT` query, records should then be fetched. The `fetchall()` function retrieves all the rows as a list of `tuples`, and `dictfetchall()` retrieves them as a list of dictionaries, as shown in the following example:

```
>>> self.env.cr.execute("SELECT id, login FROM res_users WHERE login=%s OR
id=%s", ('demo', 1))
>>> self.env.cr.fetchall()
[(6, 'demo'), (1, '__system__')]
```

It's also possible to run **Data Manipulation Language** (**DML**) instructions, such as UPDATE and INSERT. Since the server keeps data caches, they may become inconsistent with the actual data in the database. Because of that, when using raw DML, the caches should be cleared afterward by using self.env.cache.invalidate().

Caution!
Executing SQL directly in the database can lead to inconsistent data. You should use it only if you're sure of what you are doing.

Summary

In this chapter, we learned how to work with model data and perform CRUD operations—creating, reading, updating, and deleting data. This is the foundation to implement our business logic and automation.

To experiment with the ORM API, we used the Odoo interactive shell. Our commands run in an environment accessible through self.env. The environment provides access to the model registry and has a context that can provide relevant information for the commands executed, such as the current language, lang, and timezone, tz.

Recordsets are created using the search(<domain>) or browse([<ids<]) ORM methods. They can then be iterated to access each singleton (an individual record). We can then use object-like dot-notation on singletons to get and set values on records.

Other than the direct value assignment on singletons, we can also use write(<dict>) to update all elements in a recordset with a single command. The create(<dict>), copy(<dict>) and unlink() commands are used to create, duplicate, and delete records.

Recordsets can by inspected and manipulated. Inspection operators include in and not in. Composition operators include | for union, and & for intersection and slicing. Transformations available include .ids, to extract the list of IDs, .mapped(<field>), .filtered(<func>), or .sorted(<func>).

Finally, low-level SQL operations and transaction control are possible through the Cursor object exposed in self.env.cr.

In the next chapter, we will add the business logic layer for our models, implementing model methods that use the ORM API to automate actions.

Business Logic – Supporting Business Processes

In the previous chapters, we learned about the model layer, how to build the application data structures, and then how to use the ORM API to store and explore that data. In this chapter, we'll be leveraging what we learned about models and recordset handling to implement business logic patterns that are common in applications.

We'll discuss the following topics in this chapter:

- Using stages for document centered workflows
- The ORM method decorators; `@api.multi`, `@api.one`, and `@api@model`
- On change methods, for immediate reaction to users
- Using the ORM built-in methods, such as `create`, `write`, and `unlink`
- The message and activity features, provided by the `mail` add-on module
- Creating a wizard to assist users to do non-trivial actions
- Using log messages for better system observability
- Raising exceptions to give feedback to the user when things go wrong
- Unit tests to automate the quality checks on your code
- Development tools, aiding developer work, such as debugging

Technical requirements

In this chapter, we create a new `library_checkout` add-on module that depends on the `library_app` and `library_member` add-on modules created in previous chapters.

The code for these add-on modules can be found in the book's GitHub repository, at `https://github.com/PacktPublishing/Odoo-12-Development-Essentials-Fourth-Edition`:

- The `library_app` module can be found in the `ch06/` subdirectory
- The `library_member` module can be found in the `ch04/` subdirectory

Both of these add-on modules should be available in the add-ons path we are using, so that they can be installed and used.

Learning project – the library_checkout module

In previous chapters, we prepared the master data structures for the library application. Now we want to add the ability for library members to borrow books. This means we can keep track of book availability and book returns.

Each book checkout request has a life cycle, from the moment it's being drafted, to the moment the books are returned. It's a simple workflow that can be represented as a Kanban board, where the several stages are presented as columns and the work items and checkout requests flow from the left-hand column to the right, until they are completed.

In this chapter, we will focus on the data model and business logic to support this feature. The user interface will be discussed in `Chapter 10`, *Backend Views – Designing the User Interface*, and the Kanban views in `Chapter 11`, *Kanban Views and Client - Side Qweb*.

The library checkout model will have the following:

- The library member borrowing the books (required)
- The request date (defaults to today)
- The librarian responsible for the request (defaults to the current user)
- Checkout lines, with the books requested (one or more)

To support and document the checkout's life cycle, we will also have the following:

- Stage of the request—draft, open, borrowed, returned, or cancelled
- Checkout date, when the books were borrowed
- Closed date, when the books were returned

We will start by creating the new `library_checkout` module and implementing an initial version of the library checkout model. It doesn't introduce anything new compared to the previous chapters. It's provide a foundation to build the new features discussed in this chapter.

We should create a new `library_checkout` directory in the same directory as the other add-on modules of the library project:

1. Begin by adding the `__manifest__.py` file, with this content, as follows:

```
{ 'name': 'Library Book Borrowing',
  'description': 'Members can borrow books from the library.',
  'author': 'Daniel Reis',
  'depends': ['library_member'],
 'data': [
 'security/ir.model.access.csv',
 'views/library_menu.xml',
 'views/checkout_view.xml',
 ],
}
```

2. Add the `__init__.py` file in the `module` directory, with the following:

```
from . import models
```

3. Add the `models/__init__.py` file containing the following:

```
from . import library_checkout
```

4. Add the actual code file, `models/library_checkout.py`, as follows:

```
from odoo import api, exceptions, fields, models


class Checkout(models.Model):
    _name = 'library.checkout'
    _description = 'Checkout Request'
    member_id = fields.Many2one(
        'library.member',
        required=True)
    user_id = fields.Many2one(
        'res.users',
        'Librarian',
        default=lambda s: s.env.uid)
    request_date = fields.Date(
        default=lambda s: fields.Date.today())
    line_ids = fields.One2many(
```

```
                    'library.checkout.line',
                    'checkout_id',
                    string='Borrowed Books',)


        class CheckoutLine(models.Model):
            _name = 'library.checkout.line'
            _description = 'Borrow Request Line'
            checkout_id = fields.Many2one('library.checkout')
            book_id = fields.Many2one('library.book')
```

Next we should add the data files, adding the access rule, the menu items, and some basic views, so that the module is minimally usable.

5. The following is the `security/ir.model.access.csv` file:

```
id,name,model_id:id,group_id:id,perm_read,perm_write,perm_create,pe
rm_unlink
checkout_user,Checkout
User,model_library_checkout,library_app.library_group_user,1,1,1,0
checkout_line_user,Checkout Line User
,model_library_checkout_line,library_app.library_group_user,1,1,1,1
checkout_manager,Checkout Manager
,model_library_checkout,library_app.library_group_manager,1,1,1,1
```

6. The menu items are implemented in the following, `views/library_menu.xml`:

```xml
<odoo>
    <act_window id="action_library_checkout"
      name="Checkouts"
      res_model="library.checkout"
      view_mode="tree,form" />

    <menuitem id="menu_library_checkout"
              name="Checkout"
              action="action_library_checkout"
              parent="library_app.library_menu" />
</odoo>
```

7. The views are implemented in the following, `views/checkout_view.xml`:

```xml
<?xml version="1.0"?>
<odoo>

  <record id="view_tree_checkout" model="ir.ui.view">
    <field name="name">Checkout Tree</field>
    <field name="model">library.checkout</field>
    <field name="arch" type="xml">
```

```xml
            <tree>
                <field name="request_date" />
                <field name="member_id" />
            </tree>
        </field>
    </record>

    <record id="view_form_checkout" model="ir.ui.view">
        <field name="name">Checkout Form</field>
        <field name="model">library.checkout</field>
        <field name="arch" type="xml">
            <form>
                <sheet>
                    <group>
                        <field name="member_id" />
                        <field name="request_date" />
                        <field name="user_id" />
                        <field name="line_ids" />
                    </group>
                </sheet>
            </form>
        </field>
    </record>

</odoo>
```

Now we can install the module in our Odoo work database, and we're ready to start adding more features.

Using stages for document-centered workflows

In Odoo, we can implement workflows centered on documents. What we refer to as documents can be things such as sales orders, project tasks, or HR applicants. All of these are expected to follow a certain life cycle since they're created until they come to a conclusion. They're recorded in a document that will progress through a list of possible stages, until it is completed.

If we present the stages as columns in a board, and the documents as work items in those columns, we get a Kanban board, providing a quick view over the work in progress.

There are two approaches to implement these progress steps are usually referred to as **states** and **stages**.

States are implemented through a closed selection list of predefined options. It is convenient when implementing business rules, and models and views have special support for the `state` field, to have `required` and `invisible` attributes set, according to the current state. It has the disadvantage that the states list is predefined and closed, and so can't adapt to specific process needs.

Stages are implemented through a related model, for the stages list is open to be configured to the current process needs: it is easy to modify the list of available stages, removing, adding, or reordering them. It has the disadvantage of not being reliable for process automation; since the list of stages can be changed, automation rules can't rely on particular stage IDs or descriptions.

One way to get the best of both approaches is to map stages to states. Documents are organized into configurable stage, and are indirectly linked to a reliable state code that can be confidently used to automate business logic.

We will start by implementing the `library.checkout.stage` model in the `library_checkout/models/library_checkout_stage.py` file, shown as follows:

```python
from odoo import fields, models


class CheckoutStage(models.Model):
    _name = 'library.checkout.stage'
    _description = 'Checkout Stage'
    _order = 'sequence,name'

    name = fields.Char()
    sequence = fields.Integer(default=10)
    fold = fields.Boolean()
    active = fields.Boolean(default=True)
    state = fields.Selection(
        [('new','New'),
         ('open','Borrowed'),
         ('done','Returned'),
         ('cancel', 'Cancelled')],
        default='new',
    )
```

Here, we can see the `state` field, allowing to map each stage with one of four basic states allowed.

The `sequence` field is important. To configure the order, the stages should be presented in the Kanban board and stage selection list.

The `fold` Boolean field will be used by the Kanban board to some columns folded by default, so that their content is not immediately made available. This is usually used for the `done` and `Cancelled` stages.

Don't forget to add the new code file to the `models/__init__.py` file containing the following:

```
from . import library_checkout_stage
from . import library_checkout
```

Next, we need to add the `stage` field to the library checkout model. Edit the `library_checkout/models/library_checkout.py` file and, at the end of the `Checkout` class (after the `line_ids` field), add the following:

```
# to add in the class Checkout:
@api.model
def _default_stage(self):
    Stage = self.env['library.checkout.stage']
    return Stage.search([], limit=1)

 @api.model
 def _group_expand_stage_id(self, stages, domain, order):
     return stages.search([], order=order)

stage_id = fields.Many2one(
    'library.checkout.stage',
    default=_default_stage,
    group_expand='_group_expand_stage_id')
state = fields.Selection(related='stage_id.state')
```

`stage_id` is a many-to-one relation with the stages model. We also added the `state` field. It is a `related` field that simply makes available the stage's `state` field in this model, so that it can be used in views.

The stage default value is computed by the `_default_stage()` helper function that returns the first record in the stages model. Since the stage model is properly ordered by sequence, it'll return the one with the lowest sequence number.

The `group_expand` parameter overrides the way grouping on the field works. The default, and expected, behavior for grouping operations is to only see the stages that are being used, and the stages with no checkout document won't be shown. But in this case, we would prefer something different; we would like to see all available stages, even if they have no documents. The `_group_expand_stage_id()` helper function returns the list of group's records that the grouping operation should use. In this case, it returns all existing stages, regardless of having library checkouts in that stage or not.

Changed in Odoo 10

The `group_expand` field attribute was introduced in Odoo 10 but isn't described in the official documentation. Usage examples can be found in the Odoo source code, for example, in the Project app: `https://github.com/odoo/odoo/blob/12.0/addons/project/models/project.py`.

Since we added a new model, we also need to add the corresponding access security to the`security/ir.model.access.csv` file, shown as follows:

```
checkout_stage_user,Checkout Stage
User,model_library_checkout_stage,library_app.library_group_user,1,0,0,0
checkout_stage_manager,Checkout Stage
Manager,model_library_checkout_stage,library_app.library_group_manager,1,1,
1,1
```

We need some stages to work with, so let's add some default data to the module. Create the

`data/library_checkout_stage.xml` file with the following code:

```xml
<odoo noupdate="1">
    <record id="stage_10" model="library.checkout.stage">
        <field name="name">Draft</field>
        <field name="sequence">10</field>
        <field name="state">new</field>
    </record>
    <record id="stage_20" model="library.checkout.stage">
        <field name="name">Borrowed</field>
        <field name="sequence">20</field>
        <field name="state">open</field>
    </record>
    <record id="stage_90" model="library.checkout.stage">
        <field name="name">Completed</field>
        <field name="sequence">90</field>
        <field name="state">done</field>
    </record>
    <record id="stage_95" model="library.checkout.stage">
        <field name="name">Cancelled</field>
        <field name="sequence">95</field>
        <field name="state">cancel</field>
    </record>
</odoo>
```

Before this can take effect, it needs to be added to the
`library_checkout/__manifest__.py` file, as follows:

```
'data': [
  'security/ir.model.access.csv',
  'views/library_menu.xml',
  'views/checkout_view.xml',
  'data/library_checkout_stage.xml',
],
```

The ORM method decorators

In the Odoo Python code encountered so far, we can see that decorators, such as
`@api.multi`, are frequently used in model methods. These are important for the ORM and
allow it to give those methods specific uses.

Let's review the ORM decorators we have available and when each should be used.

Methods for recordsets – @api.multi

Most of the time, we want a custom method to perform some actions on a recordset. For
this, we should use `@api.multi`, and in that case, the self argument will be the recordset to
work with. The method's logic will usually include a `for` loop iterating on it. This is surely
the most frequently used decorator.

> If no decorator is used on a model method, it will default to `@api.multi`
> behavior.

Methods for singleton records – @api.one

In some cases, the method is prepared to work with a single record (a singleton). Here, we
could use the `@api.one` decorator that's still available, but announced as deprecated since
Odoo 9. It wraps the decorated method, doing the `for` loop iteration, calling the decorated
method with it one record at a time, and then returning a list with the results. So, inside an
`@api.one` decorated method, `self` is guaranteed to be a singleton.

The return value of @api.one can be tricky; it returns a list, not the data structure returned by the actual method. For example, if the method code returns dict, the actual return value is a list of dict values. This misleading behavior was the main reason the method was deprecated.

In the case that our method is expected to work on a singleton record, we should still use @api.multi, and add at the top of the method code a line with self.ensure_one(), to ensure it is a singleton as expected.

Class static methods – @api.model

In some cases, the method is expected to work at the class level and not on particular records. In some object-oriented languages, this would be called a static method. These class-level static methods should be decorated with @api.model. In these cases, self should be used as a reference for the model, without expecting it to contain actual records.

Methods decorated with @api.model can't be used with user interface buttons. In those cases, @api.multi should be used instead.

On change methods

The on change methods are triggered from user interface form views, when the user edits a value on a particular field to perform some business logic immediately. This can be performing some validation, showing a message to the user, or changing other fields in form. The model method supporting this logic should be decorated with @api.onchange('fld1', 'fld2', ...). The decorator arguments are the names of the fields that will trigger the method when edited by the user.

A particular form disables the on change behavior, by adding the field attribute on_change="0", for example, <field name="fld1" onchange="0" />.

Inside the method, the self argument is a virtual record with the current form data. If values are set on the record, these will be changed on the user interface form. Notice that it doesn't actually write to database records, instead it provides information to change the data in the UI form.

No return value is needed, but a dict structure may be returned with a warning message to display in the user interface.

As an example, we can use this to perform some automation in the Checkout form—when the library member is changed, the request date is set to today, and a warning message is shown to the user alerting them to that.

For this, edit the `library_checkout/models/library_checkout.py` file to add the following method:

```python
@api.onchange('member_id')
def onchange_member_id(self):
    today = fields.Date.today()
    if self.request_date != today:
        self.request_date = fields.Date.today()
        return {
            'warning': {
                'title': 'Changed Request Date',
                'message': 'Request date changed to today.',
            }
        }
```

Here, we are using the `@api.onchange` decorator to trigger some logic to change on the `member_id` field, when done through the user interface. The actual method name is not relevant, but the convention is for its name to begin with `onchange_`. We update the value of the `request_date` field and return a warning message.

Inside an `onchange` method, `self` represents a single virtual record containing all of the fields currently set in the record being edited, and we can interact with them. Most of the time, this is what we want to do to automatically fill values in other fields, depending on the value set to the changed field. In this case, we're updating the `request_date` field to today.

The `onchange` methods don't need to return anything, but they can return a dictionary containing a warning or a domain key, shown as follows:

- The warning key should describe a message to show in a dialogue window, such as: `{'title': 'Message Title', 'message': 'Message Body'}`.
- The domain key can set, or change the domain attribute of other fields. This allows you to build more user-friendly interfaces, having a to-many field makes available only the options that make sense in that moment. The value for the domain key looks like this: `{'user_id': [('email', '!=', False)]}`

Other model method decorators

The following decorators are also frequently used. They are related to the internal behavior of a model and are discussed in detail in `Chapter 6`, *Models - Structuring the Application Data*.

We mention them here for your reference:

- `@api.depends(fld1, ...)` is used for computed field functions to identify on what changes the (re)calculation should be triggered. It must set values on the computed fields, otherwise it will error.
- `@api.constrains(fld1, ...)` is used for model validation functions and performs checks for when any of the mentioned fields are changed. It should not write changes in the data. If the checks fail, an exception should be raised.

Using the ORM built-in methods

The decorators discussed in the previous section allow us to add certain features to our models, such as implementing validations and automatic computations.

The ORM provides methods to perform **Create, Read, Update, and Delete (CRUD)** operations on our Model data. We will now explore these write operations and how they can be extended to support custom logic.

To read data, the main methods provided are `search()` and `browse()` and will be discussed in `Chapter 7`, *Recordsets - Working with Model Data*.

Methods for writing model data

The ORM provides three methods for the three basic write operations, shown as follows:

- `<Model>.create(values)` creates a new record on the model. It returns the created record.
- `<Recordset>.write(values)` updates field values on the recordset. It returns nothing.
- `<Recordset>.unlink()` deletes the records from the database. It returns nothing.

The `values` argument is a dictionary, mapping field names to values to write. The methods are decorated with `@api.multi`, except for the `create()` method, which is decorated with `@api.model`.

Changed in Odoo 12

The `create()` method now also allows to create records in batches. This is done by passing as argument a list of dictionary objects, instead of a single dictionary object. This is supported on `create()` methods that have the `@api.model_create_multi` decorator.

In some cases, we need to extend these methods to add some business logic to be triggered whenever these actions are executed. By placing our logic in the appropriate section of the custom method, we can have the code run before or after the main operations are executed.

We will build an example using the `Checkout` model class—add two date fields, to record when the checkout entered into an open state and when it moved to a closed state. This is something that can't be done with a computed field. We will also add a check to prevent creating checkouts already in a done state.

So we should start by adding the two new fields to the checkout class, in the following `library_checkout/models/library_checkout.py` file:

```python
# add to the Checkout Model class:
checkout_date = fields.Date(readonly=True)
close_date = fields.Date(readonly=True)
```

We can now make a custom `create()` method, to set the `checkout_date`, if in the appropriate state, and prevent the creation of checkouts in the done state, shown as follows:

```python
@api.model
def create(self, vals):
    # Code before create: should use the `vals` dict
    if 'stage_id' in vals:
        Stage = self.env['library.checkout.stage']
        new_state = Stage.browse(vals['stage_id']).state
        if new_state == 'open':
            vals['checkout_date'] = fields.Date.today()
    new_record = super().create(vals)
    # Code after create: can use the `new_record` created
    if new_record.state == 'done':
        raise exceptions.UserError(
            'Not allowed to create a checkout in the done state.')
    return new_record
```

Notice that, before the actual new record, we have no actual record available, only the dictionary with the values to use for the record creation. That's why we used browse() to get a record for the new record's stage_id, to then inspect the corresponding state value. In comparison, once the new record is created, the equivalent operation becomes simpler, using object dot notation, new_record.state.

The values dictionary can be changed before the super().create(vals) instruction, and we use that to set the checkout_date to write, when appropriate.

Changed in Odoo 11

When using Python 3, a simplified way to use super() is available and was used in the preceding code example. In Python 2, we would write super(Checkout, self).create(vals), where checkout is the name of the Python class we are in. This is still valid syntax for Python 3, but we also have available the new simplified syntax: super().create(vals).

And when a record is modified, we want to update checkout_date and close_date if the checkout is entering the appropriated states. For this we will have a custom write() method, shown as follows:

```
@api.multi
def write(self, vals):
    # Code before write: can use `self`, with the old values
    if 'stage_id' in vals:
        Stage = self.env['library.checkout.stage']
        new_state = Stage.browse(vals['stage_id']).state
        if new_state == 'open' and self.state != 'open':
            vals['checkout_date'] = fields.Date.today()
        if new_state == 'done' and self.state != 'done':
            vals['close_date'] = fields.Date.today()
    super().write(vals)
    # Code after write: can use `self`, with the updated values
    return True
```

Whenever possible, we prefer to change the values to write before the super().write(vals) instruction. For the write() method, having further write operations on the same model will lead to a recursion loop and end with an error when the worker process resources are exhausted. Please consider whether this is really needed. If it is, a technique to avoid the recursion loop is to set a flag in the context. For example, we could add code such as the following:

```
if not self.env.context.get('_library_checkout_writing'):
    self.with_context(_library_checkout_writing=True).write(
        some_values)
```

With this technique, our specific logic is guarded by an `if` statement and runs only if a specific marker is not found in the context. Furthermore, our `self.write()` operations should use `with_context` to set that marker. This combination ensures that the custom login inside the `if` statement runs only once and is not triggered on further `write()` calls, avoiding the infinite loop.

Doing so after implies running `write()` inside the `write()` method, and this can create an infinite loop. To avoid that, we need to set a marker value in the context and check it in the code to avoid running into a loop.

Consider carefully whether you really need to use extensions to the create or write methods. In most cases, we just need to perform some validation, or automatically compute some value, when the record is saved:

- For field values that are automatically calculated based on other fields, we should use computed fields. An example of this is to calculate a header total when the values of the lines are changed.
- To have field default values calculated dynamically, we can use a field default bound to a function instead of a fixed value.
- To have values set on other fields when a field is changed, we can use on change functions. An example of this is, when picking a customer, setting their currency as the document's currency that can later be manually changed by the user. Keep in mind that on change only works on form view interaction, and not on direct write calls.
- For validations, we should use constraint functions decorated with `@api.constraints(fld1, fld2, ...)`. These are like computed fields but, instead of computing values, they are expected to raise errors.

Methods for data import and export

The import and export operations, discussed in `Chapter 5`, *Import, Export, and Module Data*, are also available from the ORM API, through the following methods:

- `load([fields], [data])` is used to import data acquired from a CSV file. The first argument is the list of fields to import, and it maps directly to a CSV top row. The second argument is a list of records, where each record is a list of string values to parse and import, and it maps directly to the CSV data rows and columns. It implements the features of CSV data import, such as the external identifiers support. It is used by the web client `Import` function.

- `export_data([fields], raw_data=False)` is used by the web client `Export` function. It returns a dictionary with a data key containing the data – a list of rows. The field names can use the `.id` and `/id` suffixes used in CSV files, and the data is in a format compatible with an importable CSV file. The optional `raw_data` argument allows for data values to be exported with their Python types, instead of the string representation used in CSV.

Methods to support the user interface

The following methods are mostly used by the web client to render the user interface and perform basic interaction:

- `name_get()` returns a list of tuples (ID, name) with the text representing each record. It is used by default for computing the `display_name` value, providing the text representation of relation fields. It can be extended to implement custom display representations, such as displaying the record code and name instead of only the name.
- `name_search(name='', args=None, operator='ilike', limit=100)` returns a list of tuples (ID, name) , where the display name matches the text in the name argument. It is used in the UI while typing in a `related` field to produce the list with the suggested records matching the typed text. For example, it is used to implement product lookup both by name and by reference, while typing in a field to pick a product.
- `name_create(name)` creates a new record with only the title name to use for it. It is used in the UI for the *quick-create* feature, where you can quickly create a related record by just providing its name. It can be extended to provide specific defaults for the new records created through this feature.
- `default_get([fields])` returns a dictionary with the default values for a new record to be created. The default values may depend on variables, such as the current user or the session context.
- `fields_get()` is used to describe the model's field definitions, as seen in the view fields option of the developer menu.
- `fields_view_get()` is used by the web client to retrieve the structure of the UI view to render. It can be given the ID of the view as an argument, or the type of view we want using `view_type='form'`. For example, you may try this: `self.fields_view_get(view_type='tree')`.

The message and activity features

Odoo has available global messaging and activity planning features, provided by the Discuss application, with technical name mail.

The mail module provides the `mail.thread` abstract class that makes it simple to add the messaging features to any model, and the `mail.activity.mixin` that adds planned activity features. This was done in `Chapter 4`, *Extending Modules*, to explain how to inherit features from mixin abstract classes.

To add these features, we need to add the mail dependency to the add-on module, `library_checkout`, and then have the library checkout model class inherit from the abstract classes providing the following features.

Edit the `'depends'` key in the `library_checkout/__manifest__.py` file, to add the mail module, shown as follows:

```
'depends': ['library_member', 'mail'],
```

And edit the `library_checkout/models/library_checkout.py` file to inherit from the mixin abstract models, shown as follows:

```
class Checkout(models.Model):
    _name = 'library.checkout'
    _description = 'Checkout Request'
    _inherit = [''mail.thread', 'mail.activity']
```

After this, among other things, our model will have three new fields available. For each record (sometimes also called a document), we have the following:

- `mail_follower_ids` stores the followers and corresponding notification preferences
- `mail_message_ids` lists all of the related `messages.activity_ids` with all of the related planned activities

The followers can be either partners or channels. A **partner** represents a specific person or organization. A **channel** is not a particular person, and instead represents a subscription list.

Each follower also has a list of message types that they are subscribed to. Only the selected message types will generate notifications for them.

Message subtypes

Some types of messages are called **subtypes**. They are stored in the `mail.message.subtype` model and are accessible in the **Technical** | **Email** | **Subtypes** menu.

By default, we have the following three message subtypes available:

- **Discussions**, with `mail.mt_comment` XMLID, used for the messages created with the **Send message** link. It is intended to send a notification.
- **Activities**, with `mail.mt_activities` XMLID, used for the messages created with the **Schedule activity** link. It is not intended to send a notification.
- **Note**, with `mail.mt_note` XMLID, used for the messages created with the **Log note** link. It is not intended to send a notification.

Subtypes have the default notification settings described previously, but users are able to change them for specific documents, for example, to mute a discussion they aren't interested in.

Other than the built-in subtypes, we can also add our own subtypes to customize the notifications for our applications. Subtypes can be generic or intended for a particular model. For the latter case, we should fill in the `subtype's res_model` field with the name of the model it should apply to.

Posting messages

Our business logic can make use of this messaging system to send notifications to users. To post a message, we use the `message_post()` method. The following is an example of this:

```
self.message_post('Hello!')
```

This adds a simple text message, but sends no notification to the followers. That is because, by default, the `mail.mt_note` subtype is used for the posted messages. But we can have the message posted with the particular subtype we want. To add a message and have it send notifications to the followers, we should use the `mt_comment` subtype. Another optional attribute is the message's subject. Here, is an example using both options:

```
self.message_post('Hello again!', subject='Hello',
subtype='mail.mt_comment')
```

The message body is HTML, so we can include markup for text effects, such as <b> for bold text or <i> for italics.

 The message body will be sanitized for security reasons, so some particular HTML elements may not make it to the final message.

Adding followers

Also interesting from a business logic viewpoint is the ability to automatically add followers to a document, so that they can then get the corresponding notifications. For this, we have several methods available to add followers, listed as follows:

- `message_subscribe(partner_ids=<list of int IDs>)` adds partners
- `message_subscribe(channel_ids=<list of int IDs>)` adds channels
- `message_subscribe_users(user_ids=<list of int IDs>)` adds users

The default subtypes will be applied to each subscriber. To force subscribing a specific list of subtypes, add an additional attribute `subtype_ids=<list of int IDs>`, listing the specific subtypes to enable for the subscription.

Creating a wizard

Suppose our library users have the need to send messages to groups of borrowers. For example, they could select the oldest checkouts with borrowed book, and send them all a message requesting the return of the books. This can be implemented through a wizard. **Wizards** are forms that get input from users, then use it for further processing.

Our users will start by selecting from the checkouts list the records to consider, then select the **wizard's** option from the view top menu. This will open the wizard form, where we can write the message's subject and body. Once we click on **Send**, this message will be posted in all of the checkouts selected.

The wizard model

A wizard displays a form view to the user, usually as a dialog window, with some fields to be filled in. These will then be used for the wizard logic.

This is implemented using the same model/view architecture as for regular views, but the supporting model is based on `models.TransientModel` instead of `models.Model`. This type of model also has a database representation and stores state there, but the data is expected to be useful only until the wizard completes its work. A scheduled job regularly cleans up the old data from wizard database tables.

The `wizard/wizard/library_checkout_massmessage.py` file will define the fields we need to interact with the user: the list of checkouts to be notified, the message subject, and the message body.

First, edit the `library_checkout/__init__.py` to add an import of the code in the `wizard/` subdirectory, shown as follows:

```
from . import models
from . import wizard
```

Add the `wizard/__init__.py` file with following line of code:

```
from . import library_checkout_massmessage
```

Then, create the actual `wizard/checkout_mass_message.py` file, shown as follows:

```
from odoo import api, exceptions, fields, models

class CheckoutMassMessage(models.TransientModel):
    _name = 'library.checkout.massmessage'
    _description = 'Send Message to Borrowers'
    checkout_ids = fields.Many2many(
        'library.checkout',
        string='Checkouts')
    message_subject = fields.Char()
    message_body = fields.Html()
```

It's worth noting that one-to-many relations with regular models shouldn't be used in transient models. The reason for this is that it would require the regular model to have the inverse many-to-one relation with the transient model. But this is not allowed, since that could prevent old transient records from being cleaned up, because of the existing references in regular model records. The alternative to this is to use a many-to-many relation.

 Many-to-many relationships are stored in a dedicated table, and the rows in this table are automatically deleted when either side of the relationship gets deleted.

Transient models don't need access rules, since they are just disposable records to aid executing a process. So we don't need to add ACLs to the `security/ir.model.access.csv` file.

The wizard form

The wizard form views are the same as for regular models, except for two specific elements:

- A `<footer>` section can be used to replace the action buttons
- A `special="cancel"` button is available to interrupt the wizard without performing any action

The following is the content of our `wizard/checkout_mass_message_wizard_view.xml` file:

```xml
<?xml version="1.0"?>
<odoo>

  <record id="view_form_checkout_message" model="ir.ui.view">
    <field name="name">Library Checkout Mass Message Wizard</field>
    <field name="model">library.checkout.massmessage</field>
    <field name="arch" type="xml">

      <form>
        <group>
          <field name="message_subject" />
          <field name="message_body" />
          <field name="checkout_ids" />
        </group>
        <footer>
          <button type="object"
            name="button_send"
            string="Send Messages" />
          <button special="cancel"
            string="Cancel"
            class="btn-secondary" />
        </footer>
      </form>

    </field>
  </record>

  <act_window id="action_checkout_message"
    name="Send Messages"
```

```
            src_model="library.checkout"
            res_model="library.checkout.massmessage"
            view_type="form"
            view_mode="form"
            target="new"
            multi="True"
            />

    </odoo>
```

The `<act_window>` window action we see in the XML adds an option to the **Action** button of library checkout, using the `src_model` attribute. The `target="new"` attribute makes it open as a dialog window.

To open the wizard, we should select one or more records from the checkout list, and then choose the **Send Messages** option from the **Action** menu, which shows up at the top of the list, next to the **Filters** menu.

Right now, this opens the wizard form, but the records selected on the list are ignored. It would be nice for our wizard to show them preselected in the tasks list. When a form is presented, the `default_get()` method is called to compute the default values to be presented. This is exactly what we want, so we should use that method. Note that, when the wizard form is opened, we have an empty record and the `create()` method isn't invoked yet, which will only happen when we press a button, and so it can't be used for what we want.

Odoo views add a few elements to the context dictionary, which are available when we click through an action or jump to another view. These are as follows:

- `active_model`, with the technical name of the view's model
- `active_id`, with the ID of the form's active record (or the first record, if in a list)
- `active_ids`, with a list of the active records in a list (just one element, if in a form)
- `active_domain`, if the action is triggered from a form view

In our case, `active_ids` hold the IDs for the records selected in the **Task** list, and we can use them as the default values for the wizard's `task_ids` field, shown as follows:

```
    @api.model
    def default_get(self, field_names):
        defaults = super().default_get(field_names)
        checkout_ids = self.env.context['active_ids']
        defaults['checkout_ids'] = checkout_ids
        return defaults
```

We first use `super()` to call the standard `default_get()` computation, and then add the `checkout_id` to the defaults, with the `active_ids` value read from the environment context.

Next, we need to implement the actions to be performed on the form **Send** button.

The wizard business logic

Excluding the **Cancel** button, which just closes the form without performing any action, we have the **Send** action buttons to implement.

The method called by the button is `button_send`, and it should be defined in the `wizard/checkout_mass_message.py` file, as shown in the following code:

```
@api.multi
def button_send(self):
    self.ensure_one()
    for checkout in self.checkout_ids:
        checkout.message_post(
            body=self.message_body,
            subject=self.message_subject,
            subtype='mail.mt_comment',
        )
    return True
```

Our code only needs to handle one wizard instance at a time, so we used `self.ensure_one()` to make that clear. Here, `self` represents the browse record for the data on the wizard form.

The method iterates through the selected checkout records and posts a message for each one. The `mt_comment` subtype is used, so that the message generates a notification to the record followers.

 It is good practice for methods to always return something, at least the `True` value. The sole reason for this is that some XML-RPC protocols don't support `None` values, so those methods won't be usable with that protocol. In practice, you may not be aware of the issue because the web client uses JSON-RPC, not XML-RPC, but it is still a good practice to follow.

Using log messages

Writing messages to the log file can be useful to monitor and audit running systems. It is also helpful for code maintenance, making it easier to get debug information from running processes, without the need to change code.

For our code to be able to use logging, we first need to prepare a logger. Add the following code lines at the top of `library_checkout/wizard/checkout_mass_message.py`:

```
import logging
_logger = logging.getLogger(__name__)
```

The Python standard library `logging` module is used. The `_logger` object is initialized, using the name of the current code file, `__name__`. With this, the log messages will carry information of the file that generated them.

There are several levels available for log messages. These are as follows:

```
_logger.debug('A DEBUG message')
_logger.info('An INFO message')
_logger.warning('A WARNING message')
_logger.error('An ERROR message')
```

We can now use the logger to write messages to the log. Let's do this in the `button_send` wizard method. Add the following instruction before the ending, `return True`:

```
_logger.info(
    'Posted %d messages to Checkouts: %s',
    len(self.checkout_ids),
    str(self.checkout_ids),
)
```

With this, when you use the wizard to send messages, a message similar to this one will be shown in the server log:

```
INFO 12-library odoo.addons.library_checkout.wizard.checkout_mass_message:
Posted 2 messages to Checkouts: [3, 4]
```

Notice that we didn't use Python string interpolation for the log message. Instead of something like `_logger.info('Hello %s' % 'World')`, we used something like `_logger.info('Hello %s', 'World')`. Not using interpolation means one less task for our code to perform and makes logging more efficient. So we should always provide the variables as additional log parameters.

The timestamps of the server log messages always use UTC time. So, log messages are also printed in UTC time. This may come as a surprise, and comes from the fact that the Odoo server internally handles all dates in UTC.

For debug level log messages, we use `_logger.debug()`. For example, add the following debug log message right after the `checkout.message_post()` instruction:

```
_logger.debug(
    'Message on %d to followers: %s',
    checkout.id,
    checkout.message_follower_ids)
```

This won't display anything on the server log, since the default log level is INFO. The log level needs to be set as DEBUG for the `debug` messages to be printed to the log.

The Odoo command option, `--log-level=debug`, sets the general log level. We may also set the log level for particular modules. The Python module for our wizard is `odoo.addons.library_checkout.wizard.checkout_mass_message`, as seen in the INFO log message. To enable only the wizard's debug messages, we use the `--log-handler` option, which can be repeated several times, to the the log level of several modules, shown as follows:

```
--log-
handler=odoo.addons.library_checkout.wizard.checkout_mass_message:DEBUG
```

The complete reference to the Odoo server logging options can be found in the official documentation, at `https://www.odoo.com/documentation/12.0/reference/cmdline.html#logging`.

If you want to get into the nitty-gritty details of Python logging, the official documentation is a good place to start: `https://docs.python.org/3.5/howto/logging.html`.

Raising exceptions

When something does not work as expected, we may want to inform the user and interrupt the program with an error message. This is done by raising an exception. Odoo provides exception classes that we should use for this.

The most useful Odoo exceptions to be used in add-on modules are the following:

```
from odoo import exceptions
raise exceptions.ValidationError('Not valid message')
raise exceptions.UserError('Business logic error')
```

The `ValidationError` exception should be used for validations in Python code, such as `@api.constrains` decorated methods.

The `UserError` exception should be used in all other cases where some action should not be allowed, because it goes against business logic.

Changed in Odoo 9
The `UserError` exception was introduced, replacing the `Warning` exception, deprecated due to collision with Python builtins, but kept for Odoo backward compatibility.

As a general rule, all data manipulation done during a method execution is in a database transaction and is rolled back when an exception occurs. This means that, when an exception is raised, all of the previous data changes are canceled.

Let's look at an example using our wizard `button_send` method. If we think about it, it doesn't make any sense to run the send messages logic if no checkout document was selected. And it doesn't make sense to send messages with no message body. Let's warn the user if any of these things happen.

Edit the `button_send()` method, to add the following instruction right after the `self.ensure_one()` line:

```
if not self.checkout_ids:
    raise exceptions.UserError(
        'Select at least one Checkout to send messages to.')
if not self.message_body:
    raise exceptions.UserError(
        'Write a message body to send.')
```

Unit tests

Automated tests are generally accepted as a best practice in software. They not only help us ensure our code is correctly implemented, but more importantly, they provide a safety net for future code changes or rewrites.

In the case of dynamic programming languages, such as Python, since there's no compilation step, syntax errors can go unnoticed. This makes it even more important to have unit tests going through as many lines of code as possible.

The two goals described can provide a guiding light when writing tests. The first goal for your tests should be to provide good test coverage; designing test cases that go through all your lines of code.

This alone will usually make good progress on the second goal—to show the functional correctness of the code—since after this, we will surely have a great starting point to build additional test cases for non-obvious use cases.

Changed in Odoo 12

In previous versions, Odoo also supported tests described using YAML data files. Since Odoo 12, the YAML data file engine was removed from Odoo, and this type of file is not supported anymore. The last documentation on it is available at `https://doc.odoo.com/v6.0/contribute/15_guidelines/coding_guidelines_testing/`.

Adding unit tests

Python tests are added to addon modules in a `tests/` subdirectory. The test runner will automatically discover tests in the subdirectories with this particular name.

To add tests for the wizard logic created in the `library_checkout` add-on module, we can start by creating the `tests/test_checkout_mass_message.py` file. As usual, we will also need to add the `tests/__init__.py` file, as follows:

```
from . import test_checkout_mass_message
```

The following would be the basic skeleton for the `tests/test_checkout_mass_message.py` test code:

```
from odoo.tests.common import import TransactionCase

class TestWizard(TransactionCase):
```

```
def setUp(self, *args, **kwargs):
    super(TestWizard, self).setUp(*args, **kwargs)
    # Add test setup code here...

def test_button_send(self):
    """Send button should create messages on Checkouts"""
    # Add test code
```

Odoo provides a few classes to use for tests, listed as follows:

- The `TransactionCase` test uses a different transaction for each test, which is automatically rolled back at the end.
- The `SingleTransactionCase`, which runs all tests in a single transaction, is rolled back only at the end of the last test. This can be useful when you want the final state of each test to be the initial state for the following test.

The `setUp()` method is where we prepare data and variables to be used. We will usually store them as class attributes, so that they are available to be used in the test methods.

Tests should then be implemented as class methods, such as `test_button_send()`. The test cases method names must begin with a `test_` prefix. They are automatically discovered, and this prefix is what identifies the methods implementing test cases. Methods will be run in the order of the test function names.

When using the `TransactionCase` class, a rollback will be done at the end of each test case. The method's `docstring` is shown when the tests are run and should be used to provide a short description for the test performed.

 These test classes are wrappers around `unittest` test cases, part of the Python standard library. For more details on this, you can refer to the official documentation at `https://docs.python.org/3/library/unittest.html`.

Running tests

The tests are written, so now it's time to run them. For that, we just need to add the `--test-enable` option to the Odoo server start command, while installing or upgrading (`-i` or `-u`) the addon module.

The command will look like this:

```
$ ./odoo-bin -c 12-library.conf --test-enable -u library_checkout --stop-
after-init
```

Only the modules installed or upgraded will be tested—that's why the -u option was used. If some dependencies need to be installed, their tests will run too. If you want to avoid this, you can install the module you wish to test the usual way, and afterward, run the tests while upgrading (-u) the module to test.

The tests we have don't actually test anything yet, but they should run without failing. Having a close look at the server log, we should be able to see INFO messages reporting the test runs, such as the following:

```
INFO 12-library odoo.modules.module:
odoo.addons.library_checkout.tests.test_checkout_mass_message running
tests.
```

Setting up tests

We should begin by preparing the data to be used in the tests, in the setUp method. Here, we need to create a checkout record to be used in the wizard.

It is convenient to perform the test actions under a specific user in order to also test that access control is properly configured. This is achieved using the sudo(<user>) model method. Recordsets carry that information with them, so after being created using sudo(), later operations in the same recordset will be performed using that same context.

This is the code for the setUp method:

```
from odoo.tests.common import TransactionCase

class TestWizard(TransactionCase):

    def setUp(self, *args, **kwargs):
        super().setUp(*args, **kwargs)
        # Setup test data
        admin_user = self.env.ref('base.user_admin')
        self.Checkout = self.env['library.checkout'].sudo(admin_user)
        self.Wizard = self.env['library.checkout.massmessage']\
.sudo(admin_user)

        a_member = self.env['library.member'].create({'name': 'John'})
        self.checkout0 = self.Checkout.create({
            'member_id': a_member.id})
```

Now, we can use the `self.checkout0` record and `self.Wizard` model for our tests.

Writing test cases

Now, let's expand the `test_button_test()` method seen in our initial skeleton. The simplest tests run some code on the tested object, get a result, and then use an assert statement to compare it with an expected result.

To check the method posting a message, the test counts the number of messages before and after running the wizard to confirm whether the new message was added. To run the wizard, we need to set the `active_ids` in the context, like UI forms do, create the wizard record with the values filled in the wizard form (at least the body message), and then run the `button_send` method.

The full code looks like the following:

```
def test_button_send(self):
    "Send button creates messages on Checkouts"
    # Add test code
    msgs_before = len(self.checkout0.message_ids)

    Wizard0 = self.Wizard.with_context(active_ids=self.checkout0.ids)
    wizard0 = Wizard0.create({'message_body': 'Hello'})
    wizard0.button_send()

    msgs_after = len(self.checkout0.message_ids)
    self.assertEqual(
        msgs_after,
        msgs_before +1,
        'Expected one additional message in the Checkout.')
```

`docstring`, at the first line of the method definition, is useful to describe the test and is printed out when running the tests.

The check verifying whether the test succeeded or failed is the `self.assertEqual` statement. It compares the number of messages before and after running the wizard; we expect to find one more message than we had before. The last parameter provides a more informative message when the test fails. It is optional, but recommended.

The `assertEqual` function is just one of the assert methods available. We should use the assert function that is appropriate for each case, since this will make it easier to understand the cause of failing tests. The `unittest` documentation provides a good reference for all of the methods and is available at `https://docs.python.org/3/library/unittest.html#test-cases`.

To add a new test case, add another method to the class with its implementation. Remember that, with `TransactionCase` tests, a rollback is done at the end of each test. So, the operations done in the previous test were reverted, and we need to again populate the wizard's to-do task list. Next, we simulate the user, filling in the new deadline field, and performing the mass update. At the end, we check whether both to-do tasks ended up with the same date.

Testing exceptions

Sometimes, we need our tests to check whether an exception was generated. A common case is testing whether some validations is being done correctly.

In our case, the wizard does some validations we can test. For example, we can test that an empty body message raises an error. To check whether an exception is raised, we place the corresponding code inside a `with self.assertRaises()` block.

We first need to import the Odoo exceptions at the top of the file, shown as follows:

```
from odoo import exceptions
```

Then, we add another method with a test case to the test class, shown as follows:

```
def test_button_send_empty_body(self):
    "Send button errors on empty body message"
    wizard0 = self.Wizard.create({})
    with self.assertRaises(exceptions.UserError) as e:
        wizard0.button_send()
```

If the `button_send()` method doesn't raise an exception, the check will fail. If it does raise that exception, the check succeeds and the exception raised is stored in the e variable. We can use that to further inspect it.

Development tools

There are a few techniques developers should learn to aid them in their work. Earlier in this book, we introduced the **Developer Mode** user interface. We also have a server option available, providing some developer-friendly features. We will be describing this in more detail in this section. After that, we will discuss another relevant topic for developers: how to debug server-side code.

Server development options

The Odoo server provides the --dev option to enable some developer features to speed up our development cycle, such as the following:

- Entering the debugger when an exception is found in an add-on module
- Reloading Python code automatically once a Python file is saved, avoiding a manual server restart
- Reading view definitions directly from XML files, avoiding manual module upgrades

The --dev option accepts a comma-separated list of options, and the all option will be suitable most of the time. We can also specify the debugger we prefer to use. By default, the Python debugger, pdb, is used. Some people might prefer to install and use alternative debuggers. It is good to note that ipdb and pudb are also supported here.

Changed in Odoo 9
In Odoo versions before Odoo 9, the --debug option was available, allowing you to open the debugger on an addon module exception. Since Odoo 9, this option is no longer available and was replaced by the --dev=all option.

When working on Python code, the server needs to be restarted every time the code is changed so that it is reloaded. The --dev command-line option deals with that reloading. When the server detects that a Python file is changed, it automatically repeats the server loading sequence, making the code change immediately effective.

To use it, just add the --dev=all option to the server command, shown as follows:

```
$ ./odoo-bin -c 12-library --dev=all
```

For this to work, the `watchdog` Python package is required. It can be installed using the following `pip`:

```
$ pip install watchdog
```

Note that this is useful only for Python code changes and view architectures in XML files. For other changes, such as model data structure, a module upgrade is needed, and reloading it is not enough.

Debugging

We all know that a large part of a developer's work is to debug code. To do this, we often make use of a code editor that can set breakpoints, and run our program step by step.

If you're using Microsoft Windows as your development workstation, setting up an environment capable of running Odoo code from a source is a non-trivial task. Also, the fact that Odoo is a server that waits for client calls, and only then acts on them, makes it quite different to debug compared to client-side programs.

The Python debugger

While it may look a little intimidating for newcomers, the most pragmatic approach to debug Odoo is to use the Python integrated debugger, `pdb`. We will also introduce extensions to it that provide a richer user interface, similar to what sophisticated IDEs usually provide.

To use the debugger, the best approach is to insert a breakpoint into the code we want to inspect, typically a model method. This is done by inserting the following line in the desired place:

```
import pdb; pdb.set_trace()
```

Now, restart the server so that the modified code is loaded. As soon as the program execution reaches that line, a `(pdb)` Python prompt will be shown in the Terminal window where the server is running, waiting for our input.

This prompt works as a Python shell, where you can run any expression or command in the current execution context. This means that the current variables can be inspected and even modified. These are the most important shortcut commands available:

- h (help) displays a summary of the pdb commands available
- p (print) evaluates and prints an expression
- pp (pretty print) is useful to print data structures, such as dictionaries or lists
- l (list) lists the code around the instruction to be executed next
- n (next) steps over to the next instruction
- s (step) steps into the current instruction
- c (continue) continues execution normally
- u (up) moves up in the execution stack
- d (down) moves down in the execution stack
- bt (backtrace) shows the current execution stack

If the dev=all option is used to start the servers, when an exception is raised, the server enters a *post mortem* mode at the corresponding line. This is a pdb prompt, such as the one described earlier, allowing us to inspect the program state at the moment where the error was found.

A sample debugging session

Let's see what a simple debugging session looks like. We can start by adding a debugger breakpoint in the first line of the button_send wizard method, shown as follows:

```
def button_send(self):
    import pdb; pdb.set_trace()
    self.ensure_one()
    # ...
```

Now, restart the server, open a **Send Message** wizard form and click on the **Send** button. This will trigger the button_send method on the server, and the web client will stay in a **Loading...** state, waiting for the server's response. Looking at the Terminal window where the server is running, you will see something similar to the following:

```
> /mnt/c/Users/daniel/Documents/library-
app/library_checkout/wizard/checkout_mass_message.py(27)button_send()
-> self.ensure_one()
(Pdb)
```

This is the `pdb` debugger prompt, and the two first lines give you information about where you are in the Python code execution. The first line states the file, line number, and function name you are in, and the second line is the next line of code to be run.

During a debug session, server log messages can creep in. These won't harm our debugging, but they can disturb us. We can avoid that by reducing the verbosity of the log messages. Most of the time, these log messages will be from the `werkzeug` module. We can silence them using the `--log-handler=werkzeug:CRITICAL` option. If this is not enough, we can lower the general log level using `--log-level=warn`. Another option is to just enable the `--logfile=/path/to/log` option so that the log messages are redirected from the standard output to a disk file.

 If you get an apparently unresponsive Terminal, where what you type is not presented in the terminal, it may be related to display issues on your terminal session. There is a chance that this can be solved by typing `<enter>reset<enter>`.

If we type `h` now, we will see a quick reference of the commands available. Typing `l` shows the current line of code and the surrounding lines of code.

Typing `n` will run the current line of code and move on to the next. If we just press *Enter*, the previous command will be repeated. Do that three times, and we should be at the method's return statement.

We can inspect the content on any variable or attribute, such as the `checkout_ids` field used in the wizard, shown as follows:

```
(pdb) p self.checkout_ids
```

Any Python expressions are allowed, even variable assignments.

We can go on debugging line by line. At any point, we continue normal execution by typing `c`.

Alternative Python debuggers

While `pdb` has the advantage of being available out of the box, it can be quite terse, and a few more comfortable options exist.

The Iron Python debugger, ipdb, is a popular choice that uses the same commands as pdb, but adds improvements such as Tab completion and syntax highlighting for more comfortable use. It can be installed with the following:

```
$ sudo pip install ipdb
```

And a breakpoint is added with the following line:

```
import ipdb; ipdb.set_trace()
```

Another alternative debugger is pudb. It also supports the same commands as pdb, and works in text-only Terminals, but uses a graphical display similar to what you can find in an IDE debugger. Useful information, such as the variables in the current context and their values, is readily available on the screen in their own windows.

It can be installed either through the system package manager or through pip, as shown here:

```
$ sudo apt-get install python-pudb   # using Debian OS packages
$ sudo pip install pudb   # or using pip, possibly in a virtualenv
```

Adding a pudb breakpoint is done just the way you would expect it to be, shown as follows:

```
import pudb; pudb.set_trace()
```

But the following is a shorter and easier to remember alternative that's available:

```
import pudb; pu.db
```

Printing messages and logging

Sometimes, we just need to inspect the values of some variables or check whether some code blocks are being executed. A Python print() function can do the job perfectly without stopping the execution flow. As we are running the server in a terminal window, the printed text will be shown in the standard output, but it won't be stored to the server log if it's being written to a file.

The print() function is only being used as a development aid and should not make its way to final code, ready to be deployed. If you suspect that you need more details about the code execution, use debug level log messages instead.

Adding debug level log messages at sensitive points of our code allows us to investigate issues in a deployed instance. We would just need to elevate that server logging level to debug and then inspect the log files.

Inspecting and killing running processes

There are also a few tricks that allow us to inspect a running Odoo process.

For that, we first need to find the corresponding **process ID (PID)** . To find the PID, run another Terminal window and type the following:

```
$ ps ax | grep odoo-bin
```

The first column in the output is the PID for that process. Take a note of the PID for the process to inspect, since we will need it next.

Now, we want to send a signal to the process. The command used to do that is `kill`. By default, it sends a signal to terminate a process, but it can also send other friendlier signals.

Knowing the PID for our running Odoo server process, we can print the traces of the code currently being executed sending a SIGQUIT signal to the running process, with the following:

```
$ kill -3 <PID>
```

After this, if we look at the terminal window or log file where the server output is being written, we will see the information on several threads being run, as well as detailed stack traces on what line of code they are running. This is used by some code profiling approaches, to track where the server is spending time, and profile the code execution. Some useful information on code profiling is given in the official documentation, at `https://www.odoo.com/documentation/12.0/howtos/profilecode.html`.

Other signals we can send to the Odoo server process are `HUP`, to reload the server, and `INT` or `TERM` to force the server to shut down, shown as follows:

```
$ kill -HUP <PID>
$ kill -TERM <PID>
```

Summary

We went through an explanation of the features the ORM API, and how to use them to create dynamic applications that react to the users, which helps them to avoid errors and automate tedious tasks.

The model validations and computed fields can cover a lot of use cases, but not all. We learned how to extend the API create, write, and unlink methods to cover further use cases.

For rich user interaction, we used the `mail` core addon mixins to add features for users to communicate around documents and plan activities on them. Wizards allow the application to dialogue with the user and gather the data needed to run particular processes. Exceptions allow the application to abort incorrect operations, informing the user of the problem and rolling back intermediate changes, keeping the system consistent.

We also discussed the tools available for developers to create and maintain their applications: logging messages, debugging tools, and unit tests.

In the next chapter, we will still be working with the ORM, but looking at it from the point of view of an external application, working with the Odoo server as a backend for storing data and running business processes.

Further reading

These are the most relevant reference materials for the topics discussed in this chapter:

- ORM reference: `https://www.odoo.com/documentation/12.0/reference/orm.html#common-orm-methods`
- Message and activities features: `https://www.odoo.com/documentation/12.0/reference/mixins.html`
- Odoo tests reference: `https://www.odoo.com/documentation/12.0/reference/testing.html`
- Python `unittest` reference: `https://docs.python.org/3/library/unittest.html#module-unittest`

External API – Integrating with Other Systems

9

The Odoo server provides an external API, which is used by its web client and is available for other client applications. In this chapter, we'll learn how to use the Odoo external API from our own client programs, using Odoo's external API.

To avoid introducing additional languages the reader might not be familiar with, here we will focus on Python-based clients, although the techniques to handle the RPC calls also applies to other programming languages.

We'll describe how to use the Odoo RPC calls, and then use that knowledge to build a simple Library command-line application using Python.

The following topics will be covered in this chapter:

- Setting up Python in the client machine
- Connecting to Odoo using XML-RPC
- Running server methods using XML-RPC
- The search and read API methods
- The Library client XML-RPC interface
- The Library client user interface
- Using the `OdooRPC` library
- About the `ERPpeek` client

Technical requirements

The code in this chapter is based on the code created in Chapter 3, *Your First Odoo Application*. The necessary code can be found in the ch03/ directory of the Git repository at https://github.com/PacktPublishing/Odoo-12-Development-Essentials-Fourth-Edition.

You should have it in your addons path and install the library_app module. The code examples will assume that the Odoo database to work with is 12-library, to be consistent with the installation instructions given in Chapter 2, *Preparing the Development Environment*.

The code in this chapter can be found on the same repository, in the ch09/ directory.

Learning project – a client to catalogue books

In this chapter, we will work on a simple client application to manage the Library Book catalogue. It's the **Command-Line Interface (CLI)** application, using Odoo as the backend. The application features will be very limited, so that we can focus on the technology used to interact with the Odoo server, instead of the implementation details of our particular application.

Our simple application should be able to do the following:

- Search by title and list books
- Add new titles to the catalogue
- Correct a book title
- Remove a book from the catalogue

The application will be a Python script that expects commands to perform. A usage session will look something like this:

```
$ python3 library.py add "Moby-Dick"
$ python3 library.py list "moby"
3 Moby-Dick
$ python3 library.py set-title 3 "Moby Dick"
$ python3 library.py del 3
```

Setting up Python on the client machine

The Odoo API can be accessed externally using two different protocols: XML-RPC and JSON-RPC. Any external program capable of implementing a client for one of these protocols will be able to interact with an Odoo server. To avoid introducing additional programming languages, we will keep using Python to explore the external API.

Until now, we have been running Python code only on the server. This time, we will use Python on the client side, so it's possible you might need to do some additional setup on your workstation.

To follow the examples in this chapter, you'll need to be able to run Python files on your work computer. We will be using Python 3 for this. At this point, you should make sure you have Python 3 installed in your workstation. This can be confirmed running the `python3 --version` command in a Terminal. If not, you may refer the official website for your platform's installation package, at `https://www.python.org/downloads/`.

For Ubuntu, at this point, you probably already have Python 3 installed. If not, you can install it by running the following:

```
$ sudo apt-get install python3 python3-pip
```

If you are a Windows user and have Odoo installed on your machine, you may be wondering why you don't already have a Python interpreter and why additional installation is needed. The short answer is that the Odoo installation has an embedded Python interpreter that isn't easily used outside.

Connecting to Odoo API using XML-RPC

The simplest method to access the server is using XML-RPC. We can use the `xmlrpclib` library from Python's standard library for this. Remember that we are programming a client to connect to a server, so we need an Odoo server instance running to connect to. In our examples, we will assume that an Odoo server instance is running on the same machine (`localhost`), but you can use any reachable IP address or server name, if the server is running on a different machine.

Let's make first contact with the Odoo external API. Start a Python 3 console and type in the following:

```
>>> from xmlrpc import client
>>> srv = 'http://localhost:8069'
>>> common = client.ServerProxy('%s/xmlrpc/2/common' % srv)
>>> common.version()
{'server_version': '12.0', 'server_version_info': [12, 0, 0, 'final', 0,
''], 'server_serie': '12.0', 'protocol_version': 1}
```

Here, we import the `xmlrpc.client` library and then set up a variable with the information for the server address and listening port. Feel free to adapt these to your specific setup.

Next, we set up access to the server's public services (not requiring a login), exposed at the `/xmlrpc/2/common` endpoint. One of the methods that's available is `version()`, which inspects the server version. We use it to confirm that we can communicate with the server.

Another public method is `authenticate()`. In fact, this doesn't create a session, as you might be led to believe. This method just confirms that the username and password are accepted and returns the user ID that should be used in requests instead of the username, as shown here:

```
>>> db = '12-library'
>>> user, pwd = 'admin', 'admin'
>>> uid = common.authenticate(db, user, pwd, {})
>>> print(uid)
2
```

We start by setting, in the `db` variable, the database name we will use. In our example, it's `12-library`, but you are free to change it if you are working with a database with a different name.

If the login credentials are not correct, a `False` value is returned, instead of a user ID.

The `authenticate()` last argument is the user agent environment, used to provide the server with some metadata about the client. It's mandatory, but can be an empty dictionary.

Running server methods using XML-RPC

With XML-RPC, no session is maintained and the authentication credentials are sent with every request. This adds some overhead to the protocol, but makes it simpler to use.

Next, we set up access to the server methods that need a login to be accessed. These are exposed at the `/xmlrpc/2/object` endpoint, as shown in the following:

```
>>> api = client.ServerProxy('%s/xmlrpc/2/object' % srv)
>>> api.execute_kw(db, uid, pwd, 'res.partner', 'search_count', [[]])
42
```

Here, we are accessing the server API for the first time, performing a count on the **Partner** records. Methods are called using the `execute_kw()` method that takes the following arguments:

- The name of the database to connect to
- The connection user ID
- The user password
- The target model identifier name
- The method to call
- A list of positional arguments
- An optional dictionary with keyword arguments (not used in the example)

The preceding example calls the `search_count` method of the `res.partner` model with one positional argument, `[]`, and no keyword arguments. The positional argument is a search domain; since we are providing an empty list, it counts all of the Partners.

Frequent actions are `search` and `read`. When called from the RPC, the `search` method returns a list of IDs matching a domain. The `browse` method is not available from the RPC, and `read` should be used in its place to obtain a list of record IDs and retrieve their data, as shown in the following code:

```
>>> domain = [('is_company', '=', True)]
>>> api.execute_kw(db, uid, pwd, 'res.partner', 'search', [domain])
[14, 10, 11, 15, 12, 13, 9, 1]
>>> api.execute_kw(db, uid, pwd, 'res.partner', 'read', [[14]], {'fields':
['id', 'name', 'country_id']})
[{'id': 14, 'name': 'Azure Interior', 'country_id': [233, 'United
States']}]
```

Note that, for the `read` method, we're using one positional argument for the list of IDs, `[14]`, and one keyword argument, `fields`. We can also notice that many-to-one relational fields, such as `country_id`, are retrieved as a pair, with the related record's ID and display name. That's something to keep in mind when processing the data in your code.

The `search` and `read` combination is so frequent that a `search_read` method is provided to perform both operations in a single step. The same result from the previous two steps can be obtained with the following instruction:

```
>>> api.execute_kw(db, uid, pwd, 'res.partner', 'search_read', [domain],
{'fields': ['id', 'name', 'country_id']})
```

The `search_read` method behaves like `read`, but expects a domain as a first positional argument instead of a list of IDs. It's worth mentioning that the `fields` argument on `read` and `search_read` isn't mandatory. If not provided, all fields will be retrieved. This may cause expensive computations of function fields and a large amount of data to be retrieved but probably never used, so it is generally recommended to provide an explicit list of fields.

Search and read API methods

We have seen, in `Chapter 7`, *Recordsets – Working with Model Data*, the most important model methods used to generate recordsets and how to write to them. But there are a few more model methods available for more specific actions, as shown here:

- `read([fields])` is similar to the `browse` method, but, instead of a recordset, it returns a list of rows of data with the fields given as its argument. Each row is a dictionary. It provides a serialized representation of the data that can be sent through RPC protocols and is intended to be used by client programs and not in server logic.
- `search_read([domain], [fields], offset=0, limit=None, order=None)` performs a search operation followed by a read on the resulting record list. It's intended to be used by RPC clients and saves them the extra round trip needed when doing `search` followed by `read` on the results.

All other model methods are exposed through RPC, except for the ones prefixed with an underscore, which are considered private. This means that we can use `create`, `write`, and `unlink` to modify data on the server as follows:

```
>>> x = api.execute_kw(db, uid, pwd, 'res.partner', 'create',
[{'name': 'Packt Pub'}])
>>> print(x)
51
>>> api.execute_kw(db, uid, pwd, 'res.partner', 'write',
[[x], {'name': 'Packt Publishing'}])
True
>>> api.execute_kw(db, uid, pwd, 'res.partner', 'read',
[[x], ['id', 'name']])
```

```
[{'id': 51, 'name': 'Packt Publishing'}]
>>> api.execute_kw(db, uid, pwd, 'res.partner', 'unlink', [[x]])
True
>>> api.execute_kw(db, uid, pwd, 'res.partner', 'read', [[x]])
[]
```

One limitation of the XML-RPC protocol is that it does not support `None` values. There's an XML-RPC extension that supports `None` values, but whether this is available will depend on the particular XML-RPC library being used on your client. Methods that don't return anything may not be usable through XML-RPC, since they are implicitly returning `None`. This is why methods should always finish with at least a `return True` statement. Another alternative is to use JSON-RPC instead, also supported. The OdooRPC library allows for this, and we will use it later in this chapter, in the *Using the OdooRPC library* section.

It is worth repeating that the Odoo external API can be used by most programming languages. In the official documentation, we can find practical examples for Ruby, PHP, and Java. It is available at `https://www.odoo.com/documentation/12.0/webservices/odoo.html`.

 The Model methods prefixed with an underscore are considered private and aren't exposed through XML-RPC.

The Library client XML-RPC interface

Let's start with the implementation of out Library client application. We will split it into two files: one dealing with the interface with the server backend, `library_api.py`, and another dealing with the application's user interface, `library.py`. We will then provide alternative implementation for the backend interface, using the existing library, OdooRPC.

We will create a class to set up the connection with an Odoo server, and read/write Library Book data. It should expose the basic CRUD methods:

- `search_read()` to retrieve book data
- `create()` to create books
- `write()` to update books
- `unlink()` to delete a book

Choose a directory to host the application files and create the `library_api.py` file. We start by adding the class constructor, as follows:

```
from xmlrpc import client

class LibraryAPI():
    def __init__(self, srv, port, db, user, pwd):
        common = client.ServerProxy(
            'http://%s:%d/xmlrpc/2/common' % (srv, port))
        self.api = client.ServerProxy(
            'http://%s:%d/xmlrpc/2/object' % (srv, port))
        self.uid = common.authenticate(db, user, pwd, {})
        self.pwd = pwd
        self.db = db
        self.model = 'library.book'
```

Here, we store all of the information needed in the created object to execute calls on a model: the API reference, `uid`, password, database name, and the model to use.

Next, we will define a helper method to execute the calls. It takes advantage of the object stored data to provide a smaller function signature, as shown next:

```
def execute(self, method, arg_list, kwarg_dict=None):
    return self.api.execute_kw(
        self.db, self.uid, self.pwd, self.model,
        method, arg_list, kwarg_dict or {})
```

Now we can use it to implement the higher-level methods.

The `search_read()` method will accept an optional list of IDs to retrieve. If none are listed, all records will be returned:

```
def search_read(self, text=None):
    domain = [('name','ilike', text)] if text else []
    fields = ['id', 'name']
    return self.execute('search_read', [domain, fields])
```

The `create()` method will create a new book with the given title and return the ID of the created record:

```
def create(self, title):
    vals = {'name': title}
    return self.execute('create', [vals])
```

The `write()` method will have the new title and book ID as arguments and will perform a write operation on that book:

```
def write(self, title, id):
    vals = {'name': title}
    return self.execute('write', [[id], vals])
```

And next we have the `unlink()` method implementation, which is quite simple:

```
def unlink(self, id):
    return self.execute('unlink', [[id]])
```

We end the file with a small piece of test code that will be executed if we run the Python file:

```
if __name__ == '__main__':
    # Sample test configurations
    srv, db, port = 'localhost' , '12-library' , 8069
    user, pwd = 'admin', 'admin'
    api = LibraryAPI(srv, port, db, user, pwd)
    from pprint import pprint
    pprint(api.search_read())
```

If we run the Python script, we should see the content of our Library Books printed out:

```
$ python3 library_api.py
[{'id': 2, 'name': 'Odoo 11 Development Cookbook'},
 {'id': 1, 'name': 'Odoo Development Essentials 11'}]
```

Now that we have a simple wrapper around our Odoo backend, let's deal with the command-line user interface.

The Library client user interface

Our goal here was to learn to write the interface between an external application and the Odoo server, and this was done in the previous section. But it would be a shame not to go the extra step and actually make it available to the end user.

To keep the setup as simple as possible, we will use Python's built-in features to implement the command-line application. Since it is part of the standard library, it does not require any additional installation.

Now, alongside the `library_api.py` file, create a new `library.py` file. It will first import Python's command-line argument parser and then the `LibraryAPI` class, as shown in the following code:

```
from argparse import ArgumentParser
from library_api import LibraryAPI
```

Next, we describe the commands the argument parser will expect; there are four commands:

- Search and list books
- Add a book
- Set (change) a book title
- Delete a book

This is the code for adding them to the command-line parser:

```
parser = ArgumentParser()
parser.add_argument(
    'command',
    choices=['list', 'add', 'set', 'del'])
parser.add_argument('params', nargs='*')   # optional args
args = parser.parse_args()
```

At this point, `args` is an object containing the arguments given to the script, `args.command` is the command provided, and `args.params` will optionally hold additional parameters to use for the command. If no or incorrect commands are given, the argument parser will handle that for us and will show the user what input is expected. For a complete reference on `argparse`, you can refer to the official documentation at `https://docs.python.org/3/library/argparse.html`.

The next step is to to perform the intended actions. We will first prepare the connection with the Odoo server:

```
srv, port, db = 'localhost', 8069, '12-library'
user, pwd = 'admin', 'admin'
api = LibraryAPI(srv, port, db, user, pwd)
```

The first line sets some fixed parameters for the server instance and database to connect to. In this example, we are connecting to an Odoo server in the same machine (`localhost`) listening on the `8069` default port, with an `12-library` available database. If want to connect to a different server and database, you should adapt these parameters accordingly.

This has a hardcoded server address and plain text password, so it's far from being the best implementation. We should have a configuration step to collect these settings from the user and possibly store them in a secure way. But we need to keep in mind that our goal here is to learn to work with the Odoo RPC, so consider this as proof of concept code, and not a finished product.

Now we will write the code to handle each of the supported commands, which will also make use of the `api` object.

We can start with the `list` command, providing a list of the books:

```
if args.command == 'list':
    books = api.search_read(args.text)
    for book in books:
        print('%(id)d %(name)s' % book)
```

Here, we use the `LibraryAPI.search_read()` method to retrieve the list of Book records from the server. We then iterate through each element in the list and print it out. We use Python's string formatting to present each `book` record, a key-value dictionary, to the user.

Next, we have the add command. This will make use of the additional parameters, for the book titles:

```
if args.command == 'add':
    for title in args.params:
        new_id = api.create(title)
        print('Book added with ID %d.' % new_id)
```

Since the hard work was already done in the `LibraryAPI` object, here we just need to call the `write()` method and show the result to the end user.

The `set` command allows to change the title of an existing book. It should have two parameters, the new title and the ID of the book:

```
if args.command == 'set-title':
    if len(params) != 2:
        print("set command requires a Title and ID.")
        return
    book_id title = int(args.params[0]), args.params[1]
    api.write(title, book_id)
    print('Title set for Book ID %d.' % book_id)
```

Finally, we have the implementation for the `del` command, which should delete a Book record. At this point, this should be no challenge for us:

```
if args.command == 'del':
    for param in params:
        api.unlink(int(param))
        print('Book with ID %s deleted.' % param)
```

At this point, the basic API CLI is finished, and the reader can try some commands on it the verify how it is working. For example, we should now be able to run the example commands shown at the beginning of this chapter, in the *Learning project: a Client to catalogue books* section. Accessing the data in the Library app using the regular web client would also be helpful to confirm that the CLI app is working as expected.

This is a quite basic application, and you probably could think of a few ways to improve it while going through the code. But remember that the point here is to make an example of interesting ways to leverage the Odoo RPC API.

Using the OdooRPC library

Another relevant client library to be considered is `OdooRPC`. It is a more modern client library that uses the JSON-RPC protocol instead of XML-RPC. In fact, the Odoo official web client uses JSON-RPC, and the original XML-RPC is supported mostly for backward compatibility.

 The `OdooRPC` library is now under the Odoo Community Association umbrella and is being actively maintained. You can learn more about it at `https://github.com/OCA/odoorpc`.

The `OdooRPC` library can be installed from PyPI:

```
$ pip3 install --user odoorpc
```

The way the Odoo API is used is not very different whether you are using JSON-RPC or XML-RPC. So, you will see that, while some details differ, the way these different client libraries are used is not very different.

The `OdooRPC` library sets up a server connection when a new `odoorpc.ODOO` object is created, and we should then use the `ODOO.login()` method to create a user session. Just like on the server side, the session has an `env` attribute with the session's environment, including the user ID, `uid`, and `context`.

We can use `OdooRPC` to provide an alternate implementation to the `library_api.py` interface with the server. It should provide the same features, but is implemented using JSON-RPC instead of XML-RPC.

Create a new `library_odoorpc.py` file alongside it, with the following code:

```
from odoorpc import ODOO

class LibraryAPI():

    def __init__(self, srv, port, db, user, pwd):
        self.api = ODOO(srv, port=port)
        self.api.login(db, user, pwd)
        self.uid = self.api.env.uid
        self.model = 'library.book'
        self.Model = self.api.env[self.model]

    def execute(self, method, arg_list, kwarg_dict=None):
        return self.api.execute(
            self.model,
            method, *arg_list, **kwarg_dict)
```

The `OdooRPC` library implements `Model` and `Recordset` objects that mimic the behavior of the server-side counterparts. The goal is that programming the client should be about the same as programming in the server. The methods used by our client will make use of this, through the Library Book Model stored in the `self.Model` attribute.

The `execute()` method implemented here won't be used by our client and was included to allow for comparison to the other alternative implementations we discuss in this chapter.

Next, we look at the implementation for the `search_read()`, `create()`, `write()` and `unlink()` client methods. In the same file, add these methods inside the `LibraryAPI()` class:

```
    def search_read(self, text=None):
        domain = [('name','ilike', text)] if text else []
        fields = ['id', 'name']
        return self.Model.search_read(domain, fields)

    def create(self, title):
```

```
        vals = {'name': title}
        return self.Model.create(vals)

    def write(self, title, id):
        vals = {'name': title}
        self.Model.write(id, vals)

    def unlink(self, id):
        return self.Model.unlink(id)
```

Notice that the code looks like the Odoo server-side code, because it uses an API that is similar to what you could write in an Odoo add-on.

Having done this, we can try it by editing the library.py file, changing the from library_api import LibraryAPI line to from library_odoorpc import LibraryAPI. Now test drive the library.py client application, and it should perform just like before.

About the ERPpeek client

ERPpeek is a versatile tool that can be used both as an interactive **Command-Line Interface (CLI)** and as a **Python library**, with a more convenient API than the one provided by the xmlrpc library. It is available from the PyPi index and can be installed with the following:

```
$ pip3 install --user erppeek
```

Not only can ERPpeek be used as a Python library, it is also a CLI that can be used to perform administrative actions on the server. Where the Odoo shell command provided a local interactive session on the host server, the erppeek library provides a remote interactive session for a client across the network.

Opening a command line, we can have a peek at the options available, as shown here:

```
$ erppeek --help
```

Let's see a sample session, as follows:

```
$ erppeek --server='http://localhost:8069' -d 12-library -u admin
Usage (some commands):
    models(name)                       # List models matching pattern
    model(name)                        # Return a Model instance
(...)
Password for 'admin':
Logged in as 'admin'
```

```
12-library >>> model('res.users').count()
3
12-library >>> rec = model('res.partner').browse(14)
12-library >>> rec.name
'Azure Interior'
```

As you can see, a connection was made to the server, and the execution context provided a reference to the `model()` method to get model instances and perform actions on them.

The `erppeek.Client` instance used for the connection is also available through the `client` variable.

Notably, it provides an alternative to the web client to manage the addon modules installed:

- `client.modules()` lists available or installed modules
- `client.install()` performs module installation
- `client.upgrade()` performs module upgrades
- `client.uninstall()` uninstalls modules

So, ERPpeek can also provide good service as a remote administration tool for Odoo servers.

More details about ERPpeek can be found at `https://github.com/tinyerp/erppeek`.

Summary

Our goal for this chapter was to learn how the external API works and what it is capable of. We started exploring it using a simple Python XML-RPC client, but the external API can be used from any programming language. In fact, the official documentation provides code examples for Java, PHP, and Ruby.

There are a number of libraries to handle XML-RPC or JSON-RPC, some generic and some specific for use with Odoo. We showcased a particular library, `OdooRPC`.

With this, we finish the chapters dedicated to the programming API and business logic. Now, it's time to enter into the views and user interface. In the next chapter, we will see in more detail the backend views and user experience that can be provided out of the box by the web client.

Further reading

This additional reference material may complement the topics described in this chapter:

- The official documentation on Odoo web services, including code examples in programming languages other than Python: `https://www.odoo.com/documentation/12.0/webservices/odoo.html`
- The `OdooRPC` documentation: `https://pythonhosted.org/OdooRPC/`
- The `ERPpeek` documentation: `https://erppeek.readthedocs.io/en/latest/`

Backend Views – Designing the User Interface

10

This chapter will help you learn how to build the graphical interface for users to interact with the library application. You'll discover the distinct types of views and widgets available and learn how to use them to provide a good user experience.

The following topics will be covered in this chapter:

- Menu items
- Window Actions
- Form view structure
- Fields
- Buttons and smart buttons
- Dynamic view elements
- List views
- Search views
- Other view types

Technical requirements

We'll continue working with the library_checkout addon module. It already has the model layer ready, and now it needs the view layer for the user interface.

The code in this chapter is based on the code created in Chapter 8, *Business Logic – Supporting Business Processes*. The necessary code can be found in the ch08/ directory of the Git repository at https://github.com/PacktPublishing/Odoo-12-Development-Essentials-Fourth-Edition. The code in this chapter can be found on the same repository, in the ch10/ directory.

Menu items

The entry point for the user interface are the menu items. Menu items form a hierarchical structure, where the top-level items are applications, and the level below that are each application's main menu. Further sub-menu levels can be added.

Actionable menu items are linked to a windows Action that tells the web client what to do when the menu item is clicked.

Menu items are stored in the ir.ui.menu model and can be browsed through the **Settings | Technical | User Interface | Menu Items** menu.

The library_app addon module created a top-level menu for the library books, and the library_checkout addon module added the menu items for checkouts and checkout stages. They are in library_checkout/views/library_menu.xml. This is the XML for the checkout menu item:

```
<menuitem id="menu_library_checkout"
          name="Checkout"
          action="action_library_checkout"
          parent="library_app.library_menu"
/>
```

We have here a <menuitem> shortcut element, which provides an abbreviated way to define menu items and is more convenient than the raw <record model="ir.ui.menu"> element.

These are the attributes being used:

- name is the menu item title to present in the user interface.
- action is the XML ID of the Window Action to run, when clicking on the menu item.
- parent is the XML ID of the parent menu item. In this case, the parent was created in another module, so we need to reference it using the complete XML ID, <module>.<XML ID>.

We have also available the following attributes:

- `sequence` sets a number to order the presentation of the menu items, for example, `sequence="10"`
- `groups` is a comma-separated list of XML IDs of the security groups that have access to the menu item, for example, `groups="library_app.library_group_user,library_app.library_group_manager"`
- `web_icon` is the menu item's icon and is only used for top-level menu items in the enterprise edition, for example, `web_icon="library_app,static/description/icon.png"`

Window Actions

A Window Action gives instructions to the GUI client and is usually used by menu items or buttons in views. It tells the GUI which model to work on and which views to make available. These actions can filter the records to be available, using a `domain` filter, and can set default values and filters through the `context` attribute.

Window Actions are stored in the `ir.actions.act_window` model and can be browsed via the **Settings | Technical | Actions | Window Actions** menu.

In `library_checkout/views/library_menu.xml`, we can find the Window Action used in the checkout menu item. We need to make a change to it to enable the additional view types we'll add in this chapter:

```
<act_window id="action_library_checkout"
  name="Checkouts"
  res_model="library.checkout"
  view_mode="tree,form,activity,calendar,graph,pivot"
/>
```

Window Actions are usually created using the `<act_window>` shortcut, used previously. We're changing `view_mode` from `"tree, form"` to the larger `"tree,form,activity,calendar,graph,pivot"` list.

The Window Action attributes used are as follows:

- `name` is the title that will be displayed on the views opened through this action.
- `res_model` is the identifier of the target model.
- `view_mode` is a comma-separated list of the view types to make available. The first in the list is the one to open by default.

Other Window Action attributes are the following:

- `target`, if set to `new`, will open the view in a pop-up dialog window, for example, `target="new"`. By default, it's `current`, opening the view inline in the main content area.
- `context` sets context information on the target views, which can set default values or activate filters, among other things, for example, `context="{'default_user_id': uid}"`.
- `domain` is a domain expression forcing a filter for the records that can be browsed in the opened views, for example, `domain="[('user_id', '=', uid)]"`.
- `limit` is the number of records for each page, in the list view, for example, `limit="80"`.

After these changes are installed, when you select the **Checkouts** menu item and navigate to the corresponding list view, there will be additional buttons in the top-right corner, after the list and form buttons. However, these won't work until we create the corresponding views, which we'll cover later in this chapter.

Window Actions can also be used from the **Action** menu button, available at the top of the list and form views, next to the **Filters** button. For this, we need to add two more attributes to the `<act_window>` element:

- `src_model` sets the model where the action will be made available, for example, `src_model="library.checkout"`.
- `multi="true"` enables the action on the list view also, so that it can work on multiple selected records. Otherwise, it's available only in the form view, and can only be applied to one record at a time.

Form view structure

Form views can either follow a simple layout or a business document layout, similar to a paper document. We'll now see how to design these business document views and how to use the elements and widgets available.

For this, we'll revisit and expand the library checkout form created in Chapter 8, *Business Logic - Supporting Business Processes*.

Business document views

Much of the data recorded in a business application can be represented as a paper document. For a more intuitive user interface, form views can mimic these paper documents.

For example, in our app, we can think of a checkout as something that has a paper form to fill out. We'll provide a form view that follows this design.

We should edit the library_checkout/views/chceckout_view.xml file and change the form view record to have the basic skeleton of a business document view:

```xml
<record id="view_form_checkout" model="ir.ui.view">
  <field name="model">library.checkout</field>
  <field name="arch" type="xml">
    <form>
      <header>
        <!-- To add buttons and status widget -->
      </header>
      <sheet>
        <!-- To add form content -->
      </sheet>
      <!-- Discuss widgets -->
      <div class="oe_chatter">
        <field name="message_follower_ids"
            widget="mail_followers" />
        <field name="activity_ids"
            widget="mail_activity" />
        <field name="message_ids"
            widget="mail_thread" />
      </div>
    </form>
  </field>
</record>
```

The view name is optional and automatically generated if missing. For simplicity, we took advantage of that and omitted the `<field name="name">` element from the view record.

We can see that business document views usually use three main areas:

- The **header** status bar
- The **sheet** for the main content
- A bottom communication section, also known as **chatter**

The communication section at the bottom uses the social network widgets provided by the `mail` addon module. To be able to use them, our model should inherit the `mail.thread` and `mail.activity.mixin` models, as we saw in `Chapter 8`, *Business Logic – Supporting Business Processes*:

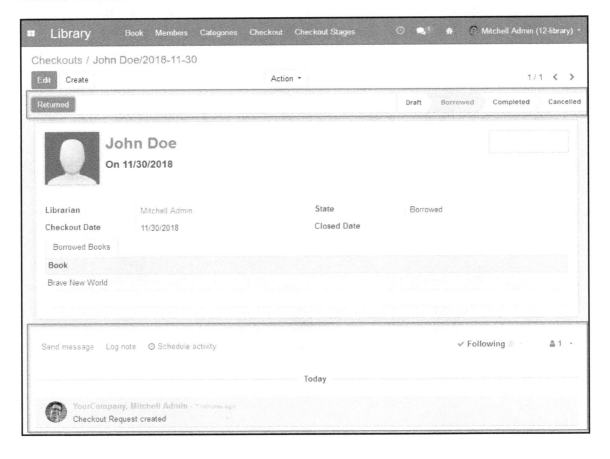

The header

The header at the top usually features the life cycle or steps that the document will move through and the related action buttons. These action buttons are regular form buttons, and the most important next steps can be highlighted.

Header buttons

Editing the `<header>` section in the form view, we'll add a button to make it easier to set a returned checkout as done:

```
<header>
  <field name="state" invisible="True" />
  <button name="button_done"
     type="object"
     string="Return Books"
     attrs="{'invisible':
             [('state', 'in', ['new', 'done'])]}"
     class="oe_highlight" />
</header>
```

Here, we add a **Return Books** button to the header that calls the `button_done` model method when clicked. Note that `class="oe_highlight"` can be used to highlight actions to the user. For example, when having several buttons to choose from, we can highlight the main or more usual action to perform next.

The `attrs` attribute is used to make this button invisible for the New and Done states. The condition to do this uses the `state` field, which will not be shown on the form. But, for the condition to work, we need all values it uses to be loaded in the web client. Since we're not planning to make the `state` field available to the end users, we need to add it as an invisible field.

> The fields used in a `domain` or `attrs` expression must be loaded into the view, and there must be a `<field>` element for them. If the field isn't supposed to be seen by the users, we must have it loaded with an invisible field element.

In this particular case, since we're using a `state` field, the same effect can be achieved by the `states` field attribute. While it's not as flexible as the `attrs` attribute, it's more concise. Instead of `attrs=...`, we could have used the following:

```
<button name="button_done"
    type="object"
    string="Returned"
    states="open,cancel"
    class="oe_highlight" />
```

The `attrs` and `states` element visibility features can also be used on other view elements, such as fields. We'll explore them in more detail later in this chapter.

For our button to work, we need to implement the method being called. In the `library_checkout/models/library_checkout.py` file, add this method to the checkout class:

```
def button_done(self):
    Stage = self.env['library.checkout.stage']
    done_stage = Stage.search(
        [('state', '=', 'done')],
        limit=1)
    for checkout in self:
        checkout.stage_id = done_stage
    return True
```

It first finds the `done` stage record to use, and then for each record in the `self` recordset, sets it's `stage_id` value to the done stage.

The stage pipeline

Next, we'll add to the header a status bar widget, showing the stage the document is in. Technically, it's a `<field>` element for the `stage_id` field using the `statusbar` widget:

```
<header>
  <field name="state" invisible="True" />
  <button name="do_clear_done" type="object"
    string="Clear Done"
    states="open,cancel"
    class="oe_highlight" />
  <field name="stage_id"
    widget="statusbar"
    clickable="True"
    options="{'fold_field': 'fold'}" />
</header>
```

This adds a stage pipeline widget to the header. It uses the `statusbar` widget on a field that represents the point in the life cycle where the document is currently at. This is usually a **state** selection field or a **stage** many-to-one field. These two fields can be found across several Odoo core modules.

The `clickable` attribute allows the user to change the document stage by clicking on the status bar. We usually want to enable this, but there are also cases where we don't, such as when we need more control over the workflow and require the users to progress through the stages using only the available action buttons. This approach allows for specific validations when moving between stages.

When using a status bar widget with stages, we can have the seldom used stages hidden (folded) in a **More** stage group. The corresponding stages model must have a flag to configure the ones to hide, usually named `fold`. The `statusbar` widget should then use the `options` attribute, as shown in the preceding code, to provide this field name to the `fold_field` option.

Using states instead of stages

The stage is a many-to-one field that uses a supporting model to set up the steps of the process. Because of this, it can be dynamically configured by end users to fit their specific business process and is perfect to support Kanban boards. This is what we'll be using for the library checkouts.

The state is a selection list featuring a few rather stable steps in a process, such as **New**, **In Progress**, and **Done**. It's not configurable by end users but, since it's static, it's much easier to be used in business logic. View fields even have special support for states: the `states` field attribute allows it to be made available to the user only when the record is in certain states.

 Historically, stages were introduced later than states. Both have coexisted, but the trend in Odoo core is for stages to replace states. But, as seen in the preceding explanation, states still provide some features that stages don't.

It's still possible to benefit from the best of both worlds by mapping the stages into states. In the checkout model we did this by adding a state field in the checkout stages model and making it available in the checkout documents through a related field.

In case the model works with states instead of stages, we can also use the status bar pipeline. In this case, to list the states to be made available in the status bar, we use the `statusbar_visible` attribute instead of the `fold_field` option.

Using it would look like this:

```
<field name="state"
    widget="statusbar"
    clickable="True"
    statusbar_visible="draft,open,done" />
```

Notice that we can't use this in our actual library checkout, because it's stage driven, not state driven.

The document sheet

The sheet canvas is the main area of the form where the actual data elements are placed. It's designed to look like an actual paper document, and it's common to see that the records in Odoo are referred to as documents.

Usually, a document sheet structure will have these areas:

- A document title and subtitle at the top-left
- A button box at the top-right corner
- Other document header fields
- A notebook at the bottom, for additional fields organized into tabs or pages

Document lines usually go in the notebook's first page. After the sheet, we usually have the chatter widget, with the document followers, discussion messages, and planned activities.

Let's go through each of these areas.

Title and subtitle

Fields outside a `<group>` element don't automatically have labels rendered for them. This will be the case for the title elements, so the `<label for="..."/>` element should be used to render it. At the expense of some extra work, this has the advantage of giving us more control over the label display.

Regular HTML, including CSS-style elements, can also be used to make the title shine. Usually, titles are placed inside <div> with the oe_title class.

Here is the <sheet> element expanded to include the title plus some additional fields as subtitles:

```
<sheet>
  <field name="member_image" widget="image" class="oe_avatar" />
  <div class="oe_title">
    <label for="name" class="oe_edit_only"/>
    <h1><field name="name"/></h1>
    <h3>
      <span class="oe_read_only">By</span>
      <label for="user_id" class="oe_edit_only"/>
      <field name="user_id" class="oe_inline" />
    </h3>
  </div>
  <!-- More elements will be added from here... -->
</sheet>
```

Here, we can see that we use regular HTML elements, such as div, span, h1, and h3.

The <label> element allows us to control when and where the field labels will be shown. The for attribute identifies the field we should get the label text from. Another possibility is to use the string attribute to provide a specific text to use for the label. Our example also uses the class="oe_edit_only" attribute so that it's visible only in edit mode.

We can also include a a representative image next to the title, at the top-left corner of the sheet. It's used in forms view for models such as partners or products. As an example of this, we added a member_image field just before the tile section. It uses the image widget, widget="image", and a specific CSS class for this, class="oe_avatar".

That field was not added to the model yet, so we need to do it. We'll use a related field to make the member's partner image available in the checkout document. Edit the library_checkout/models/library_checkout.py file to add the field to the checkout class:

```
member_image = fields.Binary(related='member_id.partner_id.image')
```

Grouping the form content

The main content of the form should be organized using `<group>` tags.

The `<group>` tag inserts two columns in the canvas. Inside it, by default, fields will be displayed along with their label, hence taking up the two columns. So, a field plus its label takes up a line; the next field and label will take the next line, and they'll be stacked up vertically.

A common pattern in Odoo forms is to have two columns of fields with labels, side by side. To achieve that, we just need to add two `<group>` tags nested into a top one.

Continuing with our form view, we'll use this to add the main content, after the title `<div>` section:

```
<group name="group_top">
  <group name="group_col1">
    <field name="user_id" />
    <field name="checkout_date" />
  </group>
  <group name="group_col2">
    <field name="state" />
    <field name="closed_date" />
  </group>
</group>
```

It's a good practice to assign a `name` to group tags so that its easier for them to be referenced later when being extended by other modules. The `string` attribute is also allowed and, if set, is used to display a title for the section.

Changed in Odoo 11
The `string` attribute cannot be used as an anchor for inheritance because it's translated before the inheritance is applied. The `name` attribute should be used instead.

Inside a group, a `<newline>` element will force a new line, and the next element will be rendered in the group's first column.

Additional section titles can be added inside a group using the `<separator>` element, which can also have show a title label, if the `string` attribute is used.

For better control over the elements' layout, we can use the `col` and `colspan` attributes.

The `col` attribute can be used on `<group>` elements to customize the number of columns it will contain. As mentioned before, the default is two, but it can be changed to any other number. Even numbers work better, since by default each field added takes up two columns: the field label and the field value.

The following code shows how we can use a single group with `colspan="4"` to present the four fields in two columns:

```
<group name="group_top">
  <group name="group_col1"
         col="4"
         colspan="2"
         string="Group 1">
    <field name="user_id" />
    <field name="state" />
    <field name="checkout_date" />
    <field name="closed_date" />
  </group>
  <group name="group_col2" string="Group 2" />
</group>
```

We added the titles to the groups, using the `string` attribute, to make clear where they are positioned. Notice the the order of the fields is different, because fields are placed from left to right, and then from top to bottom.

The `<group>` elements can use a `colspan` attribute to set a specific number of columns they should take. By default, they take two columns, just like a field with a label. You can try playing with the `col` and `colspan` values in the preceding code and see the resulting effect on the form. For example, what would be the result of `col="6"` `colspan="4"`? Try it.

Tabbed notebooks

Another way to organize content is the `notebook` element, a container for multiple tabbed sections called pages. These can be used to keep less-used data out of sight until needed or to organize a large number of fields by topic.

We'll add a notebook element to the checkout form, with the list of the borrowed books. After the `<group name="group_top">` element added in the previous section, we should include this XML:

```
<notebook>
  <page string="Borrowed Books" name="page_lines" >
    <field name="line_ids" />
  </page>
</notebook>
```

In this case , we have only one page in our notebook. To add more, we just need additional `<page>` sections inside the `<notebook>` element. The page canvas does not render field labels by default. For that to happen, the fields should be placed inside a `<group>` section, just like for the form main canvas. In our case, we added the one-to-many `line_ids` field inside the page, and we don't need the label because we already have the page title.

The `page` element supports these attributes:

- `string` for the title of the tab (required)
- `attrs`, a dictionary mapping invisible and required attributes to expressions
- `accesskey`, an HTML access key

Fields

View fields have a few attributes available to them. Most of them have values taken from their definition in the model, but these can be overridden in the view.

Here is a quick reference for the field generic attributes:

- `name` identifies the field database name.
- `string` is the label text to be used if we want to override the label text provided by the model definition.
- `help` is tooltip text shown when you hover the pointer over the field, and it allows you to override the help text provided by the model definition.
- `placeholder` is suggestion text to display inside the field.
- `widget` allows us to override the default widget used for the field. We'll explore the available widgets in a moment.
- `options` is a JSON data structure with additional options for the widget. The values to use depend on what each widget supports.
- `class` are the CSS classes to use for the field HTML rendering.

- `nolabel="True"` prevents the automatic field label from being presented. It only makes sense for fields inside a `<group>` element and is often used along with a `<label for="...">` element.
- `invisible="True"` makes the field not visible, but its data is fetched from the server and is available on the form.
- `readonly="True"` makes the field non-editable on the form.
- `required="True"` makes the field mandatory on the form.

Some field-type specific attributes are as follows:

- `password="True"` is used for text fields. It's displayed as a password field, masking the characters typed in.
- `filename` is used for binary fields, and it's the name of the model field to be used to store the name of the uploaded file.

Labels for fields

The `<label>` element can be used to better control the presentation of a field label. One case where this is used is to present the label only when the form is in edit mode:

```
<label for="name" class="oe_edit_only" />
```

When doing this, if the field is inside a `<group>` element, we usually want to also set `nolabel="True"` on it. The `class="oe_edit_only"` code can be used to apply a CSS style, making the label visible only in edit mode.

Field widgets

Each field type is displayed in the form with the appropriate default widget. But additional alternative widgets are available to be used.

For text fields, we have the following widgets:

- `email` is used to make the email text an actionable "mail-to" address.
- `url` is used to format the text as a clickable URL.
- `html` is used to render the text as HTML content; in edit mode, it features a WYSIWYG editor to allow for the formatting of the content without the need for using the HTML syntax.

For numeric fields, we have the following widgets:

- `handle` is specifically designed for sequence fields in list views and displays a handle that allows you to drag lines to a custom order.
- `float_time` formats a float field with time quantities as hours and minutes.
- `monetary` displays a float field as the currency amount. It expects a `currency_id` companion field, but another field name can be provided with `options="{'currency_field': 'currency_id'}"`.
- `progressbar` presents a float as a progress percentage and can be useful for fields representing a completion rate.
- `percentage` and `percentpie` are widgets to use with float fields.

For relational and selection fields, we have these additional widgets:

- `many2many_tags` displays values as a list of button-like labels.
- `many2many_checkboxes` displays the selectable values as a list of checkboxes.
- `selection` uses the selection field widget for a many-to-one field.
- `radio` displays the selection field options using radio buttons.
- `priority` represents the selection field as a list of clickable stars. The selection options are usually numeric digits.
- `state_selection` shows a semaphore light for the Kanban state selection list. The normal state is represented in gray, done is represented in green, and any other state is represented in red.
- `pdf_viewer` is for binary fields (introduced in Odoo 12).

Changed in Odoo 11
The `state_selection` widget was introduced in Odoo 11 and replaces the former `kanban_state_selection`. The later one is deprecated, but for backward compatibility, it's still supported.

Relational fields

In relational fields, we can have some additional control as to what the user can do. By default, the user can create new records from these fields (also known as "quick create") and open the related record form. This can be disabled using the `options` field attribute:

```
options="{'no_open': True, 'no_create': True}"
```

The `context` and `domain` are also field attributes and are particularly useful on relational fields.

The `context` can define the default values for the related records, and `domain` can limit the selectable records. A common example is for a field to have the selection options depend on the value of another field. A `domain` field can be defined directly in the model, but it can also be overridden in the view.

In to-many fields, we can also use the `mode` attribute to change the view type used to display the records. By default, it's `tree`, but other options are `form`, `kanban`, or `graph`.

A relational field can define inline specific views to be used. These are declared as nested view definitions, inside the `<field>` element. For example, in the `line_ids` checkout, we could define specific list and form views for these lines:

```
<notebook>
  <page string="Borrowed Books" name="page_lines" >
    <field name="line_ids">
      <tree>
        <field name="book_id" />
      </tree>
      <form>
        <field name="book_id" />
      </form>
    </field>
  </page>
</notebook>
```

The line list will have the `<tree>` definition given. When we interact with a line, a form dialog pops up, and this will have the structure in the `<form>` definition.

> If we want to edit the one-to-many lines directly in the list view with the form pop up, we should use `<tree editable="top">` or `<tree editable="bottom">`.

Buttons

Buttons support these attributes:

- `string` is the button text label or the HTML `alt` text when an icon is used.

- `type` is the type of the action to perform. Possible values are as follows:
  - `object` is used for calling a Python method.
  - `action` is used to run a Window Action.

- `name` identifies the specific action to perform, according to the chosen type: either a model method name or the database ID of a Window Action to run. The `%(xmlid)d` formula can be used to translate the XML ID into the required database ID when the view is being loaded.

- `args` is used when the `type` is `object` to pass additional parameters to the method, which must be purely static JSON parameters appended to the record ID to form the arguments of the method call.

- `context` adds values to the context, which can have an effect after the windows Action is run or the Python code method called.

- `confirm` displays a confirmation message box before running the related action, displaying the text assigned to this attribute.

- `special="cancel"` is used on wizard form, to add a **Cancel** button.

- `icon` is for the icon image to be shown in the button. The icons available are from the Font Awesome set, version 4.7.0, and should be specified using the corresponding CSS class, such as `icon="fa-question"`. For more information, refer to `https://fontawesome.com/v4.7.0/icons/`.

Changed in Odoo 11
Before Odoo 11, the button icons were images originating from the GTK client library and were limited to the ones available in `addons/web/static/src/img/icons`.

Changed in Odoo 11
The workflow engine was deprecated and removed in Odoo 11. In previous versions, where workflows were supported, buttons could trigger workflow engine signals using `type="workflow"`. In this case, the `name` attribute was supposed to have a workflow signal name.

Smart buttons

It's not uncommon for document forms to have a smart button area in the top-right section. Smart buttons are shown as rectangles with a statistic indicator that can be followed through when clicked.

The UI pattern used in Odoo is to have an invisible box where smart buttons are placed. This button box is usually the first element in the `<sheet>`, added just before the `<div class="oe_title">` element (and avatar image), and looks like this:

```
<div name="button_box" class="oe_button_box">
 <!-- Smart buttons will go here... -->
</div>
```

The container for the buttons is just a `div` element with the `oe_button_box` class. In Odoo versions before 11.0, you might need to also add the `oe_right` class to ensure that the button box stays aligned to the right-hand side of the form.

For our app, we'll have a button displaying the total number of other checkouts this library member has pending to be returned; clicking on it will navigate to the list of those items.

So we want the checkout records for this member that are in the open state, excluding the current checkout. For the button statistic, we should create a computed field doing this count in the `Checkout` class of the `library_checkout/models/library_checkout.py` file:

```
num_other_checkouts = fields.Integer(
    compute='_compute_num_other_checkouts')

def _compute_num_other_checkouts(self):
    for rec in self:
        domain = [
            ('member_id', '=', checkout.rec.id),
            ('state', 'in', ['open']),
            ('id', '!=', rec.id)]
        rec.num_other_checkouts = self.search_count(domain)
```

Next, we can add the button box and the button inside it. Right at the top of the `<sheet>` section, replace the button box placeholder we added before, with the following:

```
<div name="button_box" class="oe_button_box">
  <button class="oe_stat_button"
    icon="fa-tasks"
    help="Other checkouts pending return."
    type="action"
    name="%(action_other_checkouts_button)d"
```

```
        context="{'default_member_id': member_id}" >

    <field string="To Return"
            name="num_other_checkouts"
            widget="statinfo" />
    </button>
</div>
```

The `button` element itself is a container, with fields displaying statistics. These statistics are regular fields using the `statinfo` specific widget. The field is usually a computed field defined in the underlying model. Other than fields, inside a button, we can also use static text, such as `<div>Other Checkouts</div>`. The number of other pending checkouts is presented by the `num_other checkouts` field, inside the button definition.

The smart button button must have the `class="oe_stat_button"` CSS style and should have an icon, using the `icon` attribute. It has `type="action"`, meaning that a button click will run a Window Action, identified by the `name` attribute. The `%(action_other_checkouts_button)d` expression returns the database ID for the action to run.

When clicking on the button, we want to see a list with the other checkouts from the current member. That will be done via the `action_other_checkouts_button` Window Action. This Window Action will open a library checkout list using the appropriate domain filter. The action and corresponding domain filter are processed outside the form context and have no access to the form data. So the button must set the current `member_id` value in the Context, to be used later in the Window Action.

The Window Action used must be defined before the form, so we should add it at the top of the XML file, inside the `<odoo>` root element:

```
<act_window id="action_other_checkouts_button"
  name="Open Other Checkouts"
  res_model="library.checkout"
  view_mode="tree,form"
  domain="[('member_id', '=', default_member_id),
          ('state', 'in', ['open']),
          ('id', '!=', active_id)]" />
```

Notice how we use the `default_member_id` context key for the domain filter. This particular key will also set the default value on the `member_id` field when creating new tasks after following the button link. The domain filter also needs the current ID. That one does not have to be explicitly set in the context because the web client automatically does that in the `active_id` context key.

For reference, these are the attributes that we can use when adding smart buttons:

- `class="oe_stat_button"` renders a rectangle instead of a regular button.
- `icon` sets the icon to use, chosen from the Font Awesome set. Visit `http://fontawesome.io` to browse the available icons.
- `type` and `name` are the button type and the name of the action to trigger. For smart buttons, the type will usually be `action` for a Window Action, and `name` will be the ID of the action to execute. It expects an actual database ID, so we have to use a formula to convert an XML ID into a database ID: `"%(action-xmlid)d"`. This action should open a view with the related records.
- `string` adds a label text to the button. We haven't used it here because the contained field already provides a text for it.
- `context` should be used to set default values on the target view, to be used on new records created on the view after clicking on the button.
- `help` adds a help tooltip displayed when the mouse pointer is over the button.

Dynamic view elements

View elements also support a few attributes that allow views to dynamically change their appearance or behavior, depending on field values. We may have on-change events, which are able to change values on other fields while editing data on a form, or have fields that are mandatory or visible only when certain conditions are met.

On-change events

The **on-change** mechanism allows us to change values in other form fields when a particular field is changed. For example, the on-change on a product field can set the price field to a default value whenever the product is changed.

In older versions, the on-change events were defined at the view level, but since version 8.0 they are defined directly on the model layer, without the need for any specific markup on the views. This is done with creating methods, using the `@api.onchange('field1',` `'field2',  ...)` decorator to bind on-change logic to some fields. The on-change model methods are discussed in more detail in `Chapter 8`, *Business Logic – Supporting Business Processes*, and an example is discussed there.

The on-change mechanism also takes care of the automatic recomputation of computed fields to immediately react to the user input. Using the same example as before, if the price field was changed when we changed the product, a computed total amount field would also be automatically updated using the new price information.

Dynamic attributes

Some attributes allow us to dynamically change the display of view elements, depending on the record's values.

A couple of attributes provide an easy way to control the visibility of a particular user interface element:

- groups can make an element visible depending on the security groups the current user belongs to. Only the members of the specified groups will see it. It expects a comma-separated list of group XML IDs.
- states can make an element visible depending on the record's state field. It expects a comma-separated list of state values and only works on models with an actual state field.

Other than these, we also have a flexible method available to set element visibility depending on a client-side dynamically evaluated expression. This is the attrs special attribute, expecting as a value a dictionary that maps the value of the invisible attribute to the result of an expression.

For example, to have the closed_date field not visible in the new and open states, use the following code:

```
<field name="closed_date"
       attrs="{'invisible':[('state', 'in', ['new', 'open'])]}"
/>
```

The invisible attribute is available in any element, not only fields. For example, we can use it on notebook pages and in group elements.

The attrs attribute can also set values for two other attributes: readonly and required. These only make sense for data fields to make them not editable or mandatory. This allows us to implement some basic client-side logic, such as making a field mandatory depending on other record values such as the state.

List views

At this point, list views should need little introduction, but they still have some interesting additional attributes to be discussed.

In the `library_checkout/views/checkout_view.xml` file, we'll be replacing the basic list view created in Chapter 8, *Business Logic - Supporting Business Processes*, with this improved version:

```xml
<record id="view_tree_checkout" model="ir.ui.view">
  <field name="name">Checkout Tree</field>
  <field name="model">library.checkout</field>
  <field name="arch" type="xml">
    <tree
      decoration-muted="state in ['done', 'cancel']"
      decoration-bf="state=='open'"
    >
      <field name="state" invisible="True" />
      <field name="request_date" />
      <field name="member_id" />
      <field name="checkout_date" />
      <field name="stage_id" />
      <field name="num_books" sum="# Books"/>
    </tree>
  </field>

</record>
```

The row text color and font can change dynamically, depending on the results of a Python expression evaluation. This is done through the `decoration-NAME` attributes, with the expression to evaluate based on field attributes. The `NAME` part can be `bf` or `it`, for bold and italic fonts, or any Bootstrap text contextual colors: `danger`, `info`, `muted`, `primary`, `success`, or `warning`. The Bootstrap documentation has examples of how these are presented: `https://getbootstrap.com/docs/3.3/css/#helper-classes`.

Changed in Odoo 9
The `decoration-NAME` attributes were introduced in Odoo 9. In Odoo 8, we have the `colors` and `fonts` attributes instead .

Remember that fields used in expressions must be declared in a `<field>` element, so that the web client knows that the column needs to be retrieved from the server. If we don't want to have it displayed to the user, we should use the `invisible="1"` attribute on it.

Other relevant attributes of the tree element are as follows:

- `default_order` allows us to override the model's default sort order, and its value follows the same format as an order attribute used in model definitions.
- `create`, `delete`, and `edit`, if set to `false` (in lowercase), disable the corresponding action on the list view.
- `editable` makes records editable directly on the list view. Possible values are `top` and `bottom`—the location where the new records will be added.

A list view can contain fields and buttons, and most of their attributes for forms are also valid here.

In list views, numeric fields can display summary values for their column. Add to the field one of the available aggregation attributes—`sum`, `avg`, `min`, or `max`—and assign to it the label text for the summary value. We added an example of that, on the `num_books` field:

```
<field name="num_books" sum="# Books" /
```

The `num_books` field counts the number of borrowed books in each checkout. It's a computed field, and we need to add it to the model:

```
num_books = fields.Integer(compute='_compute_num_books')

@api.depends('line_ids')
def _compute_num_books(self):
    for book in self:
        book.num_books = len(book.line_ids)
```

Search views

The search options available are defined through the `<search>` view type. We can choose the fields that can be automatically searched when typing in the search box. We can also provide predefined filters, activated with a click, and predefined grouping options to be used in list views.

Here is a possible search view for the library checkouts:

```
<record id="view_filter_checkout" model="ir.ui.view">
  <field name="model">library.checkout</field>
  <field name="arch" type="xml">
    <search>
      <field name="member_id"/>
      <field name="user_id"/>
```

```
        <filter name="filter_not_done"
                string="To Return"
                domain="[('state','=','open')]"/>
        <filter name="filter_my_checkouts"
                string="My Checkouts"
                domain="[('user_id','=',uid)]"/>
        <filter name="group_user"
                string="By Member"
                context="{'group_by': 'member_id'}"/>
    </search>
  </field>
</record>
```

Inside the `<search>` view definition, we can see two simple `<fields>` elements for the `member_id` and `user_id` fields. When the user starts typing in the search box, a suggestions drop-down list will show matches on those fields.

Then, we have two predefined filters, using domain filters. These are available for selection in the **Filters** button, below the search box. The first filters the **To Return** checkouts, which are the ones in the `open` state. The second one filters the checkout where the current user is the responsible librarian, filtering by `user_id` by the current user, available from the context `uid` key.

These filters two can be activated independently and will be joined by an `OR` operator. Blocks of filters separated with a `<separator/>` element will be joined by an `AND` operator.

The third filter only sets a `group by` context key. This tells the view to group the records by that field, `member_id` in this case.

The field elements can use the following attributes:

- `name` identifies the field to use.
- `string` is label text that is used instead of the default.
- `operator` is used to change the operator from the default one (= for numeric fields and `ilike` for the other field types).
- `filter_domain` sets a specific domain expression to use for the search, providing one flexible alternative to the operator attribute. The searched text string is referred to in the expression as self. A trivial example is: `filter_domain="[('name', 'ilike', self)]"`.
- `groups` makes the search on the field available only for users belonging to some security groups and expects a comma-separated list of XML IDs.

For the filter elements, these are the attributes available:

- `name` is an identifier to be used for later inheritance/extension, or for being enabled through Window Actions. It's not mandatory, but it's good practice to always provide it.
- `string` is the label text to be displayed for the filter. It's mandatory.
- `domain` is the domain expression to be added to the current domain.
- `context` is a context dictionary to be added to the current context. It usually sets a `group_id` key with the name of the field to group records.
- `groups` makes the search on the field available only for a list of security groups (XML IDs).

Other view types

The form, tree/list, and search views are the most frequently used view types. But there are a few more view types available to design our user interfaces.

We're already familiar with the three basic views: `form`, `tree` , and `search`. In Chapter 11, *Kanban Views and Client-Side QWeb*, we discuss in detail the `kanban` views, where we visualize the record as item cards, and even organize them in columns, to have Kanban boards.

Next, we have additional view types:

- `activity` to show an organized summary of the scheduled activities
- `calendar` to present data in a calendar format, based on selected date fields
- `diagram` to present relations between records, currently not used in Odoo

These two view type are used to show aggregated data:

- `graph` for chart presentation
- `pivot` for interactive pivot tables

There are a few more views types available only in the Odoo enterprise edition. Since we're working based on the community edition, we won't be able to try examples for these here:

- `dashboard` to present aggregate data using subviews, such as pivots and graphs
- `cohort` used to show how data changes over a period of time

- `gantt` to present date scheduling information in a Gantt chart, commonly used in project management
- `grid` to present data organized in a grid with rows and columns

The official documentation provides a good reference on all of the views and their available attributes, so there's no point in repeating that here. Instead, we'll focus on providing some basic usage examples to get you started with these views. That should provide a good platform to then further explore all that can be done with each of the views.

 Additional view types can be found as community addon modules. Under the Odoo Community Association umbrella, web client extensions are found in the `https://github.com/OCA/web` GitHub repository. For example, the `web_timeline` addon module provides a `timeline` view type, also capable of presenting scheduling information as Gantt charts, and is a community edition alternative for the `gantt` view type.

Activity views

The activity view type is a built-in scheduled activity summary board, to help users visualize activity tasks. It's provided by the `mail` addon module, so it needs to be installed to have this view type available.

To make it available, just add the `activity` view type to the view list in the Window Action `view_mode` attribute. The actual view definition will be automatically generated. We can still add it manually, but the only option we have is to change the `string` attribute, but it's not used in the UI.

For reference, the activity view definition looks like this:

```
<activity string="Activities"/>
```

Calendar views

As the name suggests, this view type presents the records in a calendar that can be viewed at different periods of time: per month, week, or day.

This is a calendar view for the library checkouts, showing the items on a calendar according to their request date:

```
<record id="view_calendar_checkout" model="ir.ui.view">
  <field name="model">library.checkout</field>
  <field name="arch" type="xml">
    <calendar date_start="request_date"
              color="user_id">
      <field name="member_id" />
      <field name="stage_id" />
    </calendar>
  </field>
</record>
```

The basic calendar attributes are as follows:

- `date_start` is the field for the start date (required).
- `date_end` is the field for the end date (optional).
- `date_delay` is the field with the duration in days, to be used instead of `date_end`.
- `all_day` provides the name of a Boolean field that is to be used to signal full day events. In these events, the duration is ignored.
- `color` is the field used to color a group of calendar entries. Each distinct value in this field will be assigned a color, and all of its entries will have the same color.
- `mode` is the default display mode for the calendar, either `day`, `week`, or `month`.

Changed in Odoo 11
The `display` calendar attribute was removed in Odoo 11. In previous versions, it could be used to customize the format of the calendar entries title text, for example, `display="[name], Stage [stage_id]"`.

Pivot views

The data can also be seen in a pivot table, a dynamic analysis matrix. For this, we have the pivot view.

Changed in Odoo 9
Pivot tables were already available in Odoo 8, as a graph view feature. In Odoo 9, they were moved to their own view type. Along with this, the pivot table features were improved, and the retrieval of pivot table data was optimized.

Data aggregations are only available for database stored fields. We want to use the `num_books` field to present some statistics on the number of borrowed books. It's a computed field and isn't being stored right now. To have it available for these views, we need to first have it stored in the database, by adding the `store=True` attribute:

```
num_books = fields.Integer(
    compute='_compute_num_books',
    store=True)
```

To also add a pivot table to the library checkouts, use this code:

```xml
<record id="view_pivot_checkout" model="ir.ui.view">
  <field name="model">library.checkout</field>
  <field name="arch" type="xml">
    <pivot>
      <field name="stage_id" type="col" />
      <field name="member_id" />
      <field name="request_date" interval="week" />
      <field name="num_books" type="measure" />
    </pivot>

  </field>
</record>
```

The graph and pivot views should contain field elements describing the axes and measures to use. Most of the available attributes are common to both the view types:

- `name` identifies the field to use in the graph, just like in other views.
- `type` is how the field will be used, as a `row` group (default), `measure`, or as `col` (only for pivot tables, used for column groups).
- `interval` is meaningful for date fields and is the time interval used to group time data by `day`, `week`, `month`, `quarter`, or `year`.

Graph views

Graph views present charts with data aggregations. We can use bar, line, and pie charts.

Now let's add the library checkout graph view:

```
<record id="view_graph_checkout" model="ir.ui.view">
  <field name="model">library.checkout</field>
  <field name="arch" type="xml">

    <graph type="bar">
      <field name="stage_id" />
      <field name="num_books" type="measure" />
    </graph>
  </field>
</record>
```

The `graph` view element can have a `type` attribute that can be set to `bar` (the default), `pie`, or `line`. In the case of `bar`, the additional `stacked="True"` can be used to make it a stacked bar chart.

The graph uses two types of fields:

- `type="row"` is the default and sets the criteria to aggregate values
- `type="measure"` is used for the fields that are to be used as metrics, the actual values being aggregated

The graph and pivot views should contain field elements describing the axes and measures to use. Most of the available graph view attributes are common to the pivot view type.

Summary

In this chapter, we learned more about Odoo views in order to build the user interface. We explained form views in detail and then provided an overview of the other view types, including list (or tree) and search view. We also learned how to add dynamic behavior to view elements.

In the next chapter, we'll learn more about a specific view type not covered here: the Kanban view and the templating syntax used by it, QWeb.

Further reading

The following additional reference materials complement the topics described in this chapter:

- The official Odoo documentation:
    - **On actions:** `https://www.odoo.com/documentation/12.0/reference/actions.html`
    - **On views:** `https://www.odoo.com/documentation/12.0/reference/views.html`
- **The Font Awesome icon index:** `https://fontawesome.com/v4.7.0/icons/`

Kanban Views and Client-Side QWeb

11

QWeb is the template engine used by Odoo. It's XML-based and used to generate HTML fragments and pages. It enables richer Kanban views, reports, and the CMS website pages.

Here, you will learn about the QWeb syntax and how to use it to create your own Kanban views and custom reports. Let's get started by learning more about Kanban boards.

The following topics will be covered in this chapter:

- What Kanban boards are
- Designing Kanban views
- The QWeb template language
- Inheritance on Kanban views
- Adding custom CSS and JavaScript assets

Technical requirements

We will continue working with the `library_checkout` add-on module, based on the code created in `Chapter 10`, *Backend Views – Design the User Interface*. The necessary code can be found in the `ch10/` directory of the Git repository at https://github.com/PacktPublishing/Odoo-12-Development-Essentials-Fourth-Edition.

The code in this chapter can be found in the same repository, in the `ch11/` directory.

About Kanban boards

Kanban is a Japanese word literally meaning billboard and is associated with lean manufacturing and just-in-time manufacturing, introduced by Taiichi Ohno, an industrial engineer working at Toyota. More recently, the concept of Kanban boards has been adopted in other areas and has become popular in the software industry with the adoption of Agile methodologies.

The **Kanban board** allows you to visualize the work queue. The board is organized into columns representing the **stages** of the work process. Work items are represented by **cards** placed on the appropriate column of the board. New work items start from the leftmost column and travel through the board until they reach the rightmost column, representing completed work.

The simplicity and visual impact of Kanban boards make them excellent for supporting simple business processes. A basic example of a Kanban board can have three columns, as shown in the following diagram—**To Do**, **Doing**, and **Done**.

It can, of course, be extended to whatever specific process steps we may need:

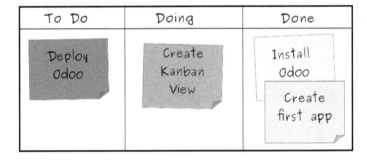

For many business use cases, a Kanban board can be a more effective way to manage the corresponding process, compared to a heavier workflow engine, such as the one featured in Odoo versions before 11.0. Odoo supports Kanban board views, along with the classic list and form views. This makes it easy to implement this type of view. Let's learn how to use it.

Kanban views

We will now add a Kanban view to our checkout model. Each checkout will be a card, and the Kanban board will be organized into stage columns. We already have a stage_id field to use for this, added in previous chapters.

Previously, in form views, we mostly used Odoo-specific XML elements, such as `<field>` and `<group>`. HTML elements, such as `<h1>` or `<div>`, were also used, but less frequently. With Kanban views, it's quite the opposite: the presentation templates are HTML-based and support only two Odoo-specific elements, `<field>` and `<button>`.

The final HTML to be presented in the web client is dynamically generated from QWeb templates. The QWeb engine processes special XML tags and attributes to produce them. This brings a lot of control over how to render the content, but also makes the view design more complex.

The Kanban view design is quite flexible, so we'll do our best to prescribe a straightforward way for you to quickly build your Kanban views. A good approach is to find an existing Kanban view similar to what you need, and inspect it to for ideas on how to build yours.

We can see two different ways to use Kanban views. One is a card list. It's used in places such as contacts, products, employee directories, or apps.

Here is how the **Contacts** Kanban view looks:

But this is not a true Kanban board. A Kanban board is expected to have the cards organized into columns, and of course the Kanban view also supports that layout. We can see examples in the **CRM** or project apps.

Here is how the **CRM | Sales | My Pipeline** looks:

The most striking difference between the two is the card organization in columns. This is achieved by the **Group By** feature, similar to what list views can do. Usually, the grouping is done on a **stage** field. One very useful feature of Kanban views is that they support dragging and dropping cards between columns, automatically assigning the corresponding value to the field the view is grouped by.

Looking at the cards in both examples, we can see some differences. In fact, their design is quite flexible, and there isn't a single way to design a Kanban card. But these two examples provide a starting point for your designs.

The **Contact** cards basically have an image on the left-hand side, and a bold title in the main area followed by a list of values. The **CRM Pipeline** cards have a bit more structure. The main card area also has a title followed by a list of relevant information, as well as a footer area. In this footer area, we can see a priority widget on the left-hand side, followed by an activities indicator, and at the right-hand side, a small image of the the responsible user. It's not visible in the image, but the cards also have an options menu at the top-right, shown when hovering the mouse pointer over it. This menu allows us to, for example, change a color indicator for the card.

We will be using this more elaborate structure as a model for the cards on our checkouts Kanban board.

Designing Kanban views

We will improve the `library_checkout` module we have been working with to add the Kanban view to the library checkouts.

For this, we'll use a new data file, `library_checkout/views/checkout_kanban_view.xml`. We need to edit the `data` key in the `__manifest__.py` descriptor file to append this new data file at the end of the list.

In `library_checkout/views/library_menu.xml`, we can find the window action used in the checkout menu item. We need to make a change to it to enable the additional view types we'll add in this chapter:

```
<act_window id="action_library_checkout"
  name="Checkouts"
  res_model="library.checkout"
  view_mode="kanban,tree,form,activity,calendar,graph,pivot"
/>
```

Here, we modify the menu action to include `kanban` at the beginning of the `view_mode` list, so that it's the default view mode used. We then add the `kanban` view record. It's similar to the other views, except that, inside the `arch` field, we have a `<kanban>` top XML element.

Next, we can create the actual XML file where our shiny new Kanban view will go, at `library_checkout/views/checkout_kanban_view.xml`:

```
<?xml version="1.0"?>
<odoo>
  <!-- Add Kanban view -->
  <record id="library_checkout_kanban" model="ir.ui.view">
    <field name="model">library.checkout</field>
    <field name="arch" type="xml">
      <kanban>
        <!-- Empty for now, but the Kanban will go here! -->
      </kanban>

    </field>
  </record>
</odoo>
```

Before starting with the Kanban views, we need to add a couple of fields to the library checkout model.

Priority, Kanban state, and color

Other than stages, a few more fields are useful and frequently used in Kanban boards:

- `priority` lets users organize their work items, signaling what should be addressed first.
- `kanban_state` signals whether a start is ready to move to the next stage or is blocked for some reason. At the model definition layer, both are selection fields. At the view layer, they have specific widgets for them that can be used on form and Kanban views.
- `color` is used to store the color the Kanban card should display and can be set using a color picker menu available on Kanban views.

To add these fields to our model, we should edit the `library_checkout/models/library_checkout.py` file:

```
# class Checkout(models.Model):
#   ...
    color = fields.Integer('Color Index')
    priority = fields.Selection(
        [('0', 'Low'),
         ('1', 'Normal'),
         ('2', 'High')],
        'Priority',
        default='1')
    kanban_state = fields.Selection(
        [('normal', 'In Progress'),
         ('blocked', 'Blocked'),
         ('done', 'Ready for next stage')],
        'Kanban State',
        default='normal')
```

We should also add these to the form view, using the special widgets available for them. The `kanban_state` field should be added before `<div oe_class="title">` and after the button box, with `<field name="kanban_stage" widget="state_selection" />`. `priority` should be added before the `name` field, inside the surrounding `<h1>` element, with `<field name="priority" widget="priority" />`. The `color` field is not usually represented in the form views.

Now that the checkout model has all of the fields we want to use, we can work on the Kanban view.

Kanban card elements

The Kanban view architecture has a `<kanban>` top element and the following basic structure:

```xml
<kanban default_group_by="stage_id" class="o_kanban_small_column" >

    <!-- Fields (to use in expressions)... -->
    <field name="stage_id" />
    <field name="id" />
    <field name="color" />
    <field name="kanban_state" />
    <field name="priority" />
    <field name="message_partner_ids" />

    <!-- Optional progress bar  -->
    <progressbar
        field="kanban_state"
        colors='{"done": "success", "blocked": "danger"}' />
    <!-- Templates with HTML snippets to use... -->
    <templates>
      <t t-name="kanban-box">
        <!-- HTML QWeb template... -->
      </t>
    </templates>
</kanban>
```

Notice the `default_group_by="stage_id"` attribute used in the `<kanban>` element. We used it so that, by default, the Kanban cards are grouped by stage, like Kanban boards should be. In simple card list Kanbans, such as the one in **Contacts**, we don't need this and would instead just use a simple `<kanban>` opening tag.

The `<kanban>` top element supports a few interesting attributes:

- `default_group_by` sets the field to use for the default column groups.
- `default_order` sets a default order to use for the Kanban items.
- `quick_create="false"` disables the quick create option (the large plus sign) available at the top of each column, to create new items by providing just a title description. The `false` value is a JavaScript literal and must be in lowercase.
- `class` adds a CSS class to the root element of the rendered Kanban view. A relevant class is `o_kanban_small_column`, making columns somewhat more compact than the default. Additional classes may be made available through additional CSS assets provided by our module.

- `group_create`, `group_edit`, `group_delete` , and `quick_create_view` can be set to `false` to disable the corresponding action on the Kanban columns. For example, `group_create="false"` removes the vertical **Add new column** bar on the right.
- `on_create` can be used to create a custom simplified form view in a popup when the user clicks on the top-left **Create** button. It should be set with the `<module>.<xml_id>` value of the intended form view.

We then see a list of fields used in templates. To be exact, only fields used exclusively in QWeb expressions need to be declared here, to ensure that their data is fetched from the server.

The QWeb engine only looks for `<field name="...">` patterns in a view to find the fields to be fetched from the model before the template is processed. QWeb attributes often use `record.field` references that won't be detected. Because of this, they need to be included before the `<templates>` section to make sure the corresponding field values are available when the template is processed.

Changed in Odoo 11
The progress bar widget was introduced. When used, a colored bar is shown at the top of each Kanban column, providing quick statistics on the status of that column's items. We can see an example in the previous screenshot, showing the **CRM Pipeline**.

The `<progressbar>` element has the following attributes:

- `field` is the field name used to color group the items in the column.
- `colors` is a dictionary, mapping each value of the group field to one of the three available colors: `danger` (red), `warning` (yellow), or `success` (green).
- `sum_field` is optional and can be used to choose the field name to use for the column total. If not set, the count of items in the column is used.

Next, we have a `<templates>` element, containing one or more QWeb templates to generate the used HTML fragments. We must have one template named `kanban-box`, which will render the Kanban cards. Additional templates can also be added, usually to define HTML fragments to be reused in the main template.

These templates use standard HTML and the QWeb templating language. QWeb provides special directives that are processed to dynamically generate the final HTML to be presented.

Changed in Odoo 12
Odoo now uses Twitter Bootstrap 4. In previous versions, Bootstrap 3 was used. These style classes are generally available wherever HTML can be rendered. You can learn more about Bootstrap at `https://getbootstrap.com`.

We will now have a closer look at the design of the QWeb templates to be used in Kanban views.

The Kanban card layout

The main content area of a Kanban card is defined inside the `kanban-box` template. This content area can also have a footer sub-container. A button opening an action menu may also be featured in the card's top-right corner.

For the footer area, we should use a `<div>` element at the bottom of the Kanban box with the `oe_kanban_bottom` CSS class. It can be further split into left and right footer areas, using the `oe_kanban_bottom_left` and `oe_kanban_bottom_right` CSS classes.

As an alternative, the Bootstrap `pull-left` and `pull-right` classes provided can be used to add left or right aligned elements anywhere in the card, including in the `oe_kanban_bottom` footer.

Here is our first iteration of the QWeb template for our Kanban card:

```
<!-- Define the kanban-box template -->
<t t-name="kanban-box">
  <!-- Set the Kanban Card color: -->
  <div t-attf-class="
    oe_kanban_color_#{kanban_getcolor(record.color.raw_value)}
    oe_kanban_global_click">
      <div class="o_dropdown_kanban dropdown">
          <!-- Top-right drop down menu here... -->
      </div>
      <div class="oe_kanban_body">
          <!-- Content elements and fields go here... -->
      </div>
      <div class="oe_kanban_footer">
        <div class="oe_kanban_footer_left">
            <!-- Left hand footer... -->
        </div>
        <div class="oe_kanban_footer_right">
            <!-- Right hand footer... -->
        </div>
```

```
      </div>
      <div class="oe_clear"/>
   </div> <!-- end of kanban color -->

</t>
```

This lays out the overall structure for the Kanban card. You may notice that the `color` field is being used in the top `<div>` element to dynamically set the card's color. We will explain the `t-attf` QWeb directive in more detail in one of the following sections.

Now let's work on the main content area and choose what to place there:

```
<div class="oe_kanban_body">
   <!-- Content elements and fields go here... -->

   <div>
     <strong>
       <a type="open"><field name="member_id" /></a>
     </strong>
   </div>
   <ul>
     <li><field name="user_id" /></li>
     <li><field name="request_date" /></li>
   </ul>

</div>
```

Most of this template is regular HTML, but we also see the `<field>` element used to render field values and the `type` attribute used in regular form view buttons, used here in an `<a>` anchor tag.

In the left-hand footer, we'll insert the priority widget:

```
<div class="oe_kanban_footer_left">
   <!-- Left hand footer... -->
   <field name="priority" widget="priority"/>
   <field name="activity_ids" widget="kanban_activity"/>
</div>
```

Here, we can see the `priority` field added, just like we do in a form view. We also add a field for the scheduled activities, using the special `kanban_activity` widget to display an indicator of pending activities.

In the right-hand footer, we'll place the Kanban state widget and the avatar for the member requesting the checkout:

```
<div class="oe_kanban_footer_right">
  <!-- Right hand footer... -->
  <field name="kanban_state"
         widget="kanban_state_selection"/>
  <img t-att-src="kanban_image(
                     'library.member',
                     'member_image',
                     record.id.raw_value)"
       t-att-title="record.member_id.value"
       t-att-alt="record.member_id.display_name.value"
       width="24"
       height="24"
       class="oe_kanban_avatar"
  />
</div>
```

The Kanban state is added using a `<field>` element with the `kanban_state_selection` widget.

The user avatar image is inserted using the HTML `<img>` tag. The image content is dynamically generated using the QWeb `t-att-` directive, which will be explained in more detail later on.

It makes use of the `kanban_image()` helper function to get the value for the `src` attribute. The `kanban_image()` Javascript function gets an image form an Odoo model, to render it in a web page. The attributes are as follows:

- The model to get the image from
- The field containing the image
- The record ID to fetch

Adding a Kanban card option menu

Kanban cards can have an option menu, placed in the top-right. Usual actions are to edit or delete the record, but it's possible to have any action that can be called from a button. We also have a widget to set the card's color.

The following is baseline HTML code for the option menu to be added at the top of the `oe_kanban_content` element:

```html
<div class="o_dropdown_kanban dropdown">
  <!-- Top-right drop down menu here... -->
  <a class="dropdown-toggle btn"
    data-toggle="dropdown" role="menu"
    href="#">
    <span class="fa fa-ellipsis-v"/>
  </a>
  <div class="dropdown-menu" role="menu">
    <!-- Edit and Delete actions, if available: -->
    <t t-if="widget.editable">
      <a role="menuitem" type="edit" class="dropdown-item">Edit</a>
    </t>
    <t t-if="widget.deletable">
      <a role="menuitem" type="delete" class="dropdown-item">Delete</a>
    </t>
    <!-- Color picker option: -->
    <ul class="oe_kanban_colorpicker" data-field="color"/>
  </div>
</div>
```

The drop-down menu is basically composed of `<li>` HTML list elements containing an `<a>` element. Some options, such as **Edit** and **Delete**, are made available only if certain conditions are met. This is done with the `t-if` QWeb directive. Later in this chapter, we explain this and other QWeb directives in more detail.

The `widget` global variable represents a `KanbanRecord()` JavaScript object, which is responsible for the rendering of the current Kanban card. Two particularly useful properties are `widget.editable` and `widget.deletable`, which allow us to check whether the corresponding actions are available.

We can also see how to show or hide an option depending on the record field values. The **Set as Done** option will only be displayed if the `is_done` field is not set.

The last option adds the color picker special widget using the `color` data field to select and change the card's background color.

Actions in Kanban views

In QWeb templates, the `<a>` tag for links can have a `type` attribute. It sets the type of action the link will perform so that links can act just like buttons in regular forms. So, in addition to the `<button>` elements, the `<a>` tags can also be used to run Odoo actions.

As in form views, the action type can be `action` or `object` and it should be accompanied by a `name` attribute, identifying the specific action to execute. Additionally, the following action types are also available:

- `open` opens the corresponding form view.
- `edit` opens the corresponding form view directly in edit mode.
- `delete` deletes the record and removes the item from the Kanban view.

The QWeb template language

The QWeb parser looks for special directives in the templates and replaces them with dynamically generated HTML. These directives are XML element attributes and can be used in any valid tag or element, such as `<div>`, `<span>`, or `<field>`.

Sometimes, we may want to use a QWeb directive but we don't want to place it in any of the XML elements in our template. For those cases, we have a `<t>` special element that can have QWeb directives, such as `t-if` or `t-foreach`, but is silent and won't have any output on the final XML/HTML produced.

The QWeb directives will frequently make use of evaluated expressions to produce different results, depending on the current record values. There are two different QWeb implementations: client-side JavaScript and server-side Python.

The reports and website pages use the server-side Python implementation of QWeb.

Kanban views use the client-side JavaScript implementation. This means that the QWeb expression used in Kanban views should be written using the JavaScript syntax, not Python.

When displaying a Kanban view, the internal steps are roughly as follows:

1. Get the XML for the templates to render.
2. Call the server `read()` method to get the data for the fields mentioned in the templates.
3. Locate the `kanban-box` template and parse it using QWeb to output the final HTML fragments.
4. Inject the HTML in the browser display (the DOM).

This is not meant to be technically exact. It's just a mind map that can be useful to understand how things work in Kanban views.

Next, we'll learn about QWeb expression evaluation and explore the available QWeb directives, using examples that enhance the checkout Kanban card.

The QWeb JavaScript evaluation context

Many of the QWeb directives use expressions that are evaluated to produce some result. When used from the client side, as is the case for Kanban views, these expressions are written in JavaScript. They're evaluated in a context that has a few useful variables available.

A `record` object is available, representing the current record, with the fields requested from the server. The field values can be accessed using either the `raw_value` or `value` attributes:

- `raw_value` is the value returned by the `read()` server method, so it's more suitable for use in condition expressions.
- `value` is formatted according to the user settings and is meant to be used for display in the user interface. This is typically relevant for date/datetime, float/monetary, and relational fields.

The QWeb evaluation context also has references available for the JavaScript web client instance. To make use of them, a good understanding of the web client architecture is needed, but we won't be able to go into that in detail. For reference purposes, the following identifiers are available in QWeb expression evaluation:

- `widget` is a reference to the current `KanbanRecord()` widget object, responsible for the rendering of the current record into a Kanban card. It exposes some helper functions we can use.
- `record` is a shortcut for `widget.record` and provides access to the fields available, using dot notation.
- `read_only_mode` indicates whether the current view is in read mode (and not in edit mode). It's a shortcut for `widget.view.options.read_only_mode`.
- `instance` is a reference to the full web client instance.

It's also noteworthy that some characters are not allowed inside expressions. The lower than sign (<) is such a case. This is because of the XML standard, where such characters have special meaning and shouldn't be used on the XML content. A negated >= operator is a valid alternative, but the common practice is to use the following alternative symbols that are available for inequality operations:

- lt is for less than.
- lte is for less than or equal to.
- gt is for greater than.
- gte is for greater than or equal to.

 The preceding comparison symbols are specific to Odoo and were introduced to overcome limitations in the XML format. They are not part of the XML standard.

Dynamic attributes by string substitution – t-attf

Our Kanban card is using the t-attf QWeb directive to dynamically set a class on the top <div> element so that the card is colored depending on the color field value. For this, the t-attf- QWeb directive was used.

The t-attf- directive dynamically generates tag attributes using string substitution. This allows for parts of larger strings generated dynamically, such as a URL address or CSS class names.

The directive looks for expression blocks that will be evaluated and replaced by the results. These are delimited either by {{ and }} or by #{ and }. The content of the blocks can be any valid JavaScript expression and can use any of the variables available for QWeb expressions, such as record and widget.

In our case, we also used the kanban_color() JavaScript function, specially provided to map color index numbers into the CSS class color names.

As an elaborate example, we'll use this directive to dynamically change the color of the user, to be in red font if the priority is high. For this, replace `<field name="user_id"/>` in our Kanban card with the following:

```
<li t-attf-class="oe_kanban_text_{{
  record.user_id.raw_value lt '2'
  ? 'black' : 'red' }}">
  <field name="user_id"/>
</li>
```

This results in either `class="oe_kanban_text_red"` or `class="oe_kanban_text_black"`, depending on the checkout's priority value. Please note that, while the `oe_kanban_text_red` CSS class is available in Kanban views, the `oe_kanban_text_black` CSS class does not exist and was used to explain the point.

> Notice the `lt` symbol used in the JavaScript expression. It's an escape expression for the < sign, not allowed in XML.

Dynamic attributes by expressions – t-att

The `t-att-` QWeb directive dynamically generates an attribute value by evaluating an expression.

Our Kanban card uses it to dynamically set some attributes on the `<img>` tag; the `title` attribute is dynamically rendered using the following:

```
t-att-title="record.member_id.value"
```

The `.value` field returns its value representation as it should be shown on the screen. For many-to-one fields, this is usually the related record's `name` value. For users, this is the username. As a result, when hovering the mouse pointer over the image, you will see the corresponding username.

When the expression evaluates to a false equivalent value, the attribute is not rendered at all. This is important for special HTML attributes such as the `checked` input field, which can have an effect even without an attribute value.

Loops – t-foreach

A block of HTML can be repeated by iterating through a loop. We can use it to add the avatars of the record followers.

Let's start by rendering just the partner IDs of the record, as follows:

```
<t t-foreach="record.message_partner_ids.raw_value" t-as="rec">
  <t t-esc="rec" />;
</t>
```

The `t-foreach` directive accepts a JavaScript expression evaluating to a collection to iterate. In most cases, this will be just the name of a to-many relation field. It's used with a `t-as` directive to set the name to be used to refer to each item in the iteration.

The `t-esc` directive used next evaluates the provided expression, just the `rec` variable name in this case, and renders it as safely escaped HTML.

In the previous example, we loop through the followers stored in the `message_parter_ids` field. Since there is limited space on the Kanban card, we could have used the `slice()` JavaScript function to limit the number of followers to display, as shown in the following:

```
t-foreach="record.message_partner_ids.raw_value.slice(0, 3)"
```

The `rec` variable holds each iteration value, a partner ID in this case. With this, we can rewrite the follower loop as follows:

```
<t t-foreach="record.message_parter_ids.raw_value.slice(0, 3)"
  t-as="rec">
  <img t-att-src="kanban_image('res.partner', 'image_small', rec)"
    class="oe_avatar" width="24" height="24" />
</t>
```

For example, this could be added next to the responsible user image, in the right-hand footer.

A few helper variables are also available. Their name has the variable name defined in `t-as` as a prefix. In our example, we used `rec`, so the helper variables available are as follows:

- `rec_index` is the iteration index, starting from zero
- `rec_size` is the number of elements of the collection
- `rec_first` is true on the first element of the iteration

- `rec_last` is true on the last element of the iteration
- `rec_even` is true on even indexes
- `rec_odd` is true on odd indexes
- `rec_parity` is either `odd` or `even`, depending on the current index
- `rec_all` represents the object being iterated over
- `rec_value`, when iterating through a `{key:value}` dictionary, holds the value (`rec` holds the key name)

For example, we could make use of the following to avoid a trailing comma on our ID list:

```
<t t-foreach="record.message_parter_ids.raw_value.slice(0, 3)"
  t-as="rec">
  <t t-esc="rec" />
  <t t-if="!rec_last">;</t>
</t>
```

Conditionals – t-if

Our Kanban view used the `t-if` directive in the card option menu to make some options available depending on some conditions. The `t-if` directive expects an expression to be evaluated in JavaScript when rendering Kanban views on the client side. The tag and its content will be rendered only if the condition evaluates to `true`.

As an example, to only display the checkout's number of books borrowed if it has a value, add the following after the `request_date` field:

```
<t t-if="record.num_books.raw_value gt 0">
  <li> <field name="num_books"/> books</li>
</t>
```

We used a `<t t-if="...">` element so that if the condition is `false`, the element produces no output. If it's `true`, only the contained `<li>` element is rendered to the output. Notice that the condition expression used the `gt` symbol instead of > to represent the greater than operator.

The `else if` and `else` conditions are also supported with the `t-elif` and `t-else` directives. Here is an example of their usage:

```
<t t-if="record.num_books.raw_value == 0">
  <li>No books.</li>
</t>
<t t-elif="record.num_books.raw_value gt 9">
```

```
    <li>A lot of books!</li>
  </t>
  <t t-else="">
    <li> <field name="num_books"/> books.</li>
  </t>
```

In Javascript expressions, the AND and OR operators are && and ||. But the ampersand symbol is not allowed in XML. We can work around this using the and and or operators.

Rendering values – t-esc and t-raw

We used the <field> element to render the field content. But field values can also be presented directly without a <field> tag.

The t-esc directive evaluates an expression and renders it as an HTML-escaped value, as shown in the following:

```
<t t-esc="record.message_parter_ids.raw_value" />
```

In some cases, and if the source data is guaranteed to be safe, t-raw can be used to render the field raw value without any escaping, as shown in the following example:

```
<t t-raw="record.message_parter_ids.raw_value" />
```

 For security reasons, it's important to avoid using t-raw as much as possible. Its usage should be strictly reserved for outputting HTML data that was specifically prepared without any user data in it or where any user data was escaped explicitly for HTML special characters.

Set values on variables – t-set

For more complex logic, we can store the result of an expression into a variable to use it later in the template. This is to be done using the t-set directive, naming the variable to set followed by the t-value directive, with the expression calculating the value to assign.

As an example, the following code renders missed deadlines in red, just as in the previous section, but uses a red_or_black variable for the CSS class to use, as shown in the following:

```
<t t-set="red_or_black"
    t-value="
      record.priority.raw_value gte '2'
```

```
        ? 'oe_kanban_text_red' : ''" />
<li t-att-class="red_or_black">
  <field name="user_id" />
</li>
```

Variables can also be assigned HTML content, as in the following example:

```
<t t-set="calendar_sign">
  <i class="fa fa-calendar"/>
</t>
<t t-raw="calendar_sign" />
```

Call and reuse other templates – t-call

QWeb templates can be reusable HTML snippets that can be inserted into other templates. Instead of repeating the same HTML blocks over and over again, we can design building blocks to compose more complex user interface views.

Reusable templates are defined inside the `<templates>` tag and identified by a top element with a `t-name` other than `kanban-box`. These other templates can then be included using the `t-call` directive. This is true for the templates declared in the same Kanban view, somewhere else in the same add-on module or in a different add-on.

The follower avatar list is something that could be isolated in a reusable snippet. Let's rework it to use a sub-template. We should start by adding another template to our XML file, inside the `<templates>` element, after the `<t t-name="kanban-box">` node, as shown in the following:

```
<t t-name="follower_avatars">    <div>
    <t t-foreach="record.message_parter_ids.raw_value.slice(0, 3)"
       t-as="rec">
      <img t-att-src="kanban_image(
        'res.partner', 'image_small', rec)"
        class="oe_avatar" width="24" height="24" />
    </t>
  </div>
</t>
```

Calling it from the `kanban-box` main template is quite straightforward. Instead of the `<div>` element containing the `for each` directive, we should use the following:

```
<t t-call="follower_avatars" />
```

To call templates defined in other add-on modules, we need to use the `module.name` full identifier, as we do with the other views. For instance, this snippet can be referred using the `library_checkout.follower_avatars` full identifier.

The called template runs in the same context as the caller, so any variable names available in the caller are also available when processing the called template.

A more elegant alternative is to pass arguments to the called template. This is done by setting variables inside the `t-call` tag. These will be evaluated and made available in the sub-template context only and won't exist in the caller context.

We could use this to have the maximum number of follower avatars set by the caller instead of being hardcoded in the sub-template. First, we need to replace the fixed value, 3, with a variable, `arg_max`, example:

```
<t t-name="follower_avatars">
  <div>
    <t t-foreach="record.message_parter_ids.raw_value.slice(0, arg_max)"
      t-as="rec">
      <img t-att-src="kanban_image('res.partner', 'image_small', rec)"
        class="oe_avatar" width="24" height="24" />
    </t>
  </div>
</t>
```

Then, define that variable's value when performing the sub-template call as follows:

```
<t t-call="follower_avatars">
  <t t-set="arg_max" t-value="3" />
</t>
```

The entire content inside the `t-call` element is also available to the sub-template through the 0 magic variable. Instead of argument variables, we can define an HTML code fragment that can be used in the sub-template with `<t t-raw="0" />`. This is especially useful for building layouts and combining/nesting QWeb templates in a modular way.

Dynamic attributes using dictionaries and lists

We've gone through the most important QWeb directives, but there are a few more we should be aware of. Let's look at a short explanation of them.

We have seen the `t-att-NAME` and `t-attf-NAME` style dynamic tag attributes. Additionally, the fixed `t-att` directive can be used. It accepts either a key-value dictionary mapping or a pair (a two-element list).

Use the following mapping:

```
<p t-att="{'class': 'oe_bold', 'name': 'Hello'}" />
```

This results in the following:

```
<p class="oe_bold" name="Hello" />
```

Use the following pair:

```
<p t-att="['class', 'oe_bold']" />
```

This results in the following:

```
<p class="oe_bold" />
```

Inheritance on Kanban views

The templates used in Kanban views and reports are extended using the regular techniques used for other views, for example, using XPath expressions. See `Chapter 4`, *Extending Modules*, for more details.

A common case is to use the `<field>` elements as selectors, then add other elements before or after them. In the case of Kanban views, the same field can be declared more than once, for example, once before the templates, and again inside the templates. Here, the selector will match the first field element and won't add our modification inside the template as intended.

To work around this, we need to use XPath expressions to make sure that the field inside the template is the one matched, for example:

```
<record id="res_partner_kanban_inherit" model="ir.ui.view">
  <field name="name">Contact Kanban modification</field>
  <field name="model">res.partner</field>
  <field name="inherit_id" ref="base.res_partner_kanban_view" />
```

```
<field name="arch" type="xml">
    <xpath expr="//t[@t-name='kanban-box']//field[@name='display_name']"
        position="before">
        <span>Name:</span>
    </xpath>
</field>
</record>
```

In the previous example, the XPath looks for a `<field name="display_name">` element inside a `<t t-name="kanban-box">` element. This rules out the same field element outside of the `<templates>` section.

For these more complex XPath expressions, we can explore the correct syntax using some command-line tools. The `xmllint` command-line utility is probably already available on your Linux system and has an `--xpath` option to perform queries on XML files.

Another option, providing nicer output, is the `xpath` command from the `libxml-xpath-perl` Debian/Ubuntu package:

```
$ sudo apt-get install libxml-xpath-perl
$ xpath -e "//record[@id='res_partner_kanban_view']" -e
"//field[@name='display_name']]" /path/to/myfile.xml
```

Custom CSS and JavaScript assets

As we have seen, Kanban views are mostly HTML and make heavy use of CSS classes. We have introduced some frequently used CSS classes provided by the standard product, but for best results, modules can also add their own CSS.

We won't go into detail here on how to write CSS code, but it's relevant to explain how a module can add its own CSS (and JavaScript) web assets. Odoo assets for the backend are declared in the `assets_backend` template. To add our module assets, we should extend that template. The XML file for this is usually placed inside a `views/` module subdirectory.

The following is a sample XML file to add a CSS and a JavaScript file to the `library_checkout` module, and it could be at `library_checkout/views/checkout_kanban_assets.xml`:

```
<odoo>
    <template id="assets_backend" inherit_id="web.assets_backend"
        name="Library Checkout Kanban Assets" >
        <xpath expr="." position="inside">
            <link rel="stylesheet"
                href="/library_checkout/static/src/css/checkout_kanban.css"/>
```

```
        <script type="text/javascript"
         src="/library_checkout/static/src/js/checkout_kanban.js">
        </script>
      </xpath>
    </template>
  </odoo>
```

As usual, it should be referenced in the __manifest__.py descriptor file. Notice that the assets are located inside a /static/src subdirectory. While this is not required, it's a generally used convention.

Summary

You learned about Kanban boards and how to build Kanban views to implement them. We also introduced QWeb templating and how it can be used to design Kanban cards. QWeb is also the rendering engine powering the CMS website, so it's growing in importance in the Odoo toolset.

Kanban views can be extended using the same XML syntax used in other views. In the case of Kanban, the XML architecture can be more complex, and we'll often need to use XPath expressions to locate the elements to extend.

Finally, advanced Kanban views can use specific CSS and Javascript. These can be added as module files that should then be included in the web client pages, by adding them in the web.assets_backend QWeb template.

In the next chapter, we'll keep using QWeb, but on the server side, to create our custom reports.

Further reading

The following additional reference materials complement the topics described in this chapter:

- The official Odoo documentation on QWeb: https://www.odoo.com/documentation/12.0/reference/qweb.html
- The Bootstrap styling documentation: https://getbootstrap.com/docs/4.1/getting-started/introduction/
- The Font Awesome icon index: https://fontawesome.com/v4.7.0/icons/

Reports and Server-Side QWeb 12

Reports are an invaluable feature for business apps. The built-in QWeb report engine is the default report engine. Reports are designed using QWeb templates to produce HTML documents that can then be converted to PDF form.

This means we can conveniently leverage what we have learned about QWeb and apply it to create business reports. In this chapter, we will be adding a report to our Library app, and will review the most important techniques to use with QWeb reports, including report computations such as totals, translation, and print paper formats.

The topics covered in this chapter are the following:

- Installing `wkhtmltopdf`
- Creating business reports
- QWeb report templates
- Presenting data in reports
- Rendering images
- Report totals
- Defining paper formats
- Enabling language translation in reports
- Reports based on custom SQL

Technical requirements

We will work with the `library_app` addon module, based on the code first created in Chapter 3, *Your First Odoo Application*, and later improved in Chapter 5, *Import, Export, and Module Data*, and Chapter 6, *Models – Structuring the Application Data*. The necessary code can be found in the `ch06/` directory of the Git repository at https://github.com/PacktPublishing/Odoo-12-Development-Essentials-Fourth-Edition.

The code in this chapter can be found in the same repository, in the `ch12/` directory.

Installing wkhtmltopdf

To correctly generate reports, the recommended version of the `wkhtmltopdf` utility needs to be installed. Its name stands for **Webkit HTML to PDF**. Odoo uses it to convert a rendered HTML page into a PDF document.

Some versions of the `wkhtmltopdf` library are known to have issues, such as not printing page headers and footers, so we need to be picky about the version to use. Since Odoo 10, version 0.12.5 is officially supported and is the officially recommended one.

 The official Odoo project keeps a wiki page with information and recommendations about `wkhtmltopdf` usage. It can be found at https://github.com/odoo/odoo/wiki/Wkhtmltopdf.

Unfortunately, the odds are that the packaged version provided for your host system, Debian/Ubuntu or any other, is not adequate. So, we should download and install the package recommended for our OS and CPU architecture. The download links can be found at https://github.com/wkhtmltopdf/wkhtmltopdf/releases.

We should first make sure that we don't have an incorrect version already installed on our system:

```
$ wkhtmltopdf --version
```

If the preceding command reports a version other than the one we want, we should uninstall it. On a Debian/Ubuntu system, this is done with the following command:

```
$ sudo apt-get remove --purge wkhtmltopdf
```

Next, we need to download the appropriate package for our system and install it. Check the correct download link at `https://github.com/wkhtmltopdf/wkhtmltopdf/releases`. For version 0.12.5, the latest Ubuntu build is for trusty Ubuntu 14.04 LTS, but it should still work with later Ubuntu versions. We installed it on a recent Ubuntu 64-bit system. The download command used was as follows:

```
$ wget "https://github.com/wkhtmltopdf/wkhtmltopdf/releases"\
"/download/0.12.5/wkhtmltox_0.12.5-1.bionic_amd64.deb" \
-O /tmp/wkhtml.deb
```

Next, we should install it. Installing a local `deb` file does not automatically install dependencies, so a second step will be needed to do that and complete the installation:

```
$ sudo dpkg -i /tmp/wkhtml.deb
```

This will probably display an error because of missing dependencies. The following command fixes that for you:

```
$ sudo apt-get -f install
```

Now, we can check the `wkhtmltopdf` library is correctly installed and confirm its version number is the one we want:

```
$ wkhtmltopdf --version
wkhtmltopdf 0.12.5 (with patched qt)
```

After this, the Odoo server start log won't display the **You need Wkhtmltopdf to print a pdf version of the report** info message.

Creating business reports

We will continue using the `library_app` module, which has been used in previous chapters, and add to it the files implementing the reports.

The report we are going to create will look like this:

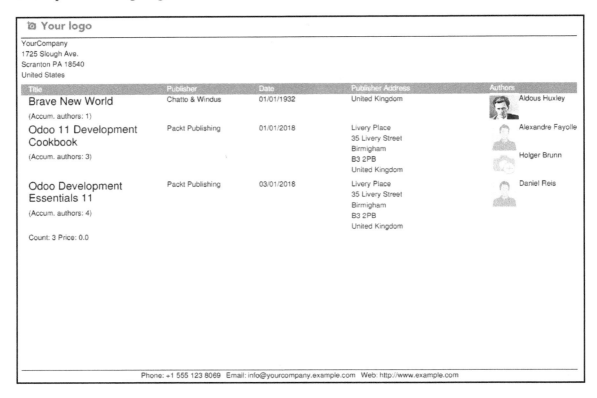

The report files should be placed inside a /reports module subdirectory. We will start by adding a reports/library_book_report.xml data file. As usual, when adding data files, remember to add it to the data key in the __manifest__.py file.

The reports/library_book_report.xml file starts off by declaring the new report as follows:

```
<?xml version="1.0"?> <odoo> <report id="action_library_book_report"
 string="Library Books"
 model="library.book" report_type="qweb-pdf"
 name="library_app.report_library_book_template" /> </odoo>
```

The <report> tag is a shortcut to write data to the ir.actions.report.xml model, which is a particular type of client action. Its data is available in the **Settings | Technical | Actions| Reports** menu option.

During the design of the report, you might prefer to leave `report_type="qweb-html"` and change it back to a `qweb-pdf` file once finished. This will make it quicker to generate and easier to inspect the HTML result from the QWeb template.

After upgrading the module with this addition, the Library Books form view will display a **Print** button at the top, to the left of the **Actions** button, containing this option to run the report.

It won't work right now, since we haven't defined the report yet. This will be a QWeb report, so it will use a QWeb template. The `name` attribute identifies the template to be used. Unlike other identifier references, the module prefix in the `name` attribute is required. We must use the full reference, `<module_name>.<identifier_name>`.

QWeb report templates

The reports will usually follow a basic skeleton, as shown in the following code. This can be added to the `reports/library_book_report.xml` file, just after the `<report>` element:

```
<template id="report_library_book_template">
  <t t-call="web.html_container">
    <t t-call="web.external_layout">
      <div class="page">

        <!-- Report header content -->
        <t t-foreach="docs" t-as="o">
          <!-- Report row content -->
        </t>
        <!-- Report footer content -->

      </div>
    </t>
  </t>
</template>
```

The most important elements here are the `t-call` directives using standard report structures. The `web.html_container` template does the basic setup to support an HTML document. The `web.external_layout` template handles the report header and footer, using the corresponding setup from the appropriate company. As an alternative, we can use the `web.internal_layout` template instead, which uses only a basic header.

Changed in Odoo 11

The support layouts for reports moved from the `report` module to the `web` module. This means that, whereas in previous Odoo versions the `report.external_layout` or `report.internal_layout` references were used, in version 11.0 they should be replaced with `web.<...>` references.

The `external_layout` template can be customized by users. Odoo 11 introduced an option for this, available from the **Settings** | **General Settings** menu, in the **Business Documents** | **Document Template** section:

There, we can **Change Document Template** to select from a few available templates, and even **Edit Layout** to customize the XML for the selected template.

This report skeleton is appropriate for the case of a list report, where each record is a line in the report. The report header area usually presents a title, and the report footer area usually presents the grand totals.

An alternative format is the document report, where each record is a page, such as a mailing letter. In this case, the appropriate report skeleton would be as follows:

```
<template id="report_todo_task_template">
  <t t-call="web.html_container">
    <t t-call="web.external_layout">

      <t t-foreach="docs" t-as="o">
        <div class="page">
          <!-- Report content -->
        </div>
      </t>
```

```
        </t>
      </t>
  </template>
```

We will be creating a list report, so we will be using the first skeleton, rather than the previous example.

Now, we have the basic skeleton for our report in place. Notice that, since reports are just QWeb templates, inheritance can be applied, just like in the other views. QWeb templates used in reports can be extended using the regular inherited views with XPATH expressions.

Presenting data in reports

Unlike Kanban views, the QWeb templates in reports are rendered on the server side and use a Python QWeb implementation. We can see this as two implementations of the same specification, and there are some differences that we need to be aware of.

To start with, QWeb expressions are evaluated using Python syntax, not JavaScript. For the simplest expressions, there may be little or no difference, but more complex operations will probably be different.

The context where expressions are evaluated is also different. For reports, we have the following variables available:

- `docs` is an iterable collection with the records to print
- `doc_ids` is a list of the IDs of the records to print
- `doc_model` identifies the model of the records, `library.book` for example
- `time` is a reference to Python's time library
- `user` is the record for the user running the report
- `res_company` is the record for the current user's company

Field values can be referenced using the `t-field` attribute, and can be complemented with the `t-options` attribute to use a specific widget to render the field content.

Changed in Odoo 11
In previous Odoo versions, the `t-field-options` attribute was used, but in Odoo 11 it was deprecated in favor of the `t-options` attribute.

For example, assuming that `doc` represents a particular record, it would look as follows:

```
<t t-field="doc.date_published"
   t-options="{'widget': 'date'}" />
```

Now, we can start designing the page content for our report.

 Unfortunately, the QWeb-supported widgets and their options are not covered by the official documentation. So, at the moment the only way to learn more about them is to read the corresponding code. You can find it at `https://github.com/odoo/odoo/blob/12.0/odoo/addons/base/models/ir_qweb_fields.py`. Look for classes inheriting from `ir.qweb.field`. The `get_available_options()` method gives insight on the supported options.

The report content is written in HTML, and makes use of Twitter Bootstrap 4 to help design the report layout. Bootstrap is widely used in web development, and a complete reference for Bootstrap can be found at `http://getbootstrap.com`.

Here is the XML we will use to render the report header. It should be placed inside the `<div class="page">` node and replaces the existing `<t t-foreach=...>` element:

```
<!-- Report header content -->
<div class="container">
  <div class="row bg-primary">
    <div class="col-3">Title</div>
    <div class="col-2">Publisher</div>
    <div class="col-2">Date</div>
    <div class="col-3">Publisher Address</div>
    <div class="col-2">Authors</div>
  </div>

  <t t-foreach="docs" t-as="o">
    <div class="row">
      <!-- Report Row Content -->
    </div>
  </t>

  <!-- Report footer content ...-->
</div>
```

The layout of the content uses the Twitter Bootstrap HTML grid system. In a nutshell, Bootstrap has a grid layout with 12 columns. The grid is in a `<div class="container">` element.

Changed in Odoo 12
Odoo now uses Bootstrap 4, which is not backward compatible with Bootstrap 3, used in previous Odoo versions. For tips on the changes from Bootstrap 3 to Bootstrap 4, see the Odoo wiki page on this topic: `https://github.com/odoo/odoo/wiki/Tips-and-tricks:-BS3-to-BS4`.

Rows can be added using `<div class="row">`. Inside a row, we have cells, each spanning a certain number of columns, that should take up the 12 columns. Each cell can be defined with the row `<div class="col-N">`, where N is the number of columns it spans.

Bootstrap 4 uses CSS flexbox in most of its components, an `wkhtmltopdf` is known to not support all of the flexbox features properly. So, if something is not working, try to use another element or approach, such as HTML tables.

Here, we are adding a header row with titles, and then we have a `t-foreach` loop iterating through each record and rendering a row for each.

Since the rendering is done on the server side, records are objects, and we can use dot notation to access fields from related data records. This makes it easy to follow through relational fields to access their data. Notice that this is not possible in client-side rendered QWeb views, such as web client kanban views.

This is the XML for the content of the record rows inside the `<div class="row">` element:

```
<!-- Report Row Content -->
<div class="col-3">
  <h4><span t-field="o.name" /></h4>
</div>
<div class="col-2">
  <span t-field="o.publisher_id" />
</div>
<div class="col-2">
  <span t-field="o.date_published"
        t-options="{'widget': 'date'}" />
</div>
<div class="col-3">
  <div t-field="o.publisher_id"
       t-options='{
         "widget": "contact",
         "fields": ["address", "email", "phone", "website"],
```

```
                "no_marker": true}' />
    </div>
    <div class="col-2">
      <!-- Render Authors -->
    </div>
```

As we can see, fields can be provided with additional options through the `t-options` attribute, containing a JSON dictionary with a `widget` key.

A sophisticated example is the `contact` widget, used to format addresses. We used it to render the publishing company address, `o.publisher_id`. By default, the `contact` widget displays addresses with some pictograms, such as a phone icon. The `no_marker="true"` option we used disables them.

Rendering images

The last column of our report will feature the list of authors with their avatars. We will loop through the followers to render each one of them, and use the Bootstrap `media` object:

```
<!-- Render authors-->
<ul class="list-unstyled">
  <t t-foreach="o.author_ids" t-as="author">
    <li class="media>
      <span t-field="author.image_small"
            t-options="{'widget': 'image'}" />
      <div class="media-body">
        <p class="mt-0">
          <span t-field="author.name" />
        </p>
      </div>
    </li>
  </t>
</ul>
```

Here, we are looping through the `author_ids`, and for each author rendering the image using a field image widget, `<t t-field="..." t-options="{'widget': 'image'}"`, and the author's name.

Report totals

A common need in reports is to provide totals. This can be done using Python expressions to compute those totals.

After the closing tag of `<t t-foreach>`, we will add a final row with the totals:

```
<!-- Report footer content -->
<div class="row">
  <div class="col-3">
    Count: <t t-esc="len(docs)" />
  </div>
  <div class="col-2" />
  <div class="col-2" />
  <div class="col-3" />
  <div class="col-2" />
</div>
```

The `len()` Python function is used to count the number of elements in a collection. Similarly, totals can also be computed using `sum()` over a list of values. For example, we could have used the following list comprehension to compute a total amount:

```
<t t-esc="sum([x.price for x in docs])" />
```

You can think of list comprehensions as embedded `for` loops.

Sometimes, we want to perform some computations as we go through the report, for example, a running total, with the total up to the current record. This can be implemented with `t-set` to define an accumulating variable and then update it on each row.

To illustrate this, we can compute the accumulated number of authors. We should start by initializing the variable, just before the `t-foreach` loop on the `docs` recordset, using the following:

```
<!-- Running total: initialize variable -->
<t t-set="author_count" t-value="0" />
```

Then, inside the loop, add the record's number of authors to the variable. We will choose to do this right after presenting the list of authors, and we will also print out the current total on every line:

```
<!-- Running total: increment and present -->
<t t-set="author_count" t-value="author_count + len(o.author_ids)" />
(Accumulated: <t t-esc="author_count"/> )
```

Defining paper formats

At this point, our report looks good in HTML, but it doesn't print out nicely on a PDF page. We might get some better results using a landscape page. So, we need to add this paper format.

At the top of the report XML file, add this record:

```
<record id="paperformat_euro_landscape"
        model="report.paperformat">
  <field name="name">European A4 Landscape</field>
  <field name="default" eval="True" />
  <field name="format">A4</field>
  <field name="page_height">0</field>
  <field name="page_width">0</field>
  <field name="orientation">Landscape</field>
  <field name="margin_top">40</field>
  <field name="margin_bottom">23</field>
  <field name="margin_left">7</field>
  <field name="margin_right">7</field>
  <field name="header_line" eval="False" />
  <field name="header_spacing">35</field>
  <field name="dpi">90</field>
</record>
```

It is a copy of the European A4 format, defined in the `base` module, in the `data/report_paperformat_data.xml` file, but changing the orientation from portrait to landscape. The defined paper formats can be seen from the web client through the **Settings | Technical | Reporting | Paper Format** menu.

Now, we can use it in our report. The default paper format is defined in the company setup, but we can also specify the paper format to be used by a specific report. That is done using a `paperfomat` attribute in the report action.

Let's edit the action used to open our report, to add this attribute:

```
<report id="action_library_book_report"
    string="Library Books"
    model="library.book"
    report_type="qweb-pdf"
    name="library_app.report_library_book_template"
    paperformat="paperformat_euro_landscape"
/>
```

Enabling language translation in reports

To enable translations for a report, `translation` functions need to be called from a template, using a `<t t-call>` element with the `t-lang` attribute.

The `t-lang` attribute should evaluate to a language code, such as `es` or `en_US`. It needs the name of the field where the language to use can be found.

One way to do this is by using the current user's language. For this, we define an outer translation report that calls a report to translate, setting the source for the language in the `t-lang` attribute:

```
<report id="action_library_book_report_translated"
        string="Translated Library Books"
        model="library.book"
        report_type="qweb-pdf"
        name="library_app.report_library_book_translated"
        paperformat="paperformat_euro_landscape"
/>

<template id="report_library_book_translated">
  <t t-call="library_app.report_library_book_template"
     t-lang="user.lang" />
</template>
```

In this case, each book is rendered in the user's language, `user_id.lang`.

In some cases, we may need each record to be rendered in a specific language. For sales orders, we might want each one to be printed in the corresponding partner's preferred language. Suppose we wanted each book to be rendered using the corresponding publisher's language. The QWeb template for this case would look something like this:

```
<template id="report_library_book_translated">
  <t t-foreach="docs" t-as="o">
    <t t-call="library_app.report_library_book_template"
       t-lang="docs.publisher_id.lang" >
        <t t-set="docs" t-value="o" />
    </t>
  </t>
</template>
```

Here, we iterate through the records, and then for each one call the report template using the appropriate language, depending on the data in that record—in this case the publisher's language, `publisher_id.lang`.

Reports based on custom SQL

The report we built was based on a regular recordset. However, in some cases we need to transform or aggregate data in ways that are not easy or desirable to process in a QWeb template.

One approach for this is to write a SQL query to build the dataset we need, expose those results through a special model, and have our report work based on a recordset.

To showcase this, we will create a `reports/library_book_report.py` file with the following code:

```
from odoo import models, fields

class BookReport(models.Model):
    _name = 'library.book.report'
    _description = 'Book Report'
    _auto = False

    name = fields.Char('Title')
    publisher_id = fields.Many2one('res.partner')
    date_published = fields.Date()

    def init(self):
        self.env.cr.execute("""
            CREATE OR REPLACE VIEW library_book_report AS
            (SELECT *
            FROM library_book
            WHERE active = True)
        """)
```

For this file to be loaded, we need to add a `from . import reports` line to the module's top `__init__.py` file, and `from . import library_book_report` to the `reports/__init__.py` file.

The `_auto` attribute is used to disable the database table's automatic creation. We provide the alternative SQL for that in the model's `init()` method. It creates a database view, providing the data needed for the report. Our SQL query is quite simple, but the point is that we could use any valid SQL query for our view, possibly performing aggregations or computing additional data.

We still need to declare the model fields so that Odoo knows how to properly handle the data in each one.

Remember to also add security access to this new model; otherwise, we won't be able to see it. As usual, this is done by adding a line to `security/ir.model.access.csv`, such as the following one:

```
access_library_book_report,access_library_book_report,model_library_book_re
port,library_group_user,1,0,0,0
```

It is also worth noting that this is a new, different model, and does not not have the same record access rules as the library books model.

Next, we can add a new report based on this model, `reports/library_book_sql_report.xml`:

```
<odoo>

<report id="action_library_book_sql_report"
        string="Library Book SQL Report"
        model="library.book.report"
        report_type="qweb-html"
        name="library_app.report_library_book_sql"
/>

<template id="report_library_book_sql">
  <t t-call="web.html_container">
    <t t-call="web.external_layout">
      <div class="page">

        <!-- Report page content -->
        <table class="table table-striped">
          <tr>
            <th>Title</th>
            <th>Publisher</th>
            <th>Date</th>
          </tr>
          <t t-foreach="docs" t-as="o">
            <tr>
              <td class="col-xs-6">
                <span t-field="o.name" />
              </td>
              <td class="col-xs-3">
                <span t-field="o.publisher_id" />
              </td>
              <td class="col-xs-3">
                <span t-field="o.date_published"
                      t-options="{'widget': 'date'}" />
              </td>
            </tr>
```

```
        </t>
      </table>

    </div>
   </t>
  </t>
</template>

</odoo>
```

For even more complex cases, where we need to request input parameters from the user, we can use a different solution: a wizard. For this, we should create a transient model to hold the user's report parameters. Since they are generated by our code, we can implement whatever logic we may need.

It is strongly recommended to get inspiration from an existing similar report. A good example is **Leaves by Department** in the **Leaves** menu option. The corresponding transient model definition can be found at `addons/hr_holidays/wizard/hr_holidays_summary_employees.py`.

Summary

In the previous chapter, we learned about QWeb and how to use it to design a Kanban view. In this chapter, we learned about the QWeb report engine and the most important techniques when building reports with the QWeb templating language.

In the next chapter, we will keep working with QWeb, this time to build website pages. We will also learn to write web controllers, providing richer features for our web pages.

Further reading

This additional reference material complements the topics described in this chapter:

- The official Odoo documentation on the following:
    - Reports: `https://www.odoo.com/documentation/12.0/reference/reports.html`
    - QWeb language: `https://www.odoo.com/documentation/12.0/reference/qweb.html`
- The Bootstrap styling documentation: `https://getbootstrap.com/docs/4.1/getting-started/introduction/`

You can find additional learning resources on Bootstrap on the Packt Publishing tech page, `https://www.packtpub.com/tech/Bootstrap`.

13
Creating Website Frontend Features

Odoo began as a backend system, but the need for a frontend interface was soon felt. The early portal features, based on the same interface as the backend, were not very flexible or mobile-device-friendly.

To solve this gap, Odoo introduced new website features, adding a **Content Management System** (**CMS**) to the product. This allows us to build beautiful and effective frontends without the need to integrate a third-party CMS.

Here, we will learn how to develop our own frontend-oriented add-on modules, leveraging the website features provided by Odoo.

In this chapter, we will discuss the following topics:

- Learning project – the Library self-service
- Our first web page
- Building websites

Technical requirements

We will work with the `library_checkout` add-on module, last edited in Chapter 11, *Kanban Views and Client-Side QWeb*. The add-on module code can be found in the `ch11/` directory of the Git repository: `https://github.com/PacktPublishing/Odoo-12-Development-Essentials-Fourth-Edition`.

The code in this chapter can be found on the same repository, in the `ch13/` directory.

Learning project – the Library self-service

In this chapter, we will add self-service features for the Library members. Members can be assigned a login and access to their list of checkout requests. With this, we will be able to cover the essential techniques for website development: creating dynamic pages, passing parameters between pages, creating forms, and handling form data validation.

For these new library website features, we will create a new add-on module, `library_website`.

As usual, we will start by creating the add-on's `manifest` file. Create the `library_website/__manifest__.py` file with the following code:

```
{
  'name': 'Library Website',
  'description': 'Create and check book checkout requests.',
  'author': 'Daniel Reis',
  'depends': [
    'library_checkout'
  ],
  'data': [
    'security/ir.model.access.csv',
    'security/library_security.xml',
    'views/library_member.xml',
  ],
}
```

The website features will depend on `library_checkout`. We are not yet adding a dependency on the `website` core add-on module. The `website` add-on provides a useful framework to build full-featured websites, but for now we will explore the basic web capabilities that are built into the core framework, without using `website`.

We want Library Members to have a login to access their checkout requests on the Library website. For this, we will add a `user_id` field to the Library member model. This needs to be added to the model and view, before we start with the website work:

1. Add the `library_website/models/library_member.py` file:

```
from odoo import fields, models


class Member(models.Model):
    _inherit = 'library.member'
    user_id = fields.Many2one('res.users')
```

2. Add the `library_website/models/__init__.py` file:

```
from . import library_member
```

3. Add the `library_website/__init__.py` file:

```
from . import models
```

4. Add the `library_website/views/library_member.xml` file:

```xml
<?xml version="1.0"?>
<odoo>

  <record id="view_form_book" model="ir.ui.view">
    <field name="name">Book Form</field>
    <field name="model">library.book</field>
    <field name="arch" type="xml">
      <field name="card_number" position="after">
        <field name="user_id" />
      </field>
    </field>
  </record>

</odoo>
```

The users accessing these website pages will be portal users, without access to the backend menus. We need to set up the security access for this user group, otherwise they will get access errors when accessing the Library website features.

5. Add the `library_website/security/ir.model.access.csv` file, which adds read access to the Library models:

```
id,name,model_id:id,group_id:id,perm_read,perm_write,perm_creat
e,perm_unlink
access_book_portal,Book Portal
Access,library_app.model_library_book,base.group_portal,1,0,0,0
access_member_portal,Member Portal
Access,library_member.model_library_member,base.group_portal,1,
0,0,0
access_checkout_portal,Checkout Portal
Access,library_checkout.model_library_checkout,base.group_porta
l,1,0,0,0
access_stage_portal,Checkout Stage Portal
Access,library_checkout.model_library_checkout_stage,base.group
_portal,1,0,0,0
```

6. Add the `library_website/security/library_security.xml` file
   with **Record Rules** limiting the records portal users will be able to access:

```xml
<?xml version="1.0" ?>
<odoo>

    <data noupdate="1">

        <record id="member_portal_rule" model="ir.rule">
          <field name="name">Library Member Portal Access</field>
          <field name="model_id"
ref="library_member.model_library_member"/>
          <field name="domain_force">
              [('user_id', '=', user.id)]
          </field>
          <field name="groups"
eval="[(4,ref('base.group_portal'))]"/>
        </record>

        <record id="checkout_portal_rule" model="ir.rule">
          <field name="name">Library Checkout Portal Access</field>
          <field name="model_id"
              ref="library_checkout.model_library_checkout"/>
          <field name="domain_force">
              [('member_id.user_id', '=', user.id)]
          </field>
          <field name="groups"
              eval="[(4,ref('base.group_portal'))]"/>
        </record>
    </data>

</odoo>
```

`base.group_portal` is the identifier of the portal user group. When creating Portal users, we should set their **User Type** as Portal, instead of **Internal User**. This will make them belong to the portal user group and inherit the access permissions we just defined:

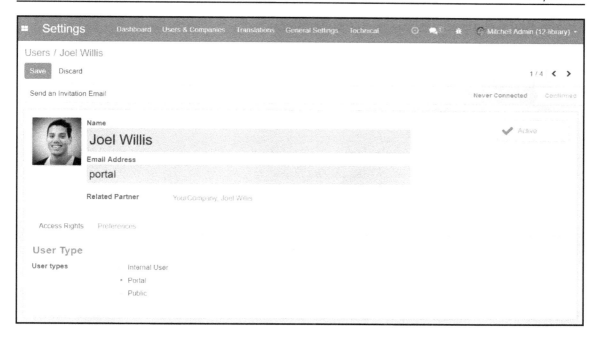

Once we create a portal user for a Library Member, we should then use it on the **User** field that we added to the Member form. That login will be able to access the corresponding member's checkout requests.

 It is safer to implement access security on the Model layer, using ACLs and **Record Rules**, instead of relying on the controller logic for that. This is because an attacker might be able to use an RPC call to access the Model API directly, bypassing the web controllers.

With this, we are ready to start implementing the Library website features. But first, we will have a brief introduction the basic website concepts, using a simple **Hello World** web page.

Our first web page

To get us started with the basics of Odoo web development, we will first implement a simple **Hello World** web page showcasing the basic concepts and techniques. Imaginative, right?

For our first web page, we only need a **controller** object.

We will begin adding it in the `controllers/hello.py` file:

1. Add the following line to the `library_website/__init__.py` file:

   ```
   from . import models
   from . import controllers
   ```

2. Add the `library_website/controllers/__init__.py` file with the following line:

   ```
   from . import hello
   ```

3. Add the actual file for the controller, `library_website/controllers/hello.py`, with the following code:

   ```
   from odoo import http

   class Hello(http.Controller):

       @http.route('/helloworld', auth='public')
       def helloworld(self):
           return('<h1>Hello World!</h1>')
   ```

The `odoo.http` module provides the Odoo web-related features. Our controllers, responsible for page rendering, should be objects that inherit from the `odoo.http.Controller` class. The actual name used for the class is not important; here, we chose to use `Hello()`. A popular choice is `Main()`.

Inside the `Controller` class, we have methods that match URL routes. These are expected to do some processing and then return a result, which is usually the HTML page to return to be user's web browser. The `odoo.http.route` decorator is what binds a method to a URL route. Our example uses the `/helloworld` route.

Once we install the new `library_website` module, we can use our web browser to open `http://localhost:8069/helloworld`, and we should be greeted with a **Hello World** message.

In this example, the processing performed by the method is trivial—it just returns a text string with the HTML markup for the **Hello World** message.

Accessing the controller with the simple URL used here and not specifying a target database can fail if there are multiple databases available on the same Odoo instance. This can be avoided by making sure the -d or --db-filter startup configurations are set, as advised in Chapter 2, *Preparing the Development Environment*.

You probably noticed the auth='public' argument used in the route decorator. This is needed for the page to be available to non-authenticated users. If we remove it, only authenticated users can see the page. If no session is active, the login screen will be shown instead.

The auth='public' parameter actually means that the request will use the special public user to run the web controller for any visitor that is not already authenticated. If they are, the loggedin user is used, instead of public.

Hello World using a QWeb template

Using Python strings to build HTML will get boring very fast. QWeb templates can do a much better job. So, let's write an improved version of our **Hello World** web page, using a template.

QWeb templates are added through XML data files, and technically they are just a type of view, alongside form or tree views. They are even stored in the same technical Model, ir.ui.view.

As usual, data files to be loaded must be declared in the manifest file, so edit the library_website/__manifest__.py file to add the key:

```
'data': [
  'security/ir.model.access.csv',
  'security/library_security.xml',
  'views/library_member.xml',
  'views/helloworld_template.xml',
],
```

Then, add the actual data file, `views/helloworld_template.xml`, with the following content:

```
<odoo>
  <template id="helloworld"
            name="Hello World Template">
    <h1>Hello again World !</h1>
  </template>
</odoo>
```

The `<template>` element is actually a shortcut to declare that `<record>` is loading data into the `ir.ui.view` Model, with `type="qweb"`.

Now, we need to modify our `Controller` method to use this template:

```
from odoo import http
from odoo.http import request

class Hello(http.Controller):

    @http.route('/helloworld', auth='public')
    def helloworld(self, **kwargs):
        return request.render('library_website.helloworld')
```

Template rendering is provided by the `request` object, through the `render()` function.

Notice that we added `**kwargs` to the method arguments. With this, any additional parameters provided by the HTTP request, such as a query string or `POST` parameters, can be captured by the `kwargs` dictionary. This makes our method more robust, since providing unexpected parameters will not cause it to produce errors.

HelloCMS!

Let's make this even more interesting, and create our own simple CMS. For this, we can have the route expect a template name (a page) in the URL and then just render it. We could then dynamically create web pages and have them served by our CMS.

It turns out that this is really easy to do:

```
@http.route('/hellocms/<page>', auth='public')
def hello(self, page, **kwargs):
    return http.request.render(page)
```

The `page` argument should match a Template External ID. If you open `http://localhost:8069/hellocms/library_website.helloworld` in your web browser, you should see our **Hello World** web page.

In fact, the built-in `website` module provides CMS features, including a more robust implementation of this, at the `/page` endpoint route.

 In `werkzeug` jargon, the endpoint is an alias of the route, and is represented by its static part (without the placeholders). For example, for our simple CMS example, the endpoint is `/hellocms`.

Most of the time, we want our pages to be integrated into the Odoo website. So, moving forward, all of our examples will be working with the `website` add-on module.

Building websites

The pages given by the previous examples are not integrated into the Odoo website; we have no page footer or site menu. The Odoo `website` add-on module conveniently provides all of these features so that we don't have to worry about them ourselves.

To use the website features, we need the `website` add-on module installed in our work instance. We should add it as a dependency to the `library_website` add-on module. The `__manifest__.py` key `depends` should look like this:

```
'depends': [
    'library_checkout',
    'website',
],
```

To use the website features, we also need to introduce some modifications on the Controller and QWeb template.

Controllers can have an the additional `website=True` argument on the route:

```
@http.route('/helloworld', auth='public', website=True)
def helloworld(self, **kwargs):
    return request.render('library_website.helloworld')
```

This `website=True` parameter is not strictly required for integration with the `website` module. We can use the website layout in our template views without adding it. However, it does make a few features available that can then be used by our web controller:

- The route will automatically become multilingual and attempt to autodetect the closest language to use from the website's installed languages. It's worth noting that this can cause rerouting and redirections.
- Any exceptions thrown by the controller will be handled by the website code, and a friendlier error page will be shown to the visitors, instead of the default error code.
- The `request.website` variable, with a browse record of the current website record, will become available on the request.
- The `public` user for any `auth=public` route will be the public user selected on the website configurations in the backend. This might be relevant for matters of localization, timezones, and so on.

If none of the preceding features is relevant for the web controller, the `website=True` parameter can be omitted. However, most website QWeb templates require data made available with `website=True`, such as the footer company information, so chances are it will be needed.

 The website data passed into the QWeb evaluation context is set in the `_prepare_qcontext` method of the `website/model/ir_ui_view.py` file.

To add the website's general layout to our templates, we should wrap our QWeb/HTML with a `t-call="website.layout"` directive, like this:

```
<template id="helloworld"
          name="Hello World" Template>
  <t t-call="website.layout">
    <h1>Hello World!</h1>
  </t>
</template>
```

`t-call` runs the QWeb template, `website.layout`, and passes to it the XML inside this `t-call` node. `website.layout` is designed to render the full website page—with menus, headers, and footers—and place passed content in the appropriate main area.

With this, the **Hello World!** example we used before should now be shown inside an Odoo website page.

Adding CSS and JavaScript assets

Our website pages might need some additional CSS or JavaScript assets. This aspect of the web pages is managed by the website, so we need a way to tell it to also use our files.

We will use some CSS to add a simple strikeout effect. For that, create the `library_website/static/src/css/library.css` file with the following content:

```css
.text-strikeout {
    text-decoration: line-through;
}
```

Next, we need to have it included in the website pages. This is done by adding them in the `website.assets_frontend` template, which is responsible for loading website-specific assets. Add the `library_website/views/website_assets.xml` data file to extend that template:

```xml
<odoo>
  <template id="assets_frontend"
    name="library_website_assets"
    inherit_id="website.assets_frontend">
      <xpath expr="." position="inside">
        <link rel="stylesheet" type="text/css"
              href="/library_website/static/src/css/library.css"/>
      </xpath>
  </template>
</odoo>
```

We will soon be using this new `text-strikeout` style class. Of course, JavaScript assets can also be added using a similar approach.

The checkout-list controller

Now that we have gone through the basics, let's work on our checkout list. We want to have a `/checkout` URL that shows us a web page with a list of checkouts.

For that, we need a controller method to prepare the data to present and a QWeb template to present it to the user.

Add the `library_website/controllers/main.py` file to the module, with the following code:

```
from odoo import http
from odoo.http import request

class Main(http.Controller):

    @http.route('/checkouts', auth='user', website=True)
    def checkouts(self, **kwargs):
        Checkout = request.env['library.checkout']
        checkouts = Checkout.search([])
        return request.render(
            'library_website.index',
            {'docs': checkouts})
```

The controller retrieves the data to be used and makes it available to the rendered template. In this case, the controller requires an authenticated session, since the route has the `auth='user'` attribute. This is the default behavior, and it's a good practice to explicitly state that a user session is required.

The logged-in user is stored in the `Environment` object, available from `request.env`. The `search()` statement uses this to filter out the appropriate checkout records.

For controllers that don't require authenticated access, the data that can be read is very limited. In those cases, we will often run part of the code in an elevated access context. For this, we can use the `sudo()` Model method; it changes the security context to the internal superuser, removing most restrictions.

While this gives us power, it also brings security risks and should be used with care. Particular attention should be given to the validation of input parameters and to the actions performed with the elevated access made. It is a good idea to keep the use of the `sudo()` recordset strictly limited to the minimum operations needed.

Going back to our code, it ends with the `request.render()` method. As before, we pass the identifier for the QWeb template to render, and a dictionary with the context available for template evaluation. In this case, we make the `docs` variable available in the template, which contains the recordset with the checkout records to render.

The checkout QWeb template

The QWeb template is added using a data file. We can use the existing `library_website/views/checkout_template.xml` data file for that and add the following code:

```
<odoo>
<template id="index" name="Checkout List">
  <t t-call="website.layout">
    <div id="wrap" class="container">
      <h1>Checkouts</h1>

      <!-- List of Checkouts -->
      <t t-foreach="docs" t-as="doc">
        <div class="row">
          <input type="checkbox" disabled="True"
            t-att-checked="'checked' if doc.stage_id.fold else None" />
          <a t-attf-href="/checkout/{{slug(doc)}}">
            <h3 t-field="doc.request_date"
              t-att-class="
                  'text-strikeout'
                  if doc.stage_id.fold
                  else ''" />
          </a>
        </div>
      </t>

    </div>
  </t>
</template>
</odoo>
```

The preceding code uses the `t-foreach` directive to iterate through the `docs` recordset.

We have a checkbox input and want it to be checked if the checkout is completed. In HTML, a checkbox is checked depending on whether it has a `checked` attribute. For this, we use the `t-att-NAME` directive to dynamically render the `checked` attribute depending on an expression. When the expression evaluates to `None` (or any other false value), QWeb will omit the attribute, which is convenient in this case.

When rendering the task name, the `t-attf` directive is used to dynamically create the URL to open the detail form for each specific task. We used the special `slug()` function to generate a human-readable URL for each record. The link won't work for now, since we haven't created the corresponding controller yet.

On each checkout record, we also use the `t-att` directive to apply the `texte-strikeout` style if the checkout is in a final state.

The checkout detail page

Each item in the checkout list has a link to the corresponding detail page. We should implement a controller for those links and a QWeb template for their presentation. At this point, this should be a straightforward exercise.

In the `library_website/controllers/main.py` file, add the the following method:

```
#class Main(http.Controller):
#...
    @http.route('/checkout/<model("library.checkout"):doc>',
                auth="user",  # default, but made explicit here
                website=True)
    def checkout(self, doc, **kwargs):
        return http.request.render(
            'library_website.checkout',
            {'doc': doc})
```

Notice that the route is using a placeholder with the `model("library.checkout")` converter, which will be mapped to the method's `doc` argument. It captures a checkout identifier from the URL, either a simple ID number or a slug representation, and converts it into the corresponding browse-record object.

For the QWeb template, we should add the following code to the `library_website/views/checkout_template.xml` data file:

```
<template id="checkout" name="Checkout Form">
<t t-call="website.layout">
  <div id="wrap" class="container">
    <h1 t-field="doc.request_date" />
    <h5>Member: <span t-field="doc.member_id" /></h5>
    <h5>Stage: <span t-field="doc.stage_id" /></h5>
  </div>
</t>
</template>
```

A noteworthy aspect here is the use of the `<t t-field>` element. It handles the proper representation of the field value, just like in the backend. It correctly presents date values and many-to-one values, for example.

Summary

You should now have a good understanding of the essentials of website features. We have seen how to use web controllers and QWeb templates to render dynamic web pages. We then learned how to use the website add-on and create our own pages for it. Finally, we introduced the website forms add-on that helped us create a web form. These should provide us with the core skills needed to create website features.

Now that we have seen the essentials of developing the main Odoo components, it's time to learn more about how to deploy our Odoo server for production use.

Further reading

These are additional reference materials that complement the topics described in this chapter, found in the official Odoo documentation:

- Web controllers: `https://www.odoo.com/documentation/12.0/reference/http.html`
- QWeb language: `https://www.odoo.com/documentation/12.0/reference/qweb.html`
- Javascript API reference: `https://www.odoo.com/documentation/12.0/reference/javascript_reference.html`
- Here is the Bootstrap styling documentation: `https://getbootstrap.com/docs/4.1/getting-started/introduction/`
- You can find additional learning resources for Bootstrap on the Packt Publishing technical page: `https://www.packtpub.com/tech/Bootstrap`

14
Deploying and Maintaining Production Instances

In this chapter, you'll learn the basics of preparing an Odoo server for use in a production environment.

Setting up and maintaining servers is a non-trivial topic in itself and should be done by specialists. The information given here is not enough to ensure an average user can create a resilient and secure environment that hosts sensitive data and services.

The goal for this chapter is to introduce the most important configuration aspects and best practices specific to Odoo deployment, so that system administrators can better prepare their Odoo server hosts.

Still, after following this chapter, the reader will be able to set up a reasonably secure Odoo server, good enough for low-profile production use. The recipes given in this chapter aren't the only valid way to deploy Odoo, either; other approaches or variants are also possible.

In this chapter, we'll discuss the following topics:

- Installing Odoo from source code, including the following:
    - Installing dependencies
    - Preparing a dedicated system user
    - Installing from source code
    - Setting up the configuration file
    - Multiprocessing workers
- Setting up Odoo as a system service, including the following:
    - Creating a `systemd` service
    - Creating an Upstart or `sysvinit` service
    - Checking the Odoo service from the command line

- Setting up an `nginx` reverse proxy
- Configuring and enforcing HTTPS, including the following :
  - Creating a self-signed SSL certificate
  - Configuring HTTPS access on `nginx`
  - Caching static content
- Server and module updates, including the following:
  - Creating a staging environment
  - Updating Odoo source code

Technical requirements

This chapter doesn't require any previous code. The code and scripts used here can be found in the `ch14/` directory of the Git repository at `https://github.com/PacktPublishing/Odoo-12-Development-Essentials-Fourth-Edition`.

Installing Odoo from source code

Odoo has a Debian or Ubuntu package available for installation. Using one will provide a working server process that automatically starts on system boot. This installation process is straightforward, and you can find all you'll need at `https://nightly.odoo.com`. You can also find the `rpm` builds for CentOS and the `.exe` installers there.

While this is an easy and convenient way to install Odoo, most integrators prefer to deploy and run version-controlled source code. This provides better control over what is deployed and makes it easier to manage changes and fixes once in production.

Installing dependencies

When using a Debian distribution, by default your login is `root` with administrator powers, and your Command Prompt shows #. On Ubuntu systems, the `root` account is disabled, and the initial user configured during the installation process is a **sudoer**, meaning it's allowed to use the `sudo` command to run commands with `root` privileges.

First, we should update the package index and then perform an upgrade to ensure that all installed programs are up to date, as follows:

```
$ sudo apt update
$ sudo apt upgrade -y
```

Next, we'll install the PostgreSQL database and make our user a database superuser with the following code:

```
$ sudo apt install postgresql -y
$ sudo su -c "createuser -s $USER" postgres
```

We'll be running Odoo from source, but before that, we need to install the required dependencies. The following are the Debian packages required:

```
$ sudo apt-get install git python3-dev python3-pip -y
$ sudo apt install build-essential libxslt-dev \
libzip-dev libldap2-dev libsasl2-dev libssl-dev
```

We should not forget to install wkhtmltox either, which is needed to print reports, as follows:

```
$ wget "https://github.com/wkhtmltopdf/wkhtmltopdf/releases/download"\
"/0.12.5/wkhtmltox-0.12.5_linux-bionic-amd64.deb" -O /tmp/wkhtml.deb
$ sudo dpkg -i /tmp/wkhtml.deb
$ sudo apt-get -fy install  # Fix dependency errors
```

Note that it's possible for the package installation to report a missing dependencies error. In this case, the last command will force the installation of those dependencies and correctly finish the installation.

Now we're only missing the Python packages required by Odoo. Many of them also have Debian or Ubuntu system packages. The official Debian installation package uses them, and you can find the package names in the Odoo source code, in the debian/control file.

However, these Python dependencies can also be installed directly from the **Python Package Index** (**PyPI**). This is a more user-friendly approach for those who prefer to install Odoo in virtualenv. The required package list is in Odoo's requirements.txt file, as is usual for Python-based projects. We can install them with the following commands:

```
$ wget https://raw.githubusercontent.com/odoo/odoo/12.0/requirements.txt
$ sudo -H pip3 install -r requirements.txt
```

On Ubuntu 18.04, the last command may print a red warning about uninstalling PyYAML and pySerial in case any older versions are already installed on your system through packages. This warning can be safely ignored.

Now that we have all dependencies, the database server, system packages, and Python packages installed, we can install Odoo.

Preparing a dedicated system user

A good security practice is to run Odoo using a dedicated user, with no special privileges on the system.

We need to create the system and database users for that, with the following code:

```
$ sudo adduser --disabled-password --gecos "Odoo" odoo
$ sudo su -c "createuser odoo" postgres
$ createdb --owner=odoo odoo-prod
```

Here, `odoo` is the username and `odoo-prod` is the name of the database supporting our Odoo instance.

The `odoo` user was made the owner of the `odoo-prod` database. This means that it has create and drop privileges over that database, including the ability to drop a full database. If you're running a multi-tenant server, you should create an `odoo`—like specific system user for each tenant.

 Odoo is designed to work correctly even if a system user is not the owner of a database. While it can complicate setup, a security-enhancing good practice is to have a master system user as the owner of databases and to create a specific system user for each of the instances to run on the server without superuser privileges.

Note that these are regular users without any administration privileges. A home directory is automatically created for the new system user. In this example, it's `/home/odoo`, and the user can refer to their own home directory with the ~ shortcut symbol. We'll use this for the user's Odoo-specific configurations and files.

We can open a session as this user using the following command:

```
$ sudo su odoo
$ exit
```

The `exit` command terminates that session and returns to the original user.

Installing from the source code

Sooner or later, your server will need upgrades and patches. A version control repository can be of great help when the time comes. We use `git` to get our code from a repository, just like we did when installing the development environment.

Next, we'll impersonate the `odoo` user and download the code into its home directory, as follows:

```
$ sudo su odoo
$ git clone https://github.com/odoo/odoo.git /home/odoo/odoo-12 \
-b 12.0 --depth=1
```

The `-b` option ensures that we get the right branch, and the `--depth=1` option ignores the change history and retrieves only the latest code revision, making the download much smaller and faster.

 `git` is often an invaluable tool when managing versions of your Odoo deployments. Note, however, that we have only scratched the surface of what can be done to manage code versions in this book. If you're not already familiar with `git`, it's worth learning more about it. A good starting point is `http://git-scm.com/doc`.

By now, we should have everything needed to run Odoo from source. We can check whether it starts correctly and then exit from the dedicated user's session with the following command:

```
$ /home/odoo/odoo-12/odoo-bin --version
Odoo Server 12.0
$ exit
```

Next, we'll set up some system-level files and directories that will be used by the system service.

Setting up the configuration file

Adding the `--save` option when starting an Odoo server saves the configuration used in the `~/.odoorc` file. We can use this file as a starting point for our server configuration, which will be stored at `/etc/odoo`, as shown in the following code:

```
$ sudo su -c "~/odoo-12/odoo-bin -d odoo-prod" \
" --db-filter='^odoo-prod$' --without-demo=all" \
" -i base --save --stop-after-init" odoo
```

This code will also contain the configuration parameters to be used by our server instance.

 The former .openerp_serverrc configuration file is still supported and is used if found. This can cause some confusion when setting up Odoo 10 or later in a machine that was also used to run older Odoo versions. In this case, you may find that the --save option updates the .openerp_serverrc file instead of .odoorc.

Next, we need to place the config file in the expected location for system configuration files, the /etc directory, as follows:

```
$ sudo mkdir /etc/odoo
$ sudo cp /home/odoo/.odoorc /etc/odoo/odoo.conf
$ sudo chown -R odoo /etc/odoo
$ sudo chmod u=r,g=rw,o=r /etc/odoo/odoo.conf   # for extra hardening
```

The last command from the preceding block is optional, but it improves your security; it ensures that the user running the Odoo process can read but can't change the configuration file. With this, you won't be able to change the master database password, but for a production service this should not be a problem, as the web database manager should be disabled with the list_db=False server configuration.

We also need to create the directory where the Odoo service will store its log files. This is expected to be somewhere inside /var/log, as follows:

```
$ sudo mkdir /var/log/odoo
$ sudo chown odoo /var/log/odoo
```

Now, let's edit the configuration file and ensure that a few important parameters are configured with the following command:

```
$ sudo nano /etc/odoo/odoo.conf
```

The following are suggested values for some of the most important parameters:

```
[options]
addons_path = /home/odoo/odoo-12/odoo/addons,/home/odoo/odoo-12/addons
admin_passwd = False
db_name = odoo-prod
dbfilter = ^odoo-prod$
http_port = 8069
list_db = False
logfile = /var/log/odoo/odoo-server.log
proxy_mode = True
without_demo = all
workers = 6
```

Let's explain them:

- `addons_path` is a comma-separated list of the paths where add-on modules will be looked up. It's read from left to right, with the leftmost directories considered a higher priority.
- `admin_passwd` is the master password used to access the web client database management functions. It's critical to set this with a strong password or, even better, to set it to `False` to deactivate the function.
- `db_name` is the database instance to initialize during the server startup sequence.
- `dbfilter` is a filter for the databases to be made accessible. It's a Python-interpreted regex expression. For the user to not be prompted to select a database and for unauthenticated URLs to work properly, it should be set with `^dbname$`, for example, `dbfilter=^odoo-prod$`. It supports the `%h` and `%d` placeholders, which are replaced by the HTTP request hostname and subdomain name.
- `http_port` is the port number at which the server will listen. By default, port `8069` is used.
- `list_db = False` blocks database listing, both at the **Remote Procedure Calls (RPC)** level and in the UI, and it blocks the database management screens and the underlying RPC functions.
- `logfile` is where the server log should be written. For system services, the expected location is somewhere inside `/var/log`. If left empty, the log prints to standard output instead.
- `proxy_mode` should be set to `True` when Odoo is accessed behind a reverse proxy, as we'll do.
- `without_demo` should be set to `all` in production environments so that new databases don't have demo data on them.
- `workers` with a value of two or more enables the multiprocessing mode. We'll discuss this in more detail shortly.

 The `http_port` parameter was introduced in Odoo 11 to replace the `xmlrpc_port` parameter, which was used in the previous versions but has since been deprecated.

From a security point of view, the `admin_passwd=False` and `list_db=False` options are particularly important. They block web access to the database management features, and should be set in any production- or internet-facing Odoo server.

The following parameters can also be helpful:

- `data_dir` is the path where session data and attachment files are stored; remember to keep backups here.
- `http_interface` sets the addresses that will be listened to. By default, it listens to `0.0.0.0`, but when using a reverse proxy, it can be set to `127.0.0.1` in order to respond to local requests only. It was introduced in Odoo 11 to replace the deprecated `xmlrpc_interface` parameter.

We can check the effect of the settings made by running the server with the `-c` or `--config` option, as follows:

```
$ sudo su -c "~/odoo-12/odoo-bin -c /etc/odoo/odoo.conf" odoo
```

Running Odoo with the preceding settings won't display any output to the console, since changes are written to the log file defined in the configuration file.

To follow what is going on with the server, we need to open another Terminal window and run the following command:

```
$ sudo tail -f /var/log/odoo/odoo-server.log
```

In case we want to send the log output back to the standard output, the best solution is to use a copy of the configuration file without the `logfile` option set.

> To run multiple Terminal sessions on the same Terminal window, you can use multiplexing applications such as `tmux` or GNU Screen. You also might like to try **Byobu** (`https://help.ubuntu.com/community/Byobu`), which provides a nice user interface on top of GNU Screen or Tmux.

Multiprocessing workers

A production instance is expected to handle a significant workload. By default, the server runs one process and can use only one CPU core for processing, because of the Python language **Global Interpreter Lock (GIL)**. However, a multiprocess mode is available so that concurrent requests can be handled, taking advantage of multiple cores.

The `workers=N` option sets the number of worker processes to use. As a guideline, you can try setting it to `1+2*P`, where `P` is the number of processor cores. The best setting to use needs to be tuned for each case, as it depends on the server load and what other load-intensive services are running, such as PostgreSQL.

It's better to set workers that are too high for the load than too low. The minimum should be six due to the parallel connections used by most browsers, and the maximum is generally limited by the amount of RAM on the machine.

As a rule of thumb on normal usage patterns, the Odoo server should be able to handle `(1+2*P)*6` simultaneous users.

There are a few `limit-` configuration parameters that can be used to tune workers. Workers are recycled when they reach these limits, and the corresponding process is stopped and a new one is started. This protects the server from memory leaks and from particular processes overloading the server resources.

The official documentation already provides good advice on the tuning of the worker parameters, and you may refer to it for more detail at `https://www.odoo.com/documentation/12.0/setup/deploy.html`.

Setting up Odoo as a system service

Now we need to set up Odoo as a system service and have it started automatically when the system boots.

In Ubuntu or Debian, the `init` system is responsible for starting services. Historically, Debian (and derived operating systems) has used `sysvinit`, and Ubuntu has used a compatible system called `Upstart`. Recently, however, this has changed, and the `init` system used in both the latest Debian and Ubuntu editions is `systemd`.

This means that there are now two different ways to install a system service, and you need to pick the correct one depending on the version of your operating system.

On Ubuntu 16.04 and later, you should be using `systemd`. However, older versions are still used in many cloud providers, so there is a good chance that you might need to use it.

To check whether `systemd` is used in your system, try the following command:

```
$ man init
```

This command opens the documentation for the currently `init` system in use, so you're able to check what is being used.

Ubuntu on Windows Subsystem for Linux (WSL) is an environment good enough for development only, but may have some quirks and is entirely inappropriate for running production servers. At the time of writing, our tests revealed that while `man init` identifies the `init` system as `systemd`, installing a `systemd` service doesn't work, while installing a `sysvinit` service does.

Creating a systemd service

If the operating system you're using is recent, such as Debian 8 or Ubuntu 16.04, you should be using `systemd` for the `init` system.

To add a new service to the system, simply create a file describing it. Create a `/lib/systemd/system/odoo.service` file with the following content:

```
[Unit]
Description=Odoo
After=postgresql.service

[Service]
Type=simple
User=odoo
Group=odoo
ExecStart=/home/odoo/odoo-12/odoo-bin -c /etc/odoo/odoo.conf

[Install]
WantedBy=multi-user.target
```

The Odoo source code includes a sample `odoo.service` file inside the `debian/` directory. Instead of creating a new file, you can copy it and then make the required changes. At the very least, the `ExecStart` option should be changed according to your setup.

Next, we need to register the new service with the following code:

```
$ sudo systemctl enable odoo.service
```

To start this new service, use the following command:

```
$ sudo systemctl start odoo
```

To check its status, run the following command:

```
$ sudo systemctl status odoo
```

Finally, if you want to stop it, use the following command:

```
$ sudo systemctl stop odoo
```

Creating an Upstart or sysvinit service

If you're using an older operating system, such as Debian 7 or Ubuntu 15.04, chances are your system is `sysvinit` or `Upstart`. For the purpose of creating a system service, both should behave in the same way. Some cloud **Virtual Private Server** (**VPS**) services are still based on older Ubuntu images, so this might be aware of this scenario in case you encounter it when deploying your Odoo server.

The Odoo source code includes an `init` script used for the Debian packaged distribution. We can use it as our service `init` script with minor modifications, as follows:

```
$ sudo cp /home/odoo/odoo-12/debian/init /etc/init.d/odoo
$ sudo chmod +x /etc/init.d/odoo
```

At this point, you might want to check the content of the `init` script. The key parameters are assigned to variables at the top of the file, as illustrated in the following example:

```
PATH=/sbin:/bin:/usr/sbin:/usr/bin:/usr/local/bin
DAEMON=/usr/bin/odoo
NAME=odoo
DESC=odoo
CONFIG=/etc/odoo/odoo.conf
LOGFILE=/var/log/odoo/odoo-server.log
PIDFILE=/var/run/${NAME}.pid
USER=odoo
```

These variables should be adequate, so we'll prepare the rest of the setup with their default values in mind. However, you can of course change them to better suit your needs.

The USER variable is the system user under which the server will run. We have already created the expected `odoo` user.

The DAEMON variable is the path to the server executable. Our executable used to start Odoo is in a different location, but we can create the following symbolic link to it:

```
$ sudo ln -s /home/odoo/odoo-12/odoo-bin /usr/bin/odoo
$ sudo chown -h odoo /usr/bin/odoo
```

The CONFIG variable is the configuration file we need to use. In a previous section, we created a configuration file in the default expected location, /etc/odoo/odoo.conf.

Finally, the LOGFILE variable is the directory where log files should be stored. The expected directory is /var/log/odoo, which we created when we defined the configuration file.

Now we should be able to start and stop our Odoo service, as follows:

```
$ sudo /etc/init.d/odoo start
Starting odoo: ok
```

Stopping the service is done in a similar way with the following command:

```
$ sudo /etc/init.d/odoo stop
Stopping odoo: ok
```

In Ubuntu, the service command can also be used, as follows:

```
$ sudo service odoo start
$ sudo service odoo status
$ sudo service odoo stop
```

Now we need to make the service start automatically on system boot; this can be done with the following code:

```
$ sudo update-rc.d odoo defaults
```

After this, when we reboot our server, the Odoo service should start automatically and with no errors. It's a good time to verify that all is working as expected.

Checking the Odoo service from the command line

At this point, we can confirm whether our Odoo instance is up and responding to requests as expected.

If Odoo is running properly, we should be able to get a response from it and see no errors in the log file. We can check whether Odoo is responding to HTTP requests inside the server by using the following command:

```
$ curl http://localhost:8069
<html><head><script>window.location = '/web' +
location.hash;</script></head></html>
```

In addition, to see what is in the log file, use the following command:

```
$ sudo less /var/log/odoo/odoo-server.log
```

You can also follow what is being added to the log file live, using `tail -f` as follows:

```
$ sudo tail -f /var/log/odoo/odoo-server.log
```

Setting up an nginx reverse proxy

While Odoo itself can serve web pages, it's strongly recommended that there is a reverse proxy positioned in front of it. A reverse proxy acts as an intermediary that manages the traffic between clients sending requests and the Odoo servers responding to them. Using a reverse proxy has several benefits.

On the security side, it can do the following:

- Handle (and enforce) HTTPS protocols to encrypt traffic
- Hide the internal network characteristics
- Act as an application firewall, limiting the URLs accepted for processing

Also, on the performance side, it can provide the following significant improvements:

- Cached static content, hence reducing the load on the Odoo servers
- Compressed content to speed up loading time
- Act as a load balancer, distributing load between several servers

Apache is a popular choice when considering a reverse proxy, although `nginx` is a recent alternative with good technical arguments. Here, we'll choose to use `nginx` as a reverse proxy and show you how it can be used to perform the security and performance-side functions we've discussed.

First, we should install `nginx`. We want it to listen on the default HTTP ports, so we should ensure they aren't already taken by another service. Performing this command should result in an error, as follows:

```
$ curl http://localhost
curl: (7) Failed to connect to localhost port 80: Connection refused
```

If an error is not received, you should disable or remove the service to allow `nginx` to use those ports. For example, to stop an existing Apache server, use `sudo service apache2 stop`.

Better yet is the option of removing it from your system or reconfiguring it to listen on another port, so that the HTTP and HTTPS ports (`80` and `443`) are free to be used by `nginx`.

Once this process is complete, we can install `nginx`, which is done as follows:

```
$ sudo apt-get install nginx
$ sudo service nginx start  # start nginx, if not already started
```

To confirm that `nginx` is working correctly, we should see a **Welcome to nginx** page when visiting the server address with a browser or using `curl http://localhost` inside our server.

The `nginx` configuration files follow the same approach as Apache's—they are stored in `/etc/nginx/available-sites/` and are activated by adding a symbolic link in `/etc/nginx/enabled-sites/`. Note that you should also disable the default configuration provided by the `nginx` installation, as follows:

```
$ sudo rm /etc/nginx/sites-enabled/default
$ sudo touch /etc/nginx/sites-available/odoo
$ sudo ln -s /etc/nginx/sites-available/odoo \
/etc/nginx/sites-enabled/odoo
```

Using an editor such as `nano` or `vi`, edit the `nginx` configuration file as follows:

```
$ sudo nano /etc/nginx/sites-available/odoo
```

A basic `nginx` configuration file for an Odoo server looks like the following example:

```
upstream odoo {
  server 127.0.0.1:8069;
}
upstream odoochat {
  server 127.0.0.1:8072;
}
server {
  listen 80;

  # Add Headers for odoo proxy mode
  proxy_set_header X-Forwarded-Host $host;
  proxy_set_header X-Forwarded-For $proxy_add_x_forwarded_for;
  proxy_set_header X-Forwarded-Proto $scheme;
  proxy_set_header X-Real-IP $remote_addr;
```

```
# log
access_log /var/log/nginx/odoo.access.log;
error_log /var/log/nginx/odoo.error.log;
# Redirect longpoll requests to odoo longpolling port
location /longpolling {
  proxy_pass http://odoochat;
}
# Redirect requests to odoo backend server
location / {
  proxy_redirect off;
  proxy_pass http://odoo;
}

# common gzip
gzip_types text/css text/scss text/plain text/xml application/xml
application/json application/javascript;
gzip on;
}
```

First, we add `upstream` configuration sections for the Odoo services, listening at the default ports, 8069 and 8072. The 8069 port serves the web client and RPC requests, and 8072 serves the long polling requests used to support Odoo instant messaging features when using multiprocessing workers.

The `nginx` should receive traffic on the default HTTP port, 80, and redirect it to the `upstream odoo` services. This is defined in the `server` configuration section. Traffic for the `/longpolling` address is passed on to `upstream odoochat`, and the remaining traffic is passed on to `upstream odoo`.

Here, we also add some information to the request header that will let the Odoo backend service know that it's being proxied.

For security reasons, it's important for Odoo to ensure that the `proxy_mode` parameter is set to `True`. The reason for this is that when `nginx` acts as a proxy, all requests will appear to come from the server itself instead of the remote IP address; setting the `X-Forwarded-For` header in the proxy and enabling `--proxy-mode` solves that. However, enabling `--proxy-mode` without forcing the header at proxy-level will allow anyone to spoof their remote address.

At the end of the configuration file, we can see a couple of `gzip`-related instructions. These enable the compression of some files, improving performance.

To test whether the edited configuration is correct, use the following command:

```
$ sudo nginx -t
nginx: the configuration file /etc/nginx/nginx.conf syntax is ok
nginx: configuration file /etc/nginx/nginx.conf test is successful
```

If you find errors, verify that the configuration file is correctly typed. A common problem is for the default HTTP to be taken by another service, such as Apache or the default `nginx` website, so double-check the instructions given to ensure that this is not the case before restarting `nginx`. After this process is complete, `nginx` can reload the new configuration, as follows:

```
$ sudo /etc/init.d/nginx reload
```

If your operating system is using `systemd`, the appropriate version for the preceding command is as follows:

```
$ sudo systemctl reload nginx
```

We can now confirm that `nginx` is redirecting traffic to the backend Odoo server, as follows:

```
$ curl http://localhost
<html><head><script>window.location = '/web' +
location.hash;</script></head></html>
```

Configuring and enforcing HTTPS

Web traffic should not travel through the internet in plaintext. When exposing our Odoo web server to be used on a network, we should use the HTTPS protocol to have the traffic encrypted.

In some cases, it might be acceptable to use a self-signed certificate. Keep in mind that using a self-signed certificate can pose some security risks, however, such as man-in-the-middle attacks, and may not be allowed by some browsers.

For a more robust solution, you should use a certificate signed by a recognized certificate authority. This is particularly important if you're running a commercial or e-commerce website.

The **Let's Encrypt** service at `https://letsencrypt.org` provides free certificates. An Odoo add-on module exists to handle the automatic requesting of SSL certificates for the Odoo server, but at the time of writing, it wasn't yet ported to Odoo 12. You can learn more at `https://github.com/OCA/server-tools/tree/11.0/letsencrypt`.

Creating a self-signed SSL certificate

Next, we should install a certificate that will enable us to use SSL.

To create a self-signed certificate, use the following commands:

```
$ sudo mkdir /etc/ssl/nginx && cd /etc/ssl/nginx
$ sudo openssl req -x509 -newkey rsa:2048 \
-keyout server.key -out server.crt -days 365 -nodes
$ sudo chmod a-wx *            # make files read only
$ sudo chown www-data:root *   # access only to www-data group
```

The preceding code creates an `/etc/ssl/nginx` directory and creates a passwordless self-signed SSL certificate. When running the `openssl` command, the user will be asked for some additional information, and then a certificate and key files will be generated. Finally, the ownership of these files is given to the `www-data` user, which is used to run the web server.

Configuring HTTPS access on nginx

Now that we have an SSL certificate, we're ready to configure `nginx` to use it. To enforce HTTPS, we need to redirect all HTTP traffic. Replace the `server` directive we defined previously with the following code:

```
server {
  listen 80;
  rewrite ^(.*) https://$host$1 permanent;
}
```

Now, if we reload the `nginx` configuration and access the server with a web browser, we'll see that the `http://` address has been converted into an `https://` address.

However, this address won't return any content until we configure the HTTPS service properly; this can be done by adding the following server configuration:

```
server {
  listen 443;

  # Add Headers for odoo proxy mode
  proxy_set_header X-Forwarded-Host $host;
  proxy_set_header X-Forwarded-For $proxy_add_x_forwarded_for;
  proxy_set_header X-Forwarded-Proto $scheme;
  proxy_set_header X-Real-IP $remote_addr;

  # SSL parameters
  ssl on;
  ssl_certificate /etc/ssl/nginx/server.crt;
  ssl_certificate_key /etc/ssl/nginx/server.key;
  ssl_session_timeout 30m;
  ssl_protocols TLSv1 TLSv1.1 TLSv1.2;
  ssl_ciphers 'ECDHE-RSA-AES128-GCM-SHA256:ECDHE-ECDSA-AES128-GCM-
SHA256:ECDHE-RSA-AES256-GCM-SHA384:ECDHE-ECDSA-AES256-GCM-SHA384:DHE-RSA-
AES128-GCM-SHA256:DHE-DSS-AES128-GCM-SHA256:kEDH+AESGCM:ECDHE-RSA-AES128-
SHA256:ECDHE-ECDSA-AES128-SHA256:ECDHE-RSA-AES128-SHA:ECDHE-ECDSA-AES128-
SHA:ECDHE-RSA-AES256-SHA384:ECDHE-ECDSA-AES256-SHA384:ECDHE-RSA-AES256-
SHA:ECDHE-ECDSA-AES256-SHA:DHE-RSA-AES128-SHA256:DHE-RSA-AES128-SHA:DHE-
DSS-AES128-SHA256:DHE-RSA-AES256-SHA256:DHE-DSS-AES256-SHA:DHE-RSA-AES256-
SHA:AES128-GCM-SHA256:AES256-GCM-SHA384:AES128-SHA256:AES256-SHA256:AES128-
SHA:AES256-SHA:AES:CAMELLIA:DES-CBC3-
SHA:!aNULL:!eNULL:!EXPORT:!DES:!RC4:!MD5:!PSK:!aECDH:!EDH-DSS-DES-CBC3-
SHA:!EDH-RSA-DES-CBC3-SHA:!KRB5-DES-CBC3-SHA';
  ssl_prefer_server_ciphers on;

  # log
  access_log /var/log/nginx/odoo.access.log;
  error_log /var/log/nginx/odoo.error.log;

  # Redirect longpoll requests to odoo longpolling port
  location /longpolling {
    proxy_pass http://odoochat;
  }

  # Redirect requests to odoo backend server
  location / {
    proxy_redirect off;
    proxy_pass http://odoo;
  }
```

```
  # common gzip
  gzip_types text/css text/scss text/plain text/xml application/xml
application/json application/javascript;
  gzip on;
}
```

The preceding code will listen to the HTTPS port and use the `/etc/ssl/nginx/` certificate files to encrypt the traffic. This is similar to the server configuration section we looked at in the *Setting up an nginx reverse proxy* section.

If we reload the configuration, we should now have our Odoo service working through HTTPS, as shown in the following commands:

```
$ sudo nginx -t
nginx: the configuration file /etc/nginx/nginx.conf syntax is ok
nginx: configuration file /etc/nginx/nginx.conf test is successful
$ sudo service nginx reload  # or: sudo systemctl reload nginx
* Reloading nginx configuration nginx
...done.
$ curl -k https://localhost
<html><head><script>window.location = '/web' +
location.hash;</script></head></html>
```

The last output confirms that the Odoo web client is being served over HTTPS.

In older Odoo images, the PosBox would only work in HTTP mode; for it to work, an exception had to be added to `nginx` for the `/pos/` URL. Recent images of Odoo 10 and later include a self-signed certificate allowing HTTPS communication between PosBOx and IoT Box. The change was introduced by `https://github.com/odoo/odoo/pull/27936`.

Caching static content

We can configure `nginx` to cache the static files served, and have the repeated requests to be served directly from the `nginx` cache, without the need to pass on a request to the `upstream odoo` server.

Activating static content caching allows for a faster response time and reduces the workload for Odoo servers.

To enable this setting, add the following code before the `location /longpolling` section:

```
# cache static data
 location ~* /web/static/ {
   proxy_cache_valid 200 60m;
   proxy_buffering on;
   expires 864000;
   proxy_pass http://odoo;
 }
```

With this command, static data is now cached for 60 minutes. Further, additional requests in that interval will be responded to directly by `nginx` from the cache.

Server and module updates

Once the Odoo server is up-and-running, you'll need to install updates on Odoo. This involves two steps—getting new versions of the source code (for the server or modules) and installing them.

Creating a staging environment

If you have followed the approach described in the *Installing from the source code* section correctly, you should now be able to fetch and test new versions of source code in the staging repository. It's strongly advised that you make a copy of the production database and test any upgrades on it. If `odoo-prod` is your production database, an `odoo-stage` copy can be created with the following commands:

```
$ dropdb odoo-stage
$ createdb --owner=odoo odoo-stage
$ pg_dump odoo-prod | psql -d odoo-stage
$ sudo su odoo
$ cd ~/.local/share/Odoo/filestore/
$ cp -al odoo-prod odoo-stage  # create filestore hardlinks
$ exit
```

Before we can use the preceding copy of the database, cleanup should be done, such as deactivating scheduled actions, and email servers (both for sending and fetching messages). The specific steps needed here depend on your setup, but it's likely they can be automated by a script. Remember that the `psql` command can be used to run SQL directly from the command line, such as `psql -d odoo-stage -c "<SQL command>"`.

A database copy can be made in a much faster way using the `createdb` command, `$ createdb --owner=odoo --template=odoo-prod odoo-stage`. The caveat here is that, for it to run, there can't be any open connections to the `odoo-prod` database, so the Odoo production server needs to be stopped.

Updating Odoo source code

To get the latest Odoo source code from the GitHub repository, we use the `git pull` command. Before doing that, we can use the `git tag` command to create a tag for the current commit in use, so that it's easier to revert the code update, as follows:

```
$ sudo su odoo
$ cd ~/odoo-12
$ git tag --force 12-last-prod
$ git pull
```

For code changes to take effect, we need to restart the Odoo service. For data file changes to take effect, an upgrade to the modules is needed. As a general rule, changes to Odoo stable versions are considered code fixes, and it's therefore not often worth the risk of performing module upgrades. If you need to perform a module upgrade, however, it can be achieved using the `-u <module>` additional option, or `-u base`, which upgrades all modules.

Now it's time to start the Odoo staging server, which will use the update code on it staging database, as follows:

```
$ ~/odoo-12/odoo-bin -d odoo-stage --http-port=8080 \
-c /etc/odoo/odoo.conf  # optionally add: -u base
$ exit
```

This Odoo staging server was configured to listen on the `8080` port. We can navigate there with our web browser, using an address such as `http://localhost:8080`, to check whether the upgraded code works correctly.

If something goes wrong, we can revert the code to an earlier version with the following code:

```
$ sudo su odoo
$ cd ~/odoo-12
$ git checkout 12-last-prod
$ exit
```

If everything works as expected, it should be safe to perform an upgrade on the production service, which is usually done by restarting it. If you want to perform an actual module upgrade, the suggested approach is to stop the server, run the upgrade, and then restart the service, as follows:

```
$ sudo service odoo stop
$ sudo su -c "~/odoo-12/odoo-bin -c /etc/odoo/odoo.conf" \
" -u base --stop-after-init" odoo
$ sudo service odoo start
```

Remember to make a note of the Git reference in use by checking out the necessary version. This will enable you to rollback any changes if necessary. Keeping a backup of the database before an upgrade is also highly advised.

After this is complete, we can pull the new versions to the production repository using Git and complete the upgrade as follows:

```
$ sudo su odoo
$ cd ~/odoo-12
$ git tag --force 12-last-prod
$ git pull
$ exit
$ sudo service odoo restart  # or: sudo systemctl restart odoo
```

There's no point in updating too frequently, but it's not advised that you wait a year between updates either. Performing an update every few months is usually fine. Also note that a server restart should be enough to enable code updates—and that module upgrades aren't always necessary.

If you need a specific bug fix, however, an earlier update should be considered. Remember to also watch out for security bug disclosures on public channels such as GitHub Issues for Odoo, in particular, ones displaying the **Security** tag, at https://github.com/odoo/odoo/issues?q=is%3Aissue+label%3ASecurity, or the Odoo official mailing lists, which can be subscribed to at https://www.odoo.com/groups.

As part of the service, enterprise contract customers can expect early email notifications alerting them to this type of issue.

Summary

In this chapter, you learned about the additional steps required for setting up and running Odoo in a Debian-based production server. The most important settings in the configuration file were looked at, and you learned how to take advantage of the multiprocessing mode.

For improved security and scalability, you also learned how to use `nginx` as a reverse proxy in front of Odoo server processes.

This chapter should have covered the essentials of what's needed to run an Odoo server and provide a stable and secure service to your users.

To learn more about Odoo, you should take a look at the official documentation at `https://www.odoo.com/documentation`. Some topics are covered in more detail there, and you'll find topics not covered in this book.

There are also other published books on Odoo that you might also find useful. Packt Publishing has a few in its catalog, and in particular, *Odoo Development Cookbook* provides more advanced material on topics not discussed in this book.

Finally, Odoo is an open source product with a vibrant community. Getting involved, asking questions, and contributing is a great way not only to learn, but also to build a business network. With this in mind, we can't help mention the **Odoo Community Association** (**OCA**), which promotes collaboration and quality open source code. You can learn more about it at `odoo-comunity.org`.

Further reading

The following official Odoo titles are additional reference material that may be useful, and may complement the topics described in this chapter:

- Deploying Odoo: `https://www.odoo.com/documentation/12.0/setup/deploy.html`
- Installing Odoo: `https://www.odoo.com/documentation/12.0/setup/install.html`

Assessments

Chapter 1

1. **What are the relevant layers to consider when designing an Odoo application?**

    First focus on the Data layer, structuring the data model, the models needed and their relations. **Entity-relationship diagrams** (**ERDs**) can be a useful tool for this.

    Then think about the Presentation layer—how the user interface will be organized to fit the use cases to be supported.

    Finally, think about the Logic layer, supporting the required business rules. These can be validations, automation, or helper features.

2. **How is Developer mode enabled?**

    Developer Mode, making available the **Settings I Technical** menu and the **Debug** contextual menu, can be enabled in the main **Settings** screen, using a link in the bottom-right. This has been so since Odoo 10.0; in Odoo 9.0 and before, it is enabled from the **About** dialog, accessed from the user menu in the top-right. It can also be enabled directly on the page URL, by changing the `.../web?#...` URL to `.../web?debug#....`

3. **Where do you create a new Data model?**

    Data Models can be created and modified in the **Settings** app, in the **Technical I Database Structure I Models** menu option. To have the **Technical** menu available, you must have Developer Mode enabled. New models must have an `x_` prefix, and new fields must also have this same `x_` prefix.

4. **How do you make a new data model available for the end users to create and edit records?**

    You should create a menu item for this, and in most cases, you will also want to design proper List and Form Views. You also need to add the ACLs to a group the user belongs to, or they won't be able to see the menu and views.

5. **How do you add a field to an existing form?**

You first edit the model to add the new field, then find the base View for the form (for example, using the **Debug** menu). Then create an extension view for that base view, adding the new field.

6. **What is a Domain, and when can it be used?**

It is a filter to apply when querying records from the database.

7. **How can you set default values on the form you're navigating to?**

You do this by setting a context key with the `default_` prefix, for example, `{'default_x_name': '<Type description>'}`. This context key can be set on Window Actions, used in Menu items, and for relational fields can be set on the View's field definition.

8. **How do you give a user access to a Model?**

You first assign the ACL, for create, read, update, and delete, to a Group, and then make sure that the user belongs to that Group, directly or indirectly (indirectly belonging to another Group that inherits that one, such as Manager groups, which usually inherit from user groups).

9. **How can you add a Category field to the To-do items, with possible values selectable from an options list? (The options list is editable and can be expanded by users.)**

Create a new Model called `x_todo_category`. No additional fields needed.

Edit the `x_todo_item` Model and add a `x_category_id` field, of the many-to-one type, with a related `x_todo_category` Model.

Edit the To-do item form view to add the new field: `<field name="x_category_id" />`.

Add the ACL to the To-do User group.

10. **How can you extend the To-do Category model so that the list of Categories is specific for each user?**

It is enough to create a record rule on the To-do category for the To-do User Group. The domain to use is `[('create_uid', '=', user.id)]`.

You could also reorganize the To-do menu to have two child menu items, **Items** and **Categories**.

The **To-do** top menu item should have no action defined, the **Items** menu item should reuse the existing Action to open the to-do list, and a new Action should be used on the **Categories** menu item, opening the **To-do Category** list.

Chapter 3

1. **Is** `library-app` **a valid module name?**

It is a technically valid name, so it could be used, but it does not comply with the code conventions for Odoo, so it shouldn't be used.

2. **Should a module define access control (ACL) for all Models defined in it?**

Yes, as a general rule it should. Leaving a Model with no ACLs makes it inaccessible for the end users.

3. **Can we permit some users to only access a subset of the records in a Model?**

Yes, Record Rules allow us to define a Domain filter, and assign it to security Groups. Users in those Groups will only be able to access the records matching the Domain filter.

4. **What is the difference between a relational field and other field types?**

Relational fields store links to other records, not actual values like the other field types.

5. **What are the main view components used in an Odoo app?**

The backend view layer includes menu items, window actions, and views. All these are defined using XML data files. Menu items are usually defined with `<menuitem>` data elements, `<action>` defines Window Actions, and `<record model="ir.ui.view">` defines views.

6. **How are backend views defined?**

A backend view is defined with an XML architecture declaring the structure of the elements it is composed of.

7. **Where should business logic be implemented in an Odoo app?**

A module business logic should be implemented in the Model methods, using Python code.

8. **What is the web page templating engine used by Odoo?**

For the website/frontend views, Odoo uses the QWeb, an XML-based template engine. It allows templates to be extended by other modules, just like what can be done with the backend views.

Chapter 4

1. **How do we extend an existing Model to add a mixin, such as** mail.thread**?**

Both in-place classic extension and mixin prototype inheritance use the same _inherit Model attribute. For example, to extend x and add the y mixin, we should have the _name='x' model attribute and the _inherit = ['x', 'y'] Model attribute.

2. **What changes are needed to also have the phone field available in the member form view?**

No model changes are needed, since a phone field exists in partners, and delegation inheritance makes all partner fields also available on the member Model. We only need to add the field to the form view, for example, next to the email field: <field name=phone" />.

3. **What happens if you create a Model class with name attribute different form the inherit attribute (for example,** _name='y' **and** _inherit='x')**?**

A new y model will be created, copying all the features (data structure and methods) from Model x. If x is a database-stored Model, we will have two database tables with the same fields, but independent data records, which is not a good design practice. That's why this is usually used with abstract mixin classes that don't have an actual database representation.

4. **Can XPath be used to modify data record from other modules?**

No. XPath is used only for views, to find the element in the view structure where the extension should be done. This extension is performed at runtime, and no actual change is made to the record being extended.

5. **When inheriting a Model to extend it, can we extend a method and not use** `super()` **to call original code being inherited?**

We can, and sometimes we may have to, but we should avoid it. When not using `super()` we are completely replacing the original code, our re-implementation will have different behavior form the original one, and it may have unanticipated side-effects. Also, extensions implemented in other modules may not work as expected. If the parent method is hard to extend, it's best to propose changes to it, so that it includes extension points we can use (separating part of the logic into their own methods will make extension simpler).

6. **How can we extend the book catalog web page to add the ISBN field at the end of the line without referencing any particular field name?**

We can insert the ISBN field inside the row `div` element: `<xpath expr="//div[class='row']"><span t-field="book.isbn"/></xpath>`

Chapter 5

1. **What is the difference between an XML ID and an external ID?**

None. Both terms refer to the same thing: external identifiers.

2. **What type of data files can be used, add-on modules?**

Odoo add-on modules can use XML and CSV data files.

3. **What is wrong in this XML fragment:** `<field name="user_id">[(4, 0, [ref(base.user_demo)])]</field>`**?**

Three things are wrong: the tag content should instead be in an `eval` attribute; the `4` command expects the record references in the second element, not the third; and a single record reference is expected, not a list. The correct syntax is: `<field name="user_id" eval="[(4, ref(base.user_demo), 0)] />`

4. **Can a data file in one add-on module overwrite a record create in another module?**

Yes, in an XML file we can have a `<record>` element using the complete External ID of the record to replace (`module.identifier`).

5. **When an add-on module is upgraded, are all its data records rewritten to the module's default values?**

In most cases, yes, but there can be records loaded in a `noupdate="1"` data section that won't be rewritten on a module upgrade.

Other Books You May Enjoy

If you enjoyed this book, you may be interested in these other books by Packt:

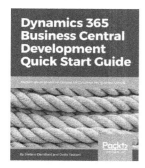

Dynamics 365 Business Central Development Quick Start Guide
Stefano Demiliani, Duilio Tacconi

ISBN: 9781789347463

- Develop solutions for Dynamics 365 Business Central
- Create a sandbox for extensions development (local or on cloud)
- Use Docker with Dynamics 365 Business Central
- Create extensions for Dynamics 365 Business Central
- Handle dependencies, translations and reporting
- Deploy extensions on-premise and to the cloud
- Create serverless processes with Dynamics 365 Business Central
- Understand source code management for AL

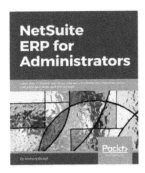

NetSuite ERP for Administrators
Anthony Bickof

ISBN: 9781788628877

- Provide executives with meaningful insights into the business
- A Framework to streamline the implementation of new and existing features
- Leverage built-in tools to optimize your efficiency and effectiveness
- Test configuration to check the implementation of role-specific permissions
- Understand how to optimize the amount of data to be shared with users
- Import data like new leads and employ current data like pricing updates
- Perform on-going maintenance and troubleshoot issues

Leave a review - let other readers know what you think

Please share your thoughts on this book with others by leaving a review on the site that you bought it from. If you purchased the book from Amazon, please leave us an honest review on this book's Amazon page. This is vital so that other potential readers can see and use your unbiased opinion to make purchasing decisions, we can understand what our customers think about our products, and our authors can see your feedback on the title that they have worked with Packt to create. It will only take a few minutes of your time, but is valuable to other potential customers, our authors, and Packt. Thank you!

Index

www.ingramcontent.com/pod-product-compliance
Lightning Source LLC
Chambersburg PA
CBHW080606060326
40690CB00021B/4610